HUMAN MOVEMENT

HUMAN
MOVEMENT

with concepts applied to children's
movement activities

MARJORIE LATCHAW / GLEN EGSTROM

University of California, Los Angeles

PRENTICE-HALL, INC., Englewood Cliffs, New Jersey

ILLUSTRATIONS BY RUE WISE

QP
303
L35

PRENTICE-HALL INTERNATIONAL, INC., London
PRENTICE-HALL OF AUSTRALIA, PTY. LTD., Sydney
PRENTICE-HALL OF CANADA, LTD., Toronto
PRENTICE-HALL OF INDIA PRIVATE LTD., New Delhi
PRENTICE-HALL OF JAPAN, INC., Tokyo

C-13-445189-9
P-13-445171-6

Library of Congress Catalog Card Number: 69-12976

Printed in the United States of America

Current printing (last digit):
10 9 8 7 6 5 4 3 2 1

PREFACE

The multiplicity and complexity of the knowledges needed by the individual in contemporary life have resulted in curricula structured on the understanding of large concepts. Concern for the conceptual development of the child is the focal point of this book.

Two large conceptual areas that should be central in children's learning are (1) human movement, and (2) biologic development. This book contributes to the understanding of concept formation in these areas by presenting scientific information that may be acquired by the child through participation in movement activities.

The facts and principles of the science of human movement are presented in nontechnical language and are accompanied by examples to clarify concepts, thus helping the teacher understand how to use movement activities in the conceptual development of the child.

Many writers have stated in their prefaces that no author produces a book alone. We acknowledge our indebtedness to our colleagues and students in the Department of Physical Education, University of California, Los Angeles; to authors, teachers, and professional colleagues and friends across the country.

We wish to express a special debt of gratitude to Camille Brown, University of California, Los Angeles, for her creative help in the organization and development of the manuscript, and for her generous contributions of ideas and materials in the areas of movement theory and exploration.

Sincere appreciation is extended to Dorothy Govas, teacher of physical education, Long Beach Unified School District, Long Beach, California, for her skillful assistance in preparing the materials on aquatics, and for her intelligent and helpful criticisms of other portions of the manuscript.

Rue Wise, of Rue Wise Studio-Gallery, Box 386, Hermosa Beach, California, is responsible for the superb drawings and sketches, and her artistry and sensitivity have contributed immeasurably to the quality of the book.

Special appreciation is extended to Donna Egstrom for her interest and perception in helping her husband meet writing deadlines, and for editing the manuscript; and to Mae Kirnbauer, teacher of kindergarten, Long Beach Unified School District, Long Beach, California, for reading and criticizing the scientific materials from the viewpoint of a teacher, for whom this book is written.

THE AUTHORS

CONTENTS

PART TWO

MOVEMENT ACTIVITIES FOR CHILDREN

HUMAN MOVEMENT

PART ONE

SCIENCE OF HUMAN MOVEMENT

1   AN OVERVIEW

The child is a moving, dynamic organism which is growing and developing, exploring and evaluating, selecting and rejecting from the surrounding environments. Adults who participate in the child-world are continuously amazed at the energy-in-action that is a child. Twisting, leaping, shouting, laughing, striking, pushing, screaming, he moves vigorously into the tasks of his day.

For the teacher, the challenge of childhood is a never-ending source of wonderment. Like a rolling stone, one who fraternizes with children can gather no moss. Volatile and tempestuous, yet serene in contemplation of a space-world, moving over his earth-world with large movements or small movements, quickly or slowly, with or without restraint, a child is movement.

The child's lungs urge him to move, that they may inflate and deflate with ever-increasing effectiveness. The child's heart and other muscles demand energetic movement for healthy growth. The organic systems thus are dependent on movement, and movement is dependent upon the well-being of the total organism.

The child must have an environment that fulfills his movement needs. He can leap into the air only if a surface supports the downward push of his feet. He can swim only if water is available for his propulsive movement. He can lift, push, climb, dive, or stretch only if his environment makes it possible. Conversely, he uses movement to control his environment. He chooses to move a rock and he lifts, pushes, pulls until the rock is as he wants it. He wishes to join his friends, and he moves toward them by pushing against the ground to propel himself forward in a run.

The child needs to learn how to use movement for his own best development and performance.   The haphazard movement experiences in the natural environment, the playground, the neighborhood, and the home, do not necessarily provide the "best" opportunities for movement development needed by the child.   Consequently, physical education programs are needed to provide opportunities for the "best" learning of necessary skills and concepts to meet the demands of today's world.   It is the school's responsibility to organize and conduct such programs.   In addition, these physical education programs should provide movement opportunities that insure the best *biologic* development of the individual.

Content of This Book

The material in this book includes the large conceptual areas of *human movement* and *biologic development* with application to children's movement skills: the subject matter of school physical education.

Recognizing that the teacher may not have an academic background in the physiology and mechanics of human movement, we have written this book to provide the teacher with the scientific facts and principles relating to these large conceptual areas, upon whose application the acquisition of movement skills and of improved biologic development is based.   Although human movement is a complex phenomenon, it is possible to understand and apply individual factors with relative ease.

This book, therefore, is a compilation of many of the knowledges needed by the teacher to guide the child in the development and application of movement concepts.

Use of This Book

The material in this book may be used by the teacher in the selection of program objectives and content, and in the development of more efficient and effective movement patterns in the children under his guidance.   It is not enough to recognize that the child is growing and developing.   Each child must be guided into appropriate activities that will insure his best biologic development, and will make possible the acquisition of needed movement skills and concepts.

The skills and concepts discussed in this book relate to other large conceptual areas in the total curriculum.   Concepts derived from Newtonian laws give the child further understanding of his physical world.   Knowledge of lever actions in his body gives him further understanding of other types of machines.   Muscle action as it relates to the circulatory, respiratory, and digestive systems helps him to form concepts about biologic development. As he learns to use his body effectively in many different movement situations, he may develop concepts relating to feelings of confidence, an extension of perceptions, and a more adequate self-concept.

This book, therefore, may be used by the teacher in applying the scientific facts and principles of human movement at an operational level in the school physical education program.

Organization of this Book

This book is divided into two parts: Part One, Science of Human Movement; and Part Two, Movement Activities for Children.

Part One considers the scientific material about *human movement* itself, and the interaction of movement and the organism—the effect of each on the other.   The material includes a chapter on the definition and description of human movement, and chapters on the mechanics of movement, analysis of movement skills, movement expression, and sensation and movement.   The chapters on *movement and biologic development* describe the interaction of movement and the organism; they are concerned with specific biologic factors that influence and are influenced by the individual's movement.   These chapters cover strength, endurance, flexibility, relaxation, postures, and movement and the biologic condition.

Part Two is a compilation of movement activities for elementary-age school children.   These activities are organized under traditional headings to make them readily accessible to the teacher.   Activities under each major heading are presented in order—from simple to complex—and are identified by grade level.   Preceding the description of each activity are (1) the behavioral goal, (2) concepts that may be developed by performance of the activity, (3) biologic efficiency that may be developed by the activity, and (4) the movement skill to be acquired.

In this book the term *physical education* is ". . . the school program of the study of the art and science of human movement needed in today's world designed for development through movement, and human performance restricted to expressive form and/or restricted through the use of representations of environmental reality."[1] Brown and Cassidy's cogent term, "representations of environmental reality," indicates the inclusion of facilities and equipment that provide opportunities for attainment of movement skills and concepts used in the real world.   They use the trampoline as an example for providing skill development in the use of gravitational forces of falling

---

[1] Camille Brown and Rosalind Cassidy, *Theory in Physical Education* (Philadelphia: Lea & Febiger, 1963), p. 36.

through space, propelling oneself through space, moving the body while falling, and the like.

A "behavioral goal" implies a direction of endeavor for a course of action, such as throwing a ball for distance, or performing a forward roll correctly. A behavioral goal may include achieving an outside goal, such as becoming stronger, speedier, or more flexible, by practicing a particular activity.

The term *concept* is used to mean the intellectualization of an idea or notion. The development of concepts is dependent on the developmental level and intellectual capacity of the child; and a wide range of levels of understanding exists in each age group. It has been suggested that the child's ability to understand rather complicated concepts is possible at an earlier age than that previously accepted, and Jean Piaget's studies have tended to support this view.[2] With the increased emphasis in school programs on understanding the physical world, it can be assumed that the elementary-age child is capable of understanding many of the concepts related to levers, motion, and the like. The elementary teacher is best qualified to select the concepts that are comprehensible to the children with whom he works. The concepts included with each activity in Part Two suggest a large area of subject matter, such as understandings about "strength," and the teacher may use the scientific materials in Part One to help him with the selection of specific concepts to be developed with his group of children.

The term *biology* means the science of life and all its phenomena, including origins, growth, structure, and function. Thus, the term *biologic efficiency* is used in this book to refer to the efficiency of an organism irrespective of culture. The use of the nebulous term *physical fitness* has been deliberately avoided. Brown and Cassidy state that development of the individual through movement, and movement skill development, are generally considered to mean "physical fitness."[3] Development of the individual through movement, or biologic efficiency, entails the biologic factors of strength, endurance, and flexibility development.

Movement skill development is used to mean competence in performance of a particular movement objective, such as batting a ball, swimming the crawl stroke, or performing the knee-drop on the trampoline.

The activities in this collection help boys and girls to apply, under teacher guidance, the movement concepts and skills needed for their best development in today's world. Although grade levels are designated for each activity, many of the activities are challenging to children of all ages and should be selected freely in order to reach particular behavioral goals and to develop particular skills and concepts.

For example, the children may have individual purposes—to compete

[2] John H. Flavell, *The Developmental Psychology of Jean Piaget* (Princeton, N.J.: D. Van Nostrand Co., Inc., 1963), pp. 365ff.
[3] Brown and Cassidy, *op. cit.*, p. 39.

in a track meet, to win a race, to take a three-mile hike with friends. An activity having the *behavioral goal* of running faster and longer may then be selected. The teacher may help the children to understand and apply the *concept* of how endurance is attained and maintained, and how this state affects their ability to compete in a track meet, win a race, or take a long hike. While participating in the activity, the child may learn how to improve his *movement skill* of running by using good body mechanics, and his *biologic efficiency* by improving his endurance.

2 HUMAN MOVEMENT

An object in motion is changing its position in space. This may be accomplished in a number of ways. For example, a balloon blown full of air changes its position in space by increasing its volume. If strings are tied around portions of the balloon so that it resembles an animal, it changes its position in space by changing its shape. When the balloon is tossed into the air and floats toward earth, it is changing its position in space by passing from one point to another.

Inanimate objects are subject to mechanical laws that regulate their movements. The direction, distance, and rate of speed of a moving balloon are governed by the amount of energy that thrust it into space, and by the action of the external forces that surround it as it floats. Animate, or living objects are capable of voluntary motion, which makes it possible for them to use movement for their own purposes, within the restrictions of the mechanical laws of motion. A balloon cannot change the course of its flight, but a butterfly can move in the direction it chooses; both, however, are subject to the laws of motion and gravitation.

Various combinations of individual and environmental components result in the wide range of human movements. Some of these factors are listed on the following page.

For example, an individual may hop freely, fast, and in a forward direction. He may walk jerkily, slowly, and sideward. It may be observed that the numerous combinations possible from the listing above, which is by no means complete, result in many different types of movements.

9

Forms of movement	Style of movement	Speed of movement	Direction of movement
Crawl	Free	Fast	Forward
Roll	Controlled	Slow	Upward
Walk	Sharp	Medium	Downward
Run	Floating	Quick	Sideward
Leap	Small	Sustained	Backward
Jump	Large	Other	Other
Skip			
Slide			
Gallop			
Hop			
Swim			
Throw			
Bat			
Strike			
Kick			
Catch			
Pull			
Push			
Other			

In this chapter we shall discuss several facets of movement and the human body, including basic movement, human locomotion, and overcoming inertia of external objects.

Definition of Human Movement

Human movement is a change of position in space of the body as a whole or of a body member. The child who jumps into the air and lands on both feet has changed the position in space of his body as a whole. He changes position of a body member by kicking his foot into the air. He runs from the school to the playground, moving his whole body through space as he lifts his feet, swings his arms, calls to his friends. He changes his body shape by curling up into a ball. He fills his lungs with air and increases his volume. His movement is self-regulated through the production of his own energy and is modified by his environment.

The Movers of the Body

Movement takes place in the joints of the body and is caused by muscles pulling on the bones. A muscle may be thought of as a sheet of thin fibers enclosed in a case with thickened ends. The arrangement of these fibers is such that their shortening results in a "pulling" effect on the ends of the case, which represents the cords or tendons that attach to the bone. The intensity of the tension exerted on the tendons is dependent upon the number of fibers contracting at any given time, and the frequency with which they contract.

Muscles are not capable of pushing to exert force; thus the attachments of muscles are functionally located so that most muscle-pull will exert tension across a joint, or between two bones. Most types of human movement are the result of a muscle pulling on attachments that join two bones. An example is the biceps muscle on the front (anterior) surface of the arm; the biceps crosses the elbow joint and operates to flex or bend the arm. Another illustration is provided by the muscle groups that pull to keep man in the upright position. The muscle groups that pull to hold the body erect are commonly called the antigravity muscles. They are duplicated on the right and left side of the body, and are divided into functional groups. Each of these functional groups consists of several muscles that operate together in moving a joint.

In addition the antigravity muscles and the other muscles of the body are attached so that their "pulling" force can result in lever actions which permit the individual to bend, twist, or stretch. These muscle groups can be identified in terms of the movement they cause. Muscle groups that enable the individual to bend are called flexors, and are placed so that their pull causes the angle of the two bones of the joint to grow smaller. Extensors, muscle groups that allow the individual to stretch, are placed so that their pull increases the angle at a joint. Muscle groups that cause twisting and turning are called rotators.

Even though skeletal muscles "pull" to exert force, they operate in ways that provide for the many and varied body movements. First of all, the "pull" can be halted in place at a given point, and objects can be held at that position. Such holding is accomplished through *isometric* contraction— contraction without movement. Here the muscle fibers are maintained at a constant length under tension. If you were to put the palms of your hands together and press equally hard from both sides, thus stabilizing the palms, you would be demonstrating static or isometric contraction of the muscles involved. The popular usage of isometrics for developing strength in muscles is based on this principle, the idea being to contract some muscle as though it were actually supporting a load.

Conversely, when contractions of a muscle involve movement, they are called *isotonic* contractions. For example, if you push against a book and move it across the desk, the result is isotonic contraction of the muscles used.

Isotonic contractions may be either concentric or eccentric. A concentric contraction occurs when a muscle shortens under tension. An eccentric contraction occurs when a muscle lengthens under tension. In both instances, the muscle fibers are "pulling" to create tension even though the actions appear to be opposite. An example is the holding of a pail of water in the hand with the arm at the side. To raise the pail by movement at the elbow joint one must perform a concentric contraction, with the biceps or elbow flexors shortening under tension. To lower the pail to the initial position requires the lengthening of the muscles under tension: eccentric contraction.

These types of contraction permit the muscles to function in a number of roles during activity.   Because of their manner of contracting and shortening, they may be *primarily* responsible for the observable movement of a limb. In this role, the muscle is referred to as a *prime mover,* and is so situated that tension developed in it will pull and bring about movement.   Since many efforts involve additional roles, a muscle may also function as assistant mover, fixator, stabilizer, and neutralizer.

Movements of this type remain controlled-tension type movements until enough force is exerted to cause the movement to occur at a rate faster than that at which the muscle is contracting.   At this time, the movement becomes a free swinging movement, or *ballistic*-type movement.   At the end of the ballistic phase of such a movement, the limb is slowed down and an eccentric contraction is used to regain control of the movement.   Swinging a baseball bat or a golf club are examples of ballistic-type movements.

Basic Movements

The basic movements of the human body are bending, twisting, and stretching.   In bending, the body contracts and takes up less space.   Bending may be forward, backward, or sideward; the muscle groups pull, and exert tension on the various moveable joints that perform this function. Stretching, the opposite of bending, is performed by other muscle groups that enable the individual to reach out into space.   Twisting is the rotation of the body, or a body member, around its axis, and is performed by the action of still other muscle groups.

All body movements are combinations of these three basic movements and may be thought of as the "movement patterns" of walking, running, kicking, climbing, throwing, catching, and the like.[1]   The success with which these movements can be carried out—the movement skill or quality— is largely dependent upon the smooth summation of forces as each muscle or group of muscles makes its contribution to the movement at the appropriate time within the sequence of the activity.

Human Locomotion

Human locomotion is the act of moving the body from place to place. How this is done depends upon a number of environmental factors, and upon the nature and development of man himself.

[1] Camille Brown and Rosalind Cassidy, *Theory in Physical Education* (Philadelphia: Lea & Febiger, 1963), p. 62.

Brown and Cassidy present a taxonomy of human movement in which they list variable factors affecting any form of human movement.[2]   Variable factors of human development included in this list are: (1) individual structure, both skeletal and muscular; (2) individual purpose or motivation; (3) elements of biologic efficiency, such as strength, endurance, flexibility, relaxation, and general health; (4) anthropometric conditions such as height, weight, and body proportions; (5) movement skill, rhythm, kinesthetic awareness; (6) psychological components such as self-concept and perception; and (7) individual maturation.

Environmental variable factors included in their listing are: (1) surface or media, i.e., land, water, or air; (2) sensory objects and objects of location, both animate and inanimate; (3) time-space factors; (4) human events in work, play, and subsistence; (5) materials and conditions for healthy growth and development; and (6) attitudes of valuing.

The effect of individual variations upon human movement is readily apparent.   For example, the infant's mode of locomotion is crawling, creeping, and balancing on his feet in the upright position.   As he continues to develop, he gains more control over his movement and is soon able to manage walking, running, jumping, and other adult patterns.   Individuals with structural limitations are forced to use locomotor patterns that may be distortions of patterns employed by the structurally sound individual.   Thin persons perform differently from fat persons, strong persons exhibit movement styles different from those of weak persons; and one who is secure in his outlook on life moves with an assurance that is missing in the individual with an inadequate self-concept.   There are those who perform any locomotor task with poetic grace in contrast to the awkward movers.

The environmental variables of land, water, and air affect the mode and manner of human locomotion.   Moving on land is accomplished by pushing against the surface and propelling the body forward, backward, upward, or sideward.   A firm surface that supports the body weight as the foot pushes forcefully against it permits the individual to perform leaps, jumps, fast running, and the like.   A sandy surface produces a different style of walking, running, or jumping.   The soft muddy surface, the sticky surface, the rigid concrete surface, and the rolling gravelly surface produce still different variations in locomotor patterns.

"Walking" across a horizontal ladder while being supported by the hands, and raising and lowering the body in chinning, are similar in principle to walking on the ground; the supporting surface, however, is the bar or ladder.   On land the body pushes against the ground, whereas in suspension, the body pulls against the supporting bar with movement occurring in the direction opposite from the point of application of force.

A swinging body in suspension, one hanging from a swinging trapeze, for example, behaves like a pendulum with gravity acting upon it to cause movement.   Before swinging can begin, the body must be placed in a position from which gravity can cause it to swing downward.   Then the momentum

[2] *Ibid.*, pp. 56–71.

built up in the downward swing causes the body to continue moving, into the upward swing. The speed increases as the body swings downward and decreases as it swings upward; the speed at either end of the arc is equal to zero. It is at the height of the swing, when the body is momentarily motionless, that cutoffs and other stunts are performed by the trapeze artist. At zero speed, it is possible for him to regrasp the bar or rings before they pass beyond him.

When swinging on rings or trapeze, motion may be started by: (1) pushing off from the ground, if the feet can touch the ground; (2) positioning the apparatus so that gravity will make it swing downward before one suspends oneself from it; (3) getting a push from a helper; or (4) using a pumping motion with the body.

If the speed of the rings, trapeze, or swing is too great for the child to manage successfully, the rope may be lengthened. The longer the pendulum, the slower it swings. The weight of the rings or swing-board will not affect the speed of the swing, since any falling object accelerates uniformly because of gravity at the rate of 32 feet per second/per second.

In the water the body's center of balance is called the center of buoyancy. Since the body is less dense than the water, its displaces water until an amount equal to the weight of the body has been displaced. The remainder of the body then floats. The center of buoyancy is the center of gravity of the displaced water. In swimming, as in walking or chinning, the first problem is to overcome body inertia and to start the movement. This is accomplished by exerting force against the water, thus propelling the body in the direction opposite from that in which the force is applied. The depth and turbulence of the water also influence locomotion. For example, it is possible to walk in shallow water, to swim underwater, to dive below the surface of the water, to tread in an upright position, and to ride a wave in body-surfing. In swiftly moving water, swimming against the current is not the same as swimming with the current.

In the air, the force of gravity acts upon the body the same as on any other unsupported object. That is, the pathway of the falling body is determined once the body is in the air. Although it is impossible to change the pathway of the fall by "swimming" movements, the individual can change the position of his body parts—he can swing his arms or legs, or he can rotate around his center of gravity. The pathway of the descent through space is controlled by the force that propelled the body into the air, whether the original movement consisted of diving from a board, rebounding from a trampoline, jumping upward, or catapulting from a swinging trapeze.

Other environmental variables include: (1) objects to be bypassed, leaped over, crawled under, around, or through; (2) space dimensions such as the walls of a room, the boundaries of a playground, or the virtually unlimited spaces of the unfenced Wyoming range; (3) time factors such as the leisurely walk of the sauntering window-shopper, the measured run of the miler, or the rapid sprint of the runner stealing third base; (4) attitudes and feelings about oneself and others described as hostility, rejection, threat, openness to experiences, acceptance, and fear; and (5) materials and conditions for healthy growth and development.[3]   Included in the fifth category are: air, food, liquids, sleep, temperature regulation, elimination of waste products, freedom from poisons, freedom from focal infection, activity, procreation, self-preservation, affection, feelings of belonging and being valued, success and recognition, perceptual clarity, realization of potentialities, and taking care of what one is born with.

Overcoming Inertia of External Objects

A part of the body may be used to put an external object in motion, striking the object with the hand or kicking it with the foot, for example.   An implement may be used as an extension of a body part, as in striking a tennis ball with a tennis racquet.   Giving impetus to an external object may be accomplished by: (1) moving the object with constant application of force as in pulling, pushing, or lifting; (2) contacting the object momentarily as in kicking, striking, or batting; and (3) developing kinetic energy in the object before releasing it, as in throwing a ball.

Kinetic energy is the energy of a moving body; it is determined by the weight and rate of motion of the moving body.   The heavier the body and the greater the velocity, the greater the kinetic energy.   *Potential energy* is the energy of position, stored energy that, when released, can perform work by moving an object.   For example, a softball bat is drawn back, ready to swing.   It has potential energy in that, if allowed to swing, it can perform work by striking a ball or anything in its pathway.   When the bat is swung, it develops speed as it moves and kinetic energy is produced.   The amount of kinetic energy produced may be determined by the formula

$$\text{kinetic energy} = \tfrac{1}{2} \, (\text{mass} \times \text{velocity}^2).$$

When the arm is drawn back in preparation for throwing a ball, it has only potential energy, the energy of position.   At the end of the throw, as the ball is released, the arm has only kinetic energy, the energy of motion.   While the arm was moving through space, the potential energy was gradually changed to kinetic energy, which was imparted to the ball on release.

The purpose of receiving impetus from a moving object, such as a thrown ball, is to cause the object to lose its kinetic energy.   The skills of receiving impetus include those of: (1) receiving impetus of one's own body, as in landing from a fall or jump; and (2) receiving impetus of external objects, as in catching a ball.   The more gradually the moving object loses its kinetic energy, the less is the shock of impact and danger of injury.   For example,

[3] Marjorie Latchaw and Camille Brown, *The Evaluation Process in Health Education, Physical Education and Recreation* (Englewood Cliffs, N.J.: Prentice-Hall, Inc., 1962), p. 13.

in landing from a jump or fall, one bends the knees, flexes the ankles, and rolls from one body part to another to cause the body to stop gradually.   In catching a ball or receiving a blow, one "gives," by moving with the object. Presenting a rigid surface to a moving object is more likely to cause injury.

The force of impact is also lessened by increasing the size of the body surface that is receiving the force.   Thus, it is better to stop a moving ball with the fingers and palms of the hands than with one finger, or to land from a fall on the large, fleshy part of the arm or thigh rather than on the elbow or knee.

In summary, human movement is a change of position of the body as a whole, or of a body member.   Movement takes place in the joints of the body and is caused by muscles pulling on bones.   The basic movements of the human body are bending, twisting, and stretching.   All body movements are combinations of these three basic movements and may be thought of as movement patterns.

Human locomotion is the act of moving the body from place to place. Individual and environmental variables affect any form of human movement.

Overcoming inertia of an external object may be accomplished by: (1) putting a stationary object in motion, as in pushing, pulling, lifting, striking, batting, kicking, and throwing; and (2) stopping a moving object by causing it to lose its kinetic energy, as in catching, blocking, or landing.

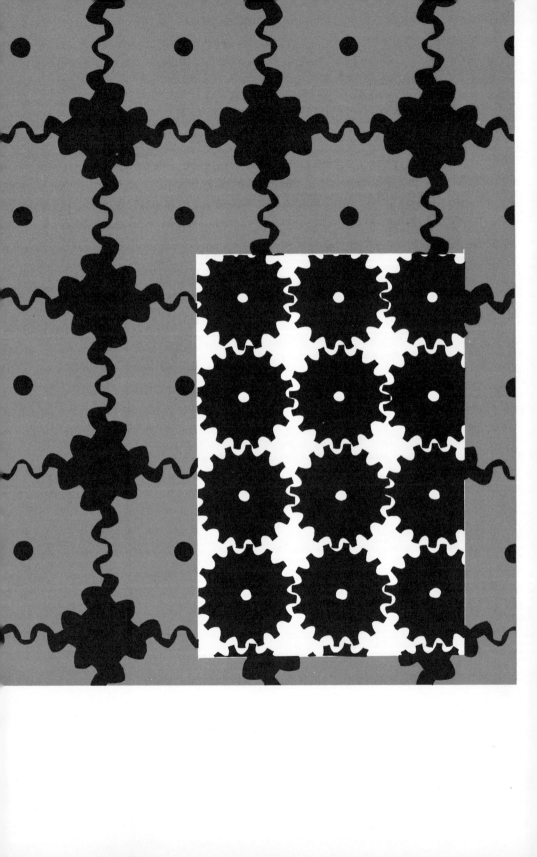

3   MECHANICS OF MOVEMENT

The human body is often referred to as a machine. It is, in fact, a computer-controlled system involving many hundreds of machines, each with a very highly specialized function. The muscles are the motors that operate the levers, pulleys, and wheels within the body in order to exert forces necessary to bring about movement. If movement is to occur, these forces must be greater than those imposed by the body weight and any other resisting forces. The amount of force applied affects the speed of movement, and the point at which the force is applied influences the direction of movement.

Usually movements are aimed at overcoming externally applied loads. These loads may result from a simple effect of gravity, as in moving one's body through space, or from the demands of overcoming inertia of other objects, as in accelerating the swing of a baseball bat to strike a hard-thrown ball.

Movement in Time-Space

All movement occurs within time and space. Force is the instigator of movement, time is the speed or rate of movement, and space governs the direction of movement; and all these factors are present when movement occurs. For example, the swimmer may move rapidly (time) through the water in a forward direction (space) by propelling himself with strong (force) arm and leg movements.   If a ball is struck on its underside with a hard blow (force), it moves upward (space) with great speed (time).   Space dimensions may be thought of as forward, backward, sideward, downward, and upward.

When time is thought of in terms of velocity and acceleration, it is possible to measure the speed of motion.   For example, if a man runs 200 feet in 10 seconds, it means that he runs an average rate of 20 feet per second. This rate of speed is his velocity.   The man, however, does not run a uniform rate of 20 feet per second.   Some seconds he runs farther than 20 feet and some seconds he runs less than 20 feet; that is, he accelerates positively and negatively.   This rate of change is his acceleration.   If at the fifth second he is running 20 feet per second and at the seventh second he is running 30 feet per second, his rate of acceleration is a positive 5 feet per second.

An object falling freely through space accelerates uniformly because of gravity.   The standard value for this acceleration is 32 feet per second/per second.   That is, at the end of the first second the object is falling at a rate of 32 feet per second, at the end of the second second it is falling 64 feet per second, the third second, 96 feet and so on.   Thus, an object that falls for 9 seconds is traveling at the rate of 288 feet per second just before it stops.   The average speed would be half the sum of the speed at the beginning and end of the fall (0 + 288 ÷ 2), or 144 feet per second.   The distance of the fall would be the average speed (144 ft. per second) times the number of seconds traveled (9), or 1296 feet.

It is possible to use these calculations for solid objects falling medium distances.   For great distances, height and air resistance may complicate computation; and airborne objects such as feathers, balloons, and parachutes may not accelerate uniformly because of air resistance.

Newton's Laws of Motion

We are bound by Newton's laws of motion whether we are in a static or dynamic condition.   Newton's first law states that objects at rest will remain at rest until acted on by an outside force; further, objects in uniform motion will continue in the same direction and at the same rate until acted upon by an external force.   This law has been called the law of inertia, and its effect can be illustrated during any ballistic movement.

A ballistic movement is one in which a limb moves faster than the muscle is contracting. During walking, for example, as the center of mass is displaced forward, the rear leg is swung forward.   The hip flexor muscles initiate this swinging; but once the movement is started, the leg swing becomes ballistic.   It continues to swing until it is slowed down by the hip extensors. Additional forces that effect such slowing are gravity during the upward pendulum swing of the leg, air resistance, and any friction occurring as the foot drags on the surface. If it were not for the application of force to slow the leg down at an appropriate time, the leg would swing too far, and a clumsy gait would result. Automobile seat belts are used to overcome the effect of this law as it operates when brakes are applied for a sudden stop. The automobile stops, but the body tends to continue to move forward.

Newton's second law states that an object, when acted upon by an external force, will experience a change in speed that will be proportional to the force applied and inversely proportional to the object's mass. This means that for a given object, application of greater force will result in greater speed. If the same amount of force is applied to two objects of different mass, the object with the smaller mass will move faster.

Newton's third law states that for every action there is an equal and opposite reaction. This can be seen when a surfer paddles his surfboard across the water. As he pulls the water back past his body, the board moves forward on the water. The more he presses on the water, the faster and farther the board moves.

Motion is of two kinds, rotatory and translatory. Rotatory motion occurs when an object turns around a center or axis; translatory motion occurs when an object moves as a whole from one place to another. For example, when a desk is pushed across the floor, its movement is translatory. If, however, the desk sticks on the floor and falls forward, the movement is rotatory; the axis is at the desk's center of gravity. Movement may be both rotatory and translatory. A person walking has translatory motion of his whole body resulting from the rotatory motion of his legs.

A moving body also develops momentum, which is determined by multiplying the mass by the velocity. Thus, the heavier the body and the greater its rate of speed, the greater the momentum. In ballistic movements such as throwing, striking, batting, and kicking, the movement is started by the muscle, which contracts and then relaxes to permit momentum to continue the movement. When performed with constant muscular contraction, these activities are awkward and unskillful rather than smooth and coordinated. Children learning ballistic skills should be encouraged to swing freely and take advantage of momentum; they thus concentrate on a relaxed movement, rather than on aiming accuracy, until the pattern is established.

Gravity and Movement

The law of gravitation states that any two bodies in the universe attract each other with a force that is directly proportional to their masses and inversely proportional to the square of their distance apart. The great mass of the earth exerts a gravitational force for the objects on it, and is responsible for the weight of the objects. The farther an object is moved from the surface of the earth, the less the earth's gravitational pull, and the less the

object weighs. This accounts for the phenomenon of "weightlessness" experienced by the astronaut. Thus, *weight* is determined by the distance of the object from earth, but its *mass* (amount of matter) remains the same wherever it is. An astronaut's weight may vary, but his mass stays the same unless something is added to or subtracted from it.

Every object has a center of gravity, the "weight center" of the body around which all body parts balance. When various parts of the body change position, as in raising the arms, standing on tip-toe, bending the knees, or leaning to the side, there is a resultant change in the center of gravity. In humans, the center of gravity is located at about the height of the hips when a person is standing erect with arms at the sides.

Let us take a look at some of the problems relating to the forces of gravity as they affect movement. Gravity always exerts force vertically toward the center of the earth, and the line of this force passes through the center of gravity of objects that it affects. Thus we find that the stability of objects on the face of the earth can be improved if: (1) the center of gravity is maintained in the line of gravity perpendicular to the base of support, (2) the base of support is widened, and (3) the center of gravity is brought closer to the base of support. If any one of these conditions is reversed, an unstable attitude occurs and the center of gravity tends to be displaced. When the line of gravitational pull passing through the center of gravity of the body falls outside the base of support, the body will fall. It is for this reason that walking has been called "a series of catastrophes nearly averted." As we take each step, the center of mass of the body is displaced forward until a loss of balance occurs. We then fall forward until the rear leg is swung forward to re-establish the base of support under the center of gravity. The farther the center of gravity is displaced forward, the faster we must adjust the base of support. When we begin running, we tend to lean forward much more for a fast start than we do for a slow start.

Consequently, when a body is in equilibrium it is in a state of balance. When one moves, one is upsetting the equilibrium of the body by changing the body position which, in turn, changes the center of gravity of the body. The control of our centers of gravity is carried on by an extremely sensitive regulatory mechanism that causes muscles to pull, thus applying force to the body levers, which thereupon make the necessary minor adjustments for equilibrium.

Levers of the Body

The lever system in the human body is well adapted to rapid movements, but less suited to movements requiring great power. This can be readily seen if we examine the types of levers present in the body. Of the three basic classes of levers, two are of sufficient relevance to merit discussion here.

The *first-class lever* is a rigid bar, with the force and resistance at the ends and the fulcrum or pivot point somewhere in-between. Inanimate examples of first-class levers are the seesaw, scissors, kitchen tongs. In the body, when the elbow is extended against resistance, the same principle may be observed. The triceps muscle shortens and applies the force, the elbow joint acts as the fulcrum, and the hand pressing against the resistance

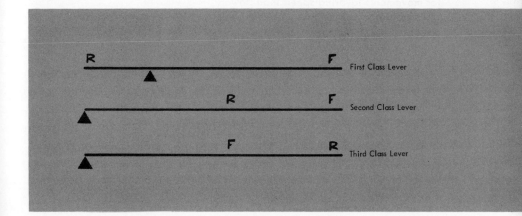

completes the pattern. Body levers are generally adapted for speed, and the point of application of force lies very near the pivot or fulcrum.

Second-class levers, such as the nutcracker or wheelbarrow, have the resistance between the fulcrum and the force. These levers are rare in the body and will not be discussed further.

Third-class levers, such as ice tongs with the axis at one end, have the force between the resistance and the fulcrum, favoring speed and range of motion. A baseball bat or tennis racquet becomes a third-class lever when it is in use, with the fulcrum at the wrist of the batter, the force at the point where the hand contacts the bat, and the resistance at the end of the bat. In the body, the third-class lever can be seen in the case of the biceps muscle during elbow flexion while an object is being lifted from the hip to the shoul-

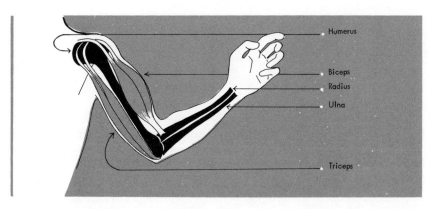

der. The fulcrum is at the elbow joint, the force is applied at the insertion of the biceps on the ulna, and the resistance is supplied by the arm and hand and gravity. Most of the levers of the body are of this type, and have the force application located near the fulcrum. This location is better suited for movements favoring speed than power.

Knowledge of the lever system leads to a better understanding of the complexity of integrated movement patterns. The effective function of the system is dependent upon a sequence of action resulting in a summation of the forces necessary to effect a desired movement.

In addition to being utilized during the application of force, the lever system may operate to absorb force from external objects. For example, an individual catches a heavy ball that has been thrown with some force. As the catch is made, levers operate to diminish the shock of the catch by sequentially reducing the speed of the ball until it comes to rest. If the levers are rigid and locked at the joints (fulcrum), or if force is being generated, the ball will strike with a shock and be difficult to control. If, on the other hand, the smooth reduction takes place from lever to lever, no shock occurs and the ball is easily caught. This is frequently called "giving" with the ball. Small children also find it advantageous to widen their stances, thus enlarging the base of support and increasing stability when catching larger, heavier balls.

During a fall, the shock of the body striking the ground should be spread to the more heavily padded segments of the body in a rolling sequence in order to avoid a sudden application of force to a small area. Many serious accidents could be avoided if individuals knew how to increase the distance and time of the fall. This is accomplished by learning to roll into a fall rather than jarring against the arm, hip, or shoulder. The shock should not be taken by placing a stiff arm out in landing, but by keeping the arms flexed and taking the shock on forearm, upper arm, shoulder, and back in sequence.

Some Guidelines Governing the Mechanics of Movement

Some general applications of the laws of motion, gravitation, and levers are summarized here. These guidelines are applied to specific skills in Chapter 4.

1. When giving impetus to an external object as in striking, throwing, pushing, and so on, the center of mass of the body should be moving in the direction of the goal. Widening the base of support by taking a stride position in the desired direction is one way to achieve this.
2. When receiving impetus from an external object as in catching, recovering from a shove, landing from a jump, and so on, the center of mass moves in the direction of the force and gradually diminishes the force. This is sometimes called giving with the ball, in catching, or landing with "rubber" legs. Lowering the center of gravity and widening the base of support by bending the knees and spreading the feet are also helpful.
3. Stability and balance can be improved when the frictional resistance is increased between the support and the body. Rubber-soled shoes and clean floors, as well as correct body position, are aids to stability. Lowering the center of gravity and widening the base of support also contribute to improved stability and balance.
4. The longer the lever, the greater the speed at the end of the lever. Implements used in sports, such as bats, racquets, hockey sticks, and golf clubs, generally increase the length of the lever in order to extend the reach. As an added benefit, they increase the amount of force that can

be applied to the external object—a circumstance owing to the greater speed at the end of the extended lever.

5. The summation of forces for effective movement is dependent upon a sequential contribution of the various levers. A force contribution occurring either early or late results in dissipation of force at the end of the sequence. For example, let us assume that a child is learning a striking movement. As he begins to shift his weight and swing one arm forward, he hesitates, waiting for the ball. This hesitation causes a reduced summation of forces and reduces the effect of the early contributions. If the hesitation halts the flow of movement even momentarily, then all previous contributions are eliminated.

Let us use batting as another example. The preparatory position is upright, with the bat drawn back, so that the muscles that are ultimately called upon to pull on the bat are put on a stretch. Just before the batter begins to swing the bat, he should start his center of mass moving in the direction of the swing. This also serves to provide for additional stretching of the musculature that ultimately contributes to the summation of forces in the swing. If the transfer of the center of mass is permitted to come to rest before the swing starts, any contribution that the movement could make to the summation of forces is eliminated, and the power of the swing becomes reduced. Thus, the effect of a hesitation or a momentary stop brings about a delay in the ultimate peak of force that could be disastrous if critical timing of peak power was important to the success of the movement. Starting the swing too soon, then slowing it down to correct the timing, also reduces the ultimate power of the swing.

Coordination and agility are terms that are frequently used to refer to timing in the performance of movement skills. Coordination usually refers to the smooth, easy sequence of movement resulting from the well-timed and controlled action of several muscle groups; agility refers to an individual's ability to move his body through various complex maneuvers with ease. Thus, sufficient coordination and agility are necessary to permit the individual to combine various joint movements into such complex patterns as running, jumping, and climbing, with a minimum loss of effectiveness.

The forces that can be summoned by the individual in the performance of a movement skill, therefore, are dependent upon: (1) coordination and agility of the mover; (2) mechanical efficiency of the levers involved, including the angle of pull; and (3) the state of nutrition and number of muscle fibers contributing to the application of force on the force arm of the lever. If the angle between the application of force and the lever arm is greater or smaller than 90 degrees, the result is reduced effectiveness for application of force by the lever.

6. To change the direction of movement of the body, the weight must be shifted to the foot that is away from the given direction of movement. Thus, the child who is standing erect and desires to move rapidly to the

right must first bend both knees slightly. A slight push against the ball of the right foot will shift the center of gravity toward the left foot. As the center of gravity moves over the base of support provided by the left foot, the right foot can be lifted from the ground and the initial step in the new direction can be taken. The more rapid the change, the lower the center of gravity is placed over the base of support. In this example, lowering the center of gravity enables a stronger push-off of the left leg as the new step is being taken.

4 MOVEMENT ANALYSIS OF SELECTED SKILLS

The subject matter of physical education includes the performance of "gross" movement skills, using all or a large part of the body: (1) basic movements, (2) skills of locomotion, and (3) skills of overcoming inertia of external objects.

Growth studies indicate that the child's neuromuscular system must mature before he is able to achieve certain types of movement skills. Before birth, the movements of the fetus lead toward the later development of postures, grasping, and locomotion. These prenatal movements continue through early infancy, and during childhood they eventually develop into many kinds of movement skills. When the child is sufficiently mature, adequate training will help him to improve his performance of the various skills.

Basic Movements of the Body

Bending, stretching, and twisting have been identified as the basic movements of the body. These movements, when combined in various fashions, result in all other patterns of movement.

Bending. Bending implies that two extremes are brought closer together. Bending can occur if one extreme is stabilized such as bending at the waist while standing or hanging, or if both extremes are free, as in the jackknife dive or standing broad jump. It can also occur at a single joint as in elbow flexion, or as the result of a change in the alignment of several joints—touching the toes, for example. Consequently, much of our ability to bend can be attributed to the fact that contracting muscles pull equally from both ends.

Stretching. Stretching occurs when extremes move away from one another. It can occur in circumstances that are the opposite of those described for bending. Thus if one end is stabilized, straightening up from a bent position is stretching. Our ability to stretch is attendant upon the facts that we have muscles on both sides of a joint, and that these muscles can operate smoothly in opposition, one relaxing while the other contracts.

Twisting. Twisting involves joints that have an axis of rotation as an inherent part of the structure. The spine, for example, can be visualized as a stack of bone wheels separated by cartilaginous intervertebral disks. The deep posterior muscles of the spine (divided half on the right and half on the left) have many attachments that can pull on the outside of the wheel causing it to rotate about its axis. The musculature on one side contracts and pulls the wheel to that side as the musculature on the opposite side is stretched. This pulling occurring in sequence results in twisting as each vertebra is rotated in sequence.

Twisting is observed typically when the feet are stationary and the shoulders move clockwise or counterclockwise, as in striking at a ball or throwing a ball. Bending, stretching, and twisting can be executed with great force and speed if necessary. Each also has an opposite movement capability that can be utilized to control the force or speed, and change its direction if desired.

The variety of movements and positions that the human body can assume is contained in the following list,[1] and is related by number to the illustration (see facing page) of the body in the anatomical position.

1. Abduction—movement away from the midline of the body.

2. Adduction—movement toward the midline of the body.

3. Circumduction—movement of a limb in a manner that describes a cone.

4. Depression—downward movement of a part.

5. Dorsiflexion—bending foot upward (flexion of the ankle).

6. Elevation—upward movement of a part.

7. Eversion—movement of the sole of the foot outward.

8. Extension—movement resulting in the increase of a joint.

[1] Gene A. Logan, J. Dunkelberg, G. Egstrom, and G. Gardner, *Student Handbook for Adapted Physical Education* (Dubuque, Iowa: William C. Brown Company, Publishers, 1960), p. 6.

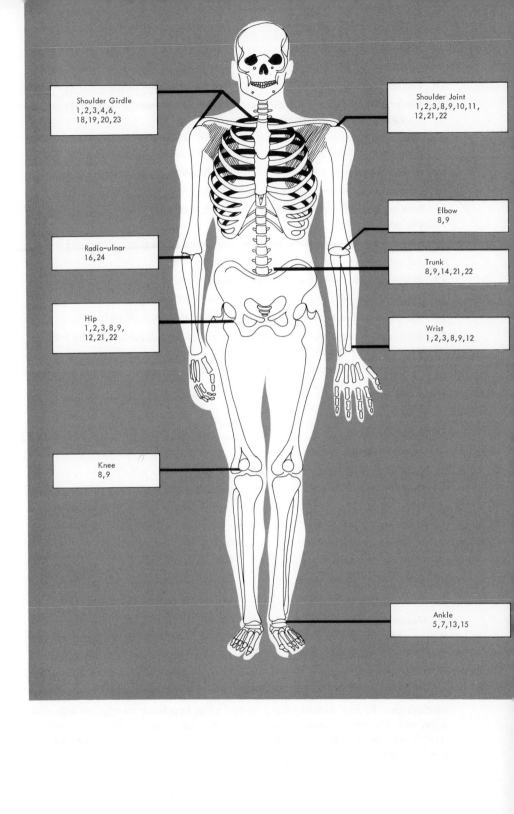

Shoulder Girdle
1,2,3,4,6,
18,19,20,23

Shoulder Joint
1,2,3,8,9,10,11,
12,21,22

Elbow
8,9

Radio-ulnar
16,24

Trunk
8,9,14,21,22

Hip
1,2,3,8,9,
12,21,22

Wrist
1,2,3,8,9,12

Knee
8,9

Ankle
5,7,13,15

9. Flexion—movement resulting in a decrease of a joint angle.

10. Horizontal abduction—movement of the arms from a front horizontal position to a side horizontal position.

11. Horizontal adduction—movement of the arms from a side horizontal position to a front horizontal position.

12. Hyperextension—movement beyond the position of extension.

13. Inversion—movement of the sole of the foot inward.

14. Lateral flexion—movement of the trunk sideways from the midline of the body.

15. Plantar flexion—bending the foot downward (extension of the ankle).

16. Pronation—turning the back of the hand forward.

17. Prone position—lying in a face-down position.

18. Protraction—forward movement of a part (shoulder girdle).

19. Retraction—backward movement of a part (shoulder girdle).

20. Rotation "downward"—rotary movement of the scapula, with the inferior angle moving medially and downward.

21. Rotation medially—movement around the axis of a bone away from the midline of the body.

22. Rotation laterally—movement around the axis of a bone away from the midline of the body.

23. Rotation "upward"—rotary movement of the scapula, with the inferior angle moving laterally and upward.

24. Supination—turning the palm of the hand forward.

25. Supine position—lying in a face-up position.

Skills of Locomotion

Maturation is a prime factor in the acquisition of various forms of locomotion skills. Once an infant is able to lift his head, sit without support, and roll from back to stomach, he may progress to some form of locomotion such as creeping or crawling. From this he rapidly moves to standing, walking with support, and then walking independently. By the age of three, his walking is quite automatic and he is able to run and jump with some degree of confidence. By five years of age, he can skip, hop occasionally, gallop, and slide; and his running and walking are highly developed. From age five or six, his improvement in locomotion is rapid, and he continues to refine already established patterns.

The most common forms of locomotion are walking, running, leaping, jumping, and hopping. Skipping, sliding, and galloping are combinations of some of these common forms. All these locomotion skills are performed on land surfaces. Skills for moving one's body in the air and in suspension, and water skills, are described in Chapters 16 and 19 respectively.

Walking. Walking is the effect of displacing the center of gravity over the base of support. The displacement brings about an increased forward momentum that is like falling. In order to prevent the fall, a leg is swung into position to provide a new stable base of support for the body weight. The degree of displacement of the center of gravity is proportional to the speed of the walk. The greater the displacement, the faster the walk, and the shorter the supporting phase. Swinging one's arms acts as a counterbalancing technique, and prevents undesirable sideward movements.

The summation of forces that occurs during the thrust from the supporting leg is most important as a contributor to forward momentum. Placing the feet straight forward takes advantage of the best functioning of the levers of the foot, ankle, and knee.

Running. When the center of gravity is displaced forward to the degree that the period of double support becomes a period of nonsupport, the individual changes from a walk to a run. This displacement can be observed as increased body lean, and is proportional to speed of running. Excessive bouncing or raising the center of gravity reduces the speed of running. Bending the knees to shorten the length of the limbs, on the other hand, increases the speed with which the legs can move. The elbows should be flexed in order to permit faster arm swings and to eliminate undersirable sideward movements.

When running, an individual who wishes to stop or change direction must slow down until he can achieve sufficient contact with the ground to enable the change of direction to take place. Moving the center of gravity to a position perpendicular or to the rear of the base of support permits a strong placement of the foot, and an increased friction surface. This, in turn, permits the use of the strong knee extensors in a lengthening contraction for deceleration. If the center of gravity is moved too far to the rear, the angle of foot placement permits slipping, and a sliding fall occurs. This effect is particularly observable on blacktop in the vicinity of sand or gravel.

Leaping. Leaping is similar to running in that the weight is transferred from one foot to the other; both movements are also characterized by a period of nonsupport. The leap, however, is performed with greater height and distance than the run. The arm swing is more forceful than it is in the run, to raise the body high in the air during the period of nonsupport.

Jumping. A jump occurs when the center of gravity is displaced vertically, or with a strong vertical component added to a horizontal displacement. Once the individual has left the ground, the path of the center of gravity is predictable and cannot be altered in flight unless acted upon by an outside force.

During the preparation for a jump, one's position should be such that the application of force by the muscles can be carried through an extended range of motion. The longer the time that force can be applied, the higher or farther the jump. The summation of forces should occur so that there is additive effect from the hip extensors, knee extensors, plantar (foot) flexors, and the flexors of the toes, especially the great toe. The arms should also be swung forcibly forward and upward to aid in height and distance.

It is important to recognize that, during the summation of forces, any slowing down or momentary stopping that destroys the linearity of the force relationship results in a shorter jump. "Hitches" in stride or in the actual jumping sequence can often be detected by careful observation. Young children, for example, frequently run too far before jumping for maximum distance. They start off sprinting, achieve their top speed, but are unable to sustain this speed to the take-off mark. As they slow down, their momentum is sacrificed and cannot be used to increase the distance of the jump.

Hopping. Hopping is executed in the standing position, with the weight centered upon one foot and the arms spread slightly for better balance. The center of gravity is displaced forward by a slight lean, and the weight-bearing foot pushes off as the body extends in a jump. As the body is airborne, the weight-bearing foot is swung forward to a position ahead of the center of gravity, and the weight is once again caught. The knee flexes to help absorb the shock and the center of gravity passes over the base of support. This makes a repetition of the extension of the body into another hop necessary. Learning to hop forward with one leg is easier if the child learns to throw both arms forward and upward as the body extends. The longer the hop, the farther forward the center of gravity must be displaced. Short hops, usually performed for height, generally require that the center of gravity be displaced vertically rather than horizontally.

Skipping, Sliding, Galloping. Skipping, sliding, and galloping are characterized by an uneven beat performed in a long-short pattern. Skipping is a combination of a step and a hop, performed as a long step and a short hop, and alternating feet after each step-hop. Sliding is a combination of two sideward steps, the opening step long and the closing step short; it is performed without alternating sides. Galloping is a combination of a step and a leap, performed as a long step and a short leap. It does not alternate sides, and the stepping leg is always in the lead. It may be performed forward, backward, or to the side.

Skills of Overcoming Inertia of External Objects

The skills of overcoming inertia of external objects include pushing and pulling, throwing, kicking, striking, batting, catching, and blocking.   These skills are used in many of the sports activities in contemporary United States. The elementary-age child is eager to acquire competence in these skill areas, which are high in cultural value.   This is particularly true of boys who may look forward to becoming varsity athletes in high school or college.

During the elementary school years, children demonstrate steady growth in the acquisition of gross motor skills, with the greatest improvement occurring "between the ninth and twelfth years."[2]   This is evidenced by their participation in many of the so-called big muscle activities, including running, jumping, swimming, throwing, catching, kicking, climbing, pushing, and the like.   Boys generally are superior to girls in throwing, kicking, striking, jumping, and running;[3] girls tend to excel boys in dancing, fancy skating, and other activities involving eye-hand coordination and balance.[4]   It is probable that these sex differences are at least partially due to social-cultural factors.

Pushing.   Pushing typically results when the force of the body is exerted against the hands which, in turn, are moving an object in a direction away from the body.   Light objects can be pushed by extending the arms while using an erect posture as the resistance.   Pushing a ball away from the body is a familiar example.

Heavier objects can be pushed more easily if the body leans in the direction of the push, and the base of support is widened.   The center of gravity of the pusher is displaced toward the object being pushed, and the stronger leg muscles can be used.   If the object is pushed at its center of gravity, all the force will be exerted toward moving the object in translatory motion, that is, moving it as a whole across the surface.   When the force is applied elsewhere than at the object's center of gravity, some of the force is dissipated in rotatory motion, with the object tending to rotate around its center of gravity.

Pulling.   Pulling generally requires that the hands grasp an object, and that the arms generate force between the object and the body in order to

---

[2] Frieda K. Merry and R. V. Merry, *The First Two Decades of Life* (New York: Harper & Row, Publishers, 1950), p. 162.

[3] Marjorie Latchaw, "Measuring Selected Motor Skills in Fourth, Fifth, and Sixth Grades," *The Research Quarterly*, American Association for Health, Physical Education and Recreation, XXV, No. 4 (December, 1954), 439–49.

[4] Frieda K. Merry and R. V. Merry, *op. cit.*, p. 163.

bring the two closer together. If the object to be pulled is heavy, the base of support of the puller is widened in order to provide a firm base for greater increments of force. Very heavy objects can be pulled more economically if the center of gravity of the puller is displaced beyond his base of support in the direction in which the individual is pulling.

For example, a boy pulling a kite can use a narrow base of support with his feet close together, and he can hold his body erect as he pulls. When pulling a loaded wagon, however, he may find it necessary to widen his base by spreading his feet apart, and to lower his center of gravity by bending his knees. If he is pulling a heavily loaded wagon, he widens his base still more, and displaces his center of gravity lower and forward, leaning in the direction of movement. Thus the body weight can be used as an anchor whose effective resistance changes as the base of support is widened, or the center of gravity lowered. When this occurs, the force for pulling is generated by the more powerful leg muscles; the arms are straight.

The strongest muscles available should be used for pulling, in order to reduce the strain on joints and ligaments. This is particularly true when the inertia of the object being pulled must first be overcome. Once the object is moving, and momentum begins to take over, less force will be necessary to keep it moving. Whenever possible, the pull should be in the direction of the desired movement. For example, in pulling a wagon, force should be exerted in a forward rather than an upward direction insofar as it is possible. This may be accomplished with relative economy by lengthening the tongue of the wagon and lowering the center of gravity of the puller.

Throwing.   Throwing an object is applying muscular force to develop momentum that can be transferred to an external object. For example, a thrown ball attains the speed of the hand and, when released, will continue in the direction of the application of force, tangent to the arc where released, until gravity or another external force alters its path. The longer the sequential development of force can be applied to the ball before its release, the farther and faster it will travel.

In a typical throwing pattern, the generation of force is preceded by a backswing that places future contributing muscles on a stretch. The forward momentum in the desired direction of the throw is begun when a step is taken with the foot away from the ball. This step causes the center of gravity to begin to move in the direction of the throw. Pushing off the back foot, and rotation of the trunk, then make their contributions, continuing to stretch the muscles across the body diagonally up to the shoulder. The elbow is then pulled forward, preceding the ball; and the final forces are added by a strong extension of the elbow, and flexion of the wrist and fingers just prior to the release. The faster the hand is moving at this point, the faster the ball will travel.

It is sometimes helpful to think of the arm as a "whip" pulling on the ball. This will insure getting the elbow in front of the ball so that the tendency to push on the ball is eliminated.

The underhand throw differs only in that the ball is held closer to the body, with a straight arm that swings like a pendulum.

Kicking. This skill is widely used in many activities, and consists of basically two types of kicks: (1) place-kicking, or kicking the ball from the ground; and (2) punting, or kicking the ball before it strikes the ground.

Kicking a ball on the ground begins when the kicker is approximately one full step from the ball. The nonkicking foot is placed near the ball so that the kicking foot is in line with the ball. The placement of the non-kicking foot will help to determine whether the ball will be kicked along the ground or up in the air. For example, the foot placement in A (see illustration) will result in a ground ball, since the kicking foot will strike the ball

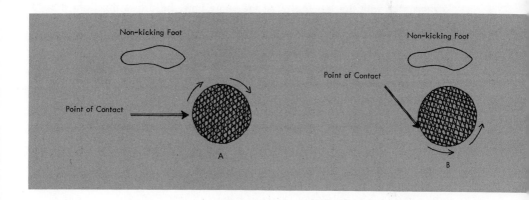

above the center of mass and cause the ball to attain top spin. The foot placement in B will result in an air flight, since the toe must strike under the center of mass of the ball, causing a reverse spin to occur as the ball rises. Notice that balance is maintained by slight flexion of the knee of the nonkicking leg, and the weight shift is followed by a slight backward lean. This lean permits additional tension to be exerted by the muscles on the front of the thigh. Strong knee extension results in a forceful kick. During the kick, the eyes are kept on the ball until it is kicked. The follow-through is accomplished with a recovery of balance.

In the punt, the ball is held in front of the body during the preparatory moves. In this sequence, the weight is shifted to the kicking leg, and the body leans so that a preliminary step with the nonkicking leg will start the body moving in the direction of the intended kick. During the step, the ball is raised to shoulder height or slightly lower, and released in line with the kicking leg. This release should be a smooth drop, not a toss. The nonkicking foot is then planted, and the kicking leg is extended and swung forcefully into the ball as the body leans away from the ball. The ball is contacted with the top of the foot, not the toe. The follow-through utilizes the returning of the kicking leg to the ground as the counterbalance for shifting the upper body back to a position over the base of support. The timing of this sequence is critical—a ball dropped too late will be kicked high, and a ball dropped too early will be kicked low, into the ground.

Striking. Striking a ball with the hand is an extension of throwing. This skill is widely used in various handball games, and in the host of "sock-ball" and volleyball games.

Striking may be initiated with a toss up to self, or a ball may be pitched to the striker by another person. When a toss-up is used by a right-handed player, the ball is lifted parallel to the body with the left hand and tossed about 18 inches above the head, slightly in front of the left shoulder. During the toss-up, the striker shifts his weight in the direction of the hit by taking a short step with the left foot. At the same time, he draws the right arm to the rear and draws the fist to a point behind his head. As the ball drops to about shoulder height, the summation of forces to strike the ball begins. The shifting of weight forward and the withdrawal of the right arm have put the body in an extended position, with the trunk rotated to the right. Because of the visual cues used to time the movements, the eyes must be kept on the ball until it is struck. When the ball is dropping to the point of contact between the shoulders and hips, the trunk is rotated hard to the left and the shoulders come around until they have rotated approximately 90 degrees, with the right elbow leading the fist as in a throwing motion, until the ball is struck with the heel of the hand that has made the fist. The heel of the hand should contact the ball at a point behind the center of mass. Changes in direction and height of flight are made by striking slightly to the right or left, and above or below the center of mass.

The follow-through permits the force of the movement to be absorbed by the extensors of the left knee and the rotators of the trunk. The recovery of balance is important, particularly if the child is expected to run immediately following the striking movement.

Except for the elimination of the toss-up the preparation for striking a pitched ball is the same, and the same mechanics apply for the contact and follow-through. Striking a ball from an underhand position differs in that the ball is held in the left hand for the right-handed striker; the right arm is swung back and then forward, close to the body, and the ball is contacted with the heel of the right hand. The shifting of weight and summation of forces are the same for striking the ball overhand or underhand.

Batting. Batting is another form of striking. In this skill a bat is used to extend the arms and to permit a greater range of movement and, consequently, a greater application of force.

The right-handed batter stands with his left side to the pitcher, head turned so that he can see the pitch. The weight is balanced over both feet. The bat is gripped with hands together, the right hand on top and closer to the heavy end of the bat, and the bat is drawn back in readiness for the swing. As the ball is pitched, the batter steps toward the ball with the left foot and begins the weight shift. As the ball comes nearer, the trunk rotates to the left, followed by the shoulders. This permits the bat to be pulled around in an arc. This arc must be coordinated so that the heavy part of the bat comes in contact with the ball in front of the body. The eyes remain on the ball until it is contacted by the bat.

Good batting technique requires that the bat be swung in an arc parallel to the ground. This can be done if the left elbow is kept approximately at shoulder height, and the end of the bat is slightly higher, until the ball is contacted. Dropping the left elbow often results in a golf-type swing; letting the heavy end of the bat get too low results in a similar pattern. The weight of the bat should be such that the batter can easily hold it parallel to the ground with his arms extended. If the bat droops, moving the grip toward the heavy end will allow the child to hold the bat easily.

Catching. Catching a moving object entails the ability to coordinate the act of receiving impetus from the moving object. The object must be gradually slowed until it can be grasped.

As the object approaches the catcher, he reaches toward it, keeping the elbows and knees slightly bent. The knees will bend more if a heavier or larger object is to be caught. The body must be in a position to permit body levers to move with the object as force is being applied to slow it down. The object should not be allowed to strike the hands when the arms are extended and elbows locked. A ball will strike the heels of the hands, and almost invariably rebound away from the grasp.

The catcher watches the object approach his hands, and usually begins moving his hands in the direction of the object's movement just as contact is made. If the object is light, the force can be absorbed in the hands and arms. Heavier or larger objects require the involvement of larger body segments such as shoulders, back, and legs. Beginners should be encouraged to catch with both hands, since the grasping action is more positive and the area for catching is enlarged.

Blocking. The skill of blocking involves the same principles used in catching. If the object to be stopped is large, it may be contacted with the shoulders or back, with knees bent and feet spread for stability. The body moves with the object, thus slowing it down gradually.

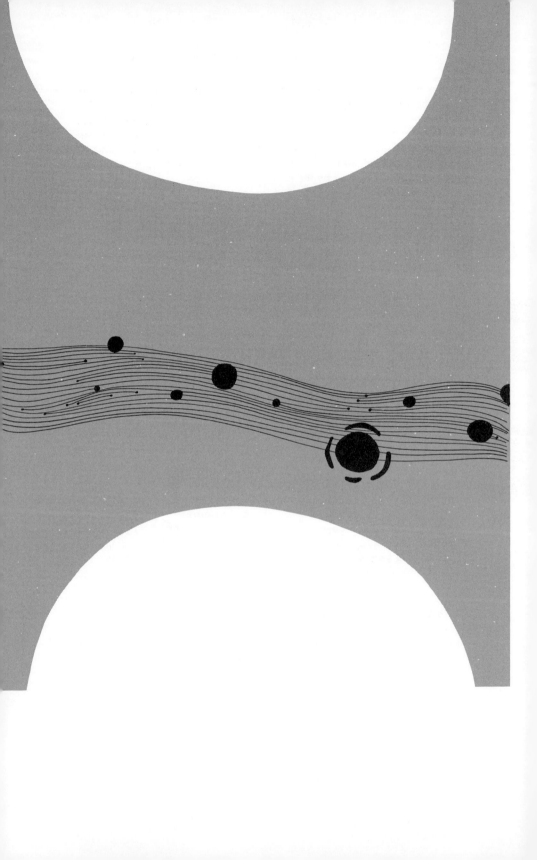

5 MOVEMENT EXPRESSION

The child moves to control his environment in order to fulfill his needs and desires. He lifts a ball and bounces it on the ground. He climbs on a bar and hangs by his knees. He pulls an orange from a tree, throws rocks in the water, forms a circle with others and skips, lifts a cup to his mouth and drinks, pedals a bicycle, pulls a wagon.

The child's purposes are easily perceived when he moves in relation to an observable object. If he lifts a cup and drinks the water, his purpose is to obtain the water in the cup. He may then drop the cup, run in larger and larger circles, flinging his arms outward, moving his head forward and backward. These movements may communicate ideas and impressions to an onlooker which he interprets in relation to his own unique experiences and meanings. This interpretation may or may not parallel the child's meanings as he moves. The observer may say, "He is a horse, running in a corral, shaking his head and snorting at the other horses." The child may be thinking, I am a drop of water fallen into the lake, making greater and greater circles in the lake, which is rippling in the wind.

A child's movements may be random, or they may be purposeful expressions of an idea or a feeling.

Definition of Movement Expression

Each individual has movements that are uniquely his own, movements that characterize his unique self-organization. These movements are nonverbal expressions of his feelings, his thoughts, his ideas. They are symbolic of ideas in the same sense that language, whether verbal expression or written symbols, is symbolic of ideas and meanings.

Gordon Allport defines expressive movement as "one's manner of performing adaptive acts. . . ." and goes on to describe every act as both expressive and adaptive (coping) to different degrees, with varying proportions of one quality or the other.[1] He further states that, in our contemporary technological society, many occupations require a high proportion of coping and a low degree of individual style or expression, as compared with the trades of artisans and cabinetmakers, dressmakers and silversmiths of former days.

This observation holds true, even in contemporary physical education programs in the United States. The movement opportunities are predetermined and are described in a "course of study," with specific activities (usually games prescribed by the culture) for each grade level. These activities include variations on basketball, softball, volleyball, and football, various stunts that must be done exactly as described or they are performed poorly, and singing games or folk dances that must be performed exactly as described or they are not "authentic"; even individual skills of throwing, kicking, and the like must be performed in "good form" for the highest level of mechanical efficiency. In many schools, unfortunately one would be hard-pressed to find any portion of a movement program that encourages individual expression.

Movement expression may be purposeful and controlled, or it may be uncontrolled.[2] Uncontrolled movement may include: (1) autistic gestures such as a sudden jerk of the arms, a twitching nose, and other mannerisms; (2) expression of feelings as displayed in a temper tantrum with flinging of arms, stamping of feet, kicking or striking, and the like; (3) unique expressive behavior as evidenced by movement style in use of time-space, such as free-flowing, rhythmic, rigid, jerky, fast, deliberate, or careless; (4) spontaneous movement below the level of awareness, caused by habitual use of the same musculature to the extent that it has come to reflect and characterize the unique personal structure of the individual.

Controlled expressive movement includes: (1) gesture for the purpose of communication, as in waving the hand to indicate "hello" or "goodbye," raising the hand with palm away from the body to signal "stop"; (2) expressive form, as exemplified in dance as an art form; (3) purposeful movement to express feelings, solve problems, or cope with the environment.

Uncontrolled self-expression as exhibited in a typical temper tantrum, expressions of fear, joy, and the like, may be observed much more readily in the child than in the adult, who has been acculturated to control his ex-

[1] Gordon W. Allport, *Pattern and Growth in Personality* (New York: Holt, Rinehart and Winston, 1961), pp. 462ff.

[2] Modified from ideas presented by Camille Brown and Rosalind Cassidy, *Theory in Physical Education* (Philadelphia: Lea & Febiger, 1963), pp. 71–3.

pression of emotion.   Autistic movements observed in gait, posture, facial expression, gesture, and speech are difficult to modify or control, however, since they are usually below the level of awareness.

Growth and Development

The newborn's movement is random, highly generalized, and usually motivated by gastrointestinal disturbances.[3]   The infant is capable of moving many body segments at the same time, although the movement is generally aimless and nonspecific.   This movement behavior may result from hunger, pain, cold, discomfort, or it may be reflex behavior, like that occurring in the grasp reflex when the hand is stimulated.   Such movement may be expressive in that the infant is responding to stimulation, but meaning is not attached to the stimuli until he is more mature.

The earliest expression of anger appears at about the tenth month, and consists of a typical temper tantrum with screaming, crying, kicking, and the like.   Emotional expression through movement helps the young child to reduce frustration through satisfying activity.   Ausubel believes that movement expression also reflects the personality of the child, his "venturesomeness, energy level, aggressiveness, sociality, and self-confidence. . . ."[4]

Before children use language, even though they can comprehend adult speech, they frequently use gesture as a form of nonverbal communication. As the child's motor mechanism matures, he uses movement for coping with the environment in addition to self-expression and communication.

The elementary school years of the child's life are movement oriented. At this age he is learning to use his body more effectively in performing movement tasks.   He is exploring and experimenting as he solves his movement problems.   He is developing characteristic movement patterns, distinctive and expressive, unique to him.

Movement Expression and Creativity

Any type of creative expression has long been synonymous with the arts. In the United States today, we tend to attribute creativity to the geniuses who produce great works of sculpture, painting, music, and poetry.   We for-

[3] David P. Ausubel, *Theory and Problems of Child Development* (New York: Grune & Stratton, 1958), pp. 205–15.
[4] *Ibid.*, p. 509.

get that the capacity for creative expression belongs to many of us, although all our inventions may not be artistic. The criteria used to judge movement expression as an art form differ from those applied to creative movement. Movement expression may or may not be art, although art is both expressive and creative.

Stoddard makes the following statement in a brilliant plea for creativity in contemporary education: "The urge to inquire, to invent, to perform, was stifled in millions of school children, now grown up, who did not get above rote learning, or at least did not stay above it. Their final culture pattern is all about us. . . . Conformity rules, not because people crave it, but because they fear deviation. . . ."[5]

The desire to inquire, to invent may be an impelling force in childhood for which the movement medium makes possible a natural outlet for creative expression. The child's imaginative impulses stimulate new movement experiences as he tries to express symbolically the pictures in his mind. Left to his own devices, he uses his body to communicate his thoughts and feelings. He may express what he sees or feels by creating a dance, a game to play with friends, or a new way of moving from one point to another.

This desire for creativity, for expressing the self by using many movement possibilities, should be fostered in elementary school physical education programs. The first provision for such a program is the establishment of an atmosphere where individualism, unpredictable behavior, curiosity, willingness to attempt the unknown, sensitivity, and even divergency are nurtured and respected.

Second, imagination should be encouraged, and allowed to move freely wherever it may go. A creative environment, rich with a variety of objects, spaces, and accompanying hosts of sensory stimuli, may help to awaken imagery that can be translated into movement.

Finally, value judgments should not be placed upon the creative process, the created object or product, or the creator. Labels such as artistic, ordinary, creative, imitative, good, bad, and mediocre, tend to stifle original behavior and lead toward conformity.

Children vary in their abilities to move freely and independently. Some may need assistance and reassurance from the teacher in coming to understand and accept the movement stimuli. Many children move fearfully, timidly, self-consciously, having already established the habit of looking for approval from others, or imitating others.

Chapter 13, *Movement Exploration,* cites activities that may serve as sources of stimuli for creative and expressive movement.

Guidelines and specific criteria that may be used by the teacher in providing an environment to nurture creative movement expression in the child are suggested as follows.

[5] George D. Stoddard, "Creativity in Education," in *Creativity and Its Cultivation,* ed. H. H. Anderson (New York: Harper & Row, Publishers, 1959), p. 181.

Guidelines	Criteria
1. The child should be free to explore without fear of censure.	1. Does the child move freely and confidently? 2. Does the child try patterns of his own making? 3. Does the teacher encourage diversity rather than conformity? 4. Is the teacher accepting? 5. Does the teacher encourage idiosyncratic expression?
2. The environment should stimulate the imagination.	1. Are many different types of objects available to the child? 2. Is the child encouraged to use objects in many different ways? 3. Is the child encouraged to use large, small, and variant spaces in many ways? 4. Are many sensory stimuli available? (See Chapter 6, *Sensation and Movement*, and Chapter 13, for use of sensory stimuli.)
3. Evaluation should be internal.	1. Does the child have adequate time to explore and develop new movements? 2. Is the child allowed to move without harassment? 3. Does the child have an opportunity to think about his movement experience? 4. Does the teacher avoid placing a label on the child's movement expression?

6 SENSATION AND MOVEMENT

Each individual lives in a private world of his own, his perceptual world. His world differs from other worlds because of his highly individualized sensory mechanisms, his particular sensory experiences, his emotions, feelings, aspirations, desires, and fulfilled and unfulfilled needs.

Although each sensory mechanism has a distinctive character, the stimulation of one sensory modality may produce sensation in other sensory modalities—hearing a certain sound, for example, may produce visual imagery. This interaction of the sensory mechanisms, *synesthesia,* helps the individual to construct a cohesive, orderly picture of his environment. The individual behaves as he does because of his world as he perceives it. He attaches meaning to sensory stimuli according to the organized perceptions he has acquired through previous experiences. His actions are determined by his own unique motives as he strives toward attainment of the human goals of survival and enrichment.

The perceived world, however, may differ from the real world. For example, perceptual time may not be actual time as measured by the clock. Time, to the child waiting while the interminable minutes of December move toward Christmas morning, may seem an eternity; yet, how rapidly the same twenty-four days seem to pass when he is vacationing with friends.

The individual's senses are his only source of communication with the outside world. He uses them to help him attain his survival needs of food, sleep, temperature regulation, safety, air, and liquids, and to attain his enrichment needs of creativity and creation, success and recognition, affection and belonging, realization of potentialities.

Definition of Sensation

Sensation is a feeling or experience produced by stimulating the sensory receptors of the visual, auditory, gustatory, olfactory, and somesthetic sense organs. Hebb further describes this as the "sum total of processes resulting from stimulation of the sense organ and remaining directly under its control. . . ."[1] When meaning is attached to the stimulus in preparation for a response, this phenomenon is termed *perception*. It is generally agreed that a sense receptor must be stimulated for perception to occur, and that perceiving requires time and investigation unless the object perceived is very familiar.

For example, one may awaken at night and hear a strange sound, a sensation caused by stimulation of the sensory receptors of the ear. In an effort to identify the sound, one may cock the head, hold his breath, and lie very quietly to eliminate other sounds. When the process of attaining the perception is complete, the response may be overt activity such as diving under the bed or screaming, or it may be simply the acquisition of knowledge about the situation.

Growth and Development

Environmental stimuli for producing rich sensory stimulation in infancy and early childhood provide the foundation for future sensory development. Hebb hypothesizes that, in the first few months of infancy, neural connections are made that influence the sense modalities. In the absence of appropriate stimulation, these basic connections may be retarded, or may never be established at all, resulting in slowed development of other perceptual functions.[2] Summarizing studies of infants reared in institutions, McCandless concludes that such studies strongly suggest the interference with intellectual and emotional development of the babies, which may be owing to a meager sensory environment.[3]

Sensation develops through the maturation of the sensory mechanisms in the presence of a wide variety of environmental stimuli. In the development of the sense modalities, the infant reacts massively to strong stimuli with

[1] D. O. Hebb, *A Textbook of Psychology* (Philadelphia: W. B. Saunders Co., 1958), p. 179 and pp. 180ff.

[2] ———, *Organization of Behavior: A Neuropsychological Theory* (New York: Science Editions, Inc., 1961).

[3] Boyd R. McCandless, *Children and Adolescents: Behavior and Development* (New York: Holt, Rinehart and Winston, 1961).

increasingly finer discriminations occurring as he matures. Sensory deprivation in infancy may retard the development of learning processes dependent upon perception, and much of the so-called higher behavior is based on the learning processes derived from early experiences.

When classifying the sense receptors of the body, we usually think of the "five senses" of sight, sound, smell, taste, and touch. The skin senses of touch, pressure, pain, and temperature, and the proprioceptive sensations (*kinesthesis*) are frequently combined under the somesthetic or body sense.

Vision. In normal adult vision, images formed on the retina of the eye and transmitted to the brain are perceived in color with varying degrees of intensity. Differences in brightness are discriminated, as are variations in size and shape. The adult is able to judge distance and distortion of images with relative accuracy.

In contrast, the infant at birth appears to see only dimly, showing little or no reaction to what he sees. This may be due to poor adaptation of the eye for distance vision. A baby two or three days old can fixate on a light with both eyes, but he does not coordinate well enough to follow it, and his field of vision seems to be limited to a few feet directly in front of him.

By six weeks the infant is responding to color, fixating longer on reds and yellows than on blues and greens, and by ten weeks of age the baby can follow a moving stimulus. By six months, he is able to react to many visual stimuli. The increasing maturity of his sense organs, with the accompanying variety of experiences, results in increased visual perception, and learning becomes intensified. He can differentiate between mother and others, between familiar and unfamiliar, and between approval and disapproval. He begins to coordinate visual perception with attempts to control his environment, reaching for things he sees, responding with pleasure to favorite objects, and withdrawing from strange situations.

It would appear, therefore, that certain visual reflexes are present at birth, but that vision is not really functional for the infant until he is roughly six weeks of age, from which time there is rapid growth in visual acuity. In the development of manipulation, the ability to focus on objects precedes the grasping attempt, success in manipulation being dependent upon satisfactory hand-eye coordination.

Hearing. The adult's auditory mechanism makes it possible for him to distinguish low and high sounds of varying intensities, qualities, and durations. The ear is less sensitive at lower frequencies than at high frequencies, but hearing in the high-frequency range steadily decreases with the aging process. The insensitivity of the ear to the lower frequencies prevents the individual from being disturbed by noises from body movements, muscle action, and other vibrations produced by walking, jumping, and the like.[4]

[4] Georg von Bekesy, "The Ear," *Scientific American* (August, 1957).

The infant is quite insensitive to all except loud or sharp sounds until about the fourth week, when he shows some reaction to the human voice. At about the twentieth week, he seems to be able to localize a sound; and by the time he is six months old, he is able to react to many sounds, even attempting to mimic occasional sounds that he hears. As with vision, his auditory responses improve steadily with maturation, and he attempts to integrate audition with other sensory stimuli.

Smell and Taste.   Smell and taste are so closely related that it is difficult to measure the sense of either in isolation from the other. In the normal adult, these senses are less used than the other senses and are relatively undeveloped, particularly in comparison to many animals who rely on them for survival.

The sensory apparatus for smell is placed high in the nasal passages; that of taste is located on the tongue, soft palate, epiglottis, and opening of the gullet. Our perception of flavor is dependent upon both the taste and smell receptors. A trained nose can detect many odors instantly and can even analyze complex mixtures of odors.

Classifying the tremendous variety of odors has been attempted at various times. A commonly described classification suggested in 1945 reduced odors to four classes corresponding to four receptors: (1) sweet; (2) sour; (3) burnt; (4) goaty. Any odor can be described by a formula that indicates each class on a scale of 1 to 8. For example, if an odor is described as 2744, it would indicate that the odor has a little of the sweet component, is strongly sour, and has some burnt and goaty components.[5]

Taste sensations are usually classified as bitter, sour, salt, and sweet, with some areas of the tongue more sensitive to certain tastes than others. The bitter sensations are located at the back of the tongue, sour toward the center and edges of the tongue. Salt and sweet receptors are at the tip and edges of the tongue.

The sense of smell is generally nonfunctional in the newborn infant, although there may be some reaction to very penetrating odors. Taste sensations appear to be present in infants. Babies prefer sweet, then sour stimuli; they avoid bitter compounds. With increasing maturation of the taste and smell organs, the baby progresses in his ability to discriminate among greater varieties of olfactory and gustatory stimuli. It is interesting that smell has cultural implications—adults in our culture, for instance, react positively to fresh, fragrant odors and negatively to pungent, goaty odors. McCandless states that these responses may be due to training in childhood; in any event, by adulthood they appear to be very resistant to change.[6]

The human adult, then, uses the senses of smell and taste less frequently than he uses the sight and sound senses. Although these two senses have

[5] Ernest C. Crocker, *Flavor* (New York: McGraw-Hill Book Company, Inc., 1945).
[6] McCandless, *op. cit.*, p. 22.

relatively less value to us than other senses, they appear to have considerable influence on our behavior. Our perceptions may be extended appreciably through response to the hosts of different olfactory and gustatory stimuli available to us.

Touch. Touch, like smell and taste, is rarely used by the human for survival. Many animals depend on touch in obtaining food, avoiding capture, and learning about their surroundings. In the human, however, the sense of touch is capable of extreme refinement, with different parts of the body having different degrees of sensitivity. Blind or deaf people often develop the tactile sense to a remarkable degree as a substitute for vision and hearing, using both pressure and vibration to inform them of the world about them.

Tactile sensitivity appears to be present in infants, and follows the cephalo-caudal course of development, beginning with the head and moving downward. The Babinski response, fanning or extension of the toes, may be produced in the newborn by stimulating the sole of the foot. By the sixth month, such stimulation produces a flexion or curling of the toes, and most other touch sensations are reasonably refined.

Discussions relating to child-rearing frequently include the roles of touch and tactile contact in the emotional development of the child. It has been suggested that the baby should be fondled and caressed, and that even the contact of rough play without injury will assist the child in developing a warm, friendly self.

Thermesthesia. Thermesthesia, or temperature perception, occurs through the skin senses; these include both heat and cold receptors, with the hypothalamus of the brain acting as a temperature regulator in the body. Heat receptors are more active in the bend of the elbow, and cold receptors in the upper lip, chin, chest, and forehead. Both heat and cold receptors are numerous in the skin of the nose and the finger tips. The skin temperature of the human averages around 81 degrees Fahrenheit (physiologic zero), and the body temperature ranges between 96 and 99 degrees.

A body immersed in cold or hot water gradually becomes accustomed to the temperature; that is, the water no longer feels so cold or hot as sensitivity to the initial change of temperature becomes dulled. After contact with cold or hot, several minutes are required for the skin to return to physiologic zero.

Infants show response to temperature changes from birth, but their ability to adjust to thermal extremes is relatively ineffective as compared to that of adults and older children.

Pain. The perception of pain is caused by the injury to the nerve receptors, modified by the personal experiences, anticipations, and cultural expectations and fears of the individual. The same stimulus may cause intense pain in one individual and little pain in another; or the same individual may react with different degrees of intensity to the same stimulus administered under different conditions. The meaning attached to the pain-producing stimulus, the emotional state of the individual, and other circumstances coloring the incident are powerful factors in determining the perception of the painful experience.

The baby at birth appears to be relatively insensitive to pain, but responses to various painful stimuli are acquired rapidly. McCandless states that by the age of six months, a baby's response to pain seems to depend very much on the handling he has received from adults; and a relatively relaxed parent is less apt to have a hyperreactive child.[7] This point of view agrees with studies cited by Melzack in which early environment appears to be a significant modality affecting the response in animals to pain-producing stimuli.[8]

Kinesthesis. Kinesthesis is the term used to describe the perception of body position, produced by stimulation of the proprioceptors or sense organs in the muscles, tendons, and joints. It is this "muscle sense" that makes an individual aware of his position when sitting, standing, lying, bending, or stretching his body or its parts. Kinesthesis helps him to know up and down, forward and backward. It helps him to adjust his position to maintain balance by rearranging muscle tensions. In addition to the kinesthetic sense, balance is affected by the vestibular apparatus of the inner ear, and by visual cues. Individuals with defective inner ears or imperfect vision learn to compensate by using their kinesthetic sense advantageously.

The kinesthetic sense may become distorted when the effect of gravity is nullified. For example, a blind individual with defective inner ears could become completely disoriented in the water, where body weight is negated by water buoyancy; and a completely normal individual can receive faulty information from his kinesthetic sense when flying in a plane, or traveling in outer space.

The kinesthetic sense provides an awareness of the degree of force used for moving the body or its parts, and causes the individual to make adaptive movements for performing a task, consciously or otherwise. Kinesthesis enables the individual to duplicate a movement, even after a long period of not performing it. For example, the adult who could ice skate as a child finds that he still has this skill, even after many years of abstinence.

From about the fourth fetal month, the kinesthetic receptors in the muscles, tendons and joints are receiving sensations that will result in later kinesthetic awareness. During infancy, the baby's need for activity is fulfilled through random, massive movement of all body parts; by six months, he is aware of being moved by others, and may have attempted independent sitting. As he

[7] *Ibid.*, p. 28.
[8] Ronald Melzack, "The Perception of Pain," *Scientific American* (February, 1961).

continues to sit, creep, crawl, stand, and move his body in many positions, his developing kinesthetic sense aids him in solving new movement problems. This development goes on through elementary school age and into adulthood.

Summary

Sensation gives us access to the outside world, although each individual's world differs from that of other individuals. A breadth of successful movement experiences during childhood, enjoyed and valued for their own sakes, may produce an extension and enrichment of the child's perceptions.

The sensory equipment of the elementary-age child is generally well-developed, particularly if the sensori-motor experiences during infancy were successful, with the accompanying development of needed neural connections. A rich sensory environment in childhood could result in movement development, which contributes to an adequate self-concept.

The child's perceptions of himself in movement influence his ability and willingness to move. He may see himself as a fast runner, a skillful performer of many activities, light on his feet, graceful and agile; or he may see himself as clumsy, inept, weak, awkward, and ridiculous in movement situations. The child must be able to explore movement possibilities without fear or threat if he is to build an adequate picture of himself as a moving person.

The child seeks many rich and varied stimuli to extend his movement experiences. A telephone ringing, a twig snapping, trucks rumbling on the freeway, a dog's sharp bark, the crash of waves on a beach, cries of birds, the whine of a jet plane—these and many other sounds may excite movement responses. The red of a sunset, a blue scarf, the smell of a rose, the sour taste of a lemon, heat and cold, stickiness, roughness, smoothness, the feel of the wind, the vibration of a motor, a seashell, a toy, a picture of boats in the harbor—all types and varieties of sensations may provide sources of movement stimulation. Such stimuli free the child to use the full possibilities of his body with its range of movements, its extraordinary eloquence, its beauty of expression.

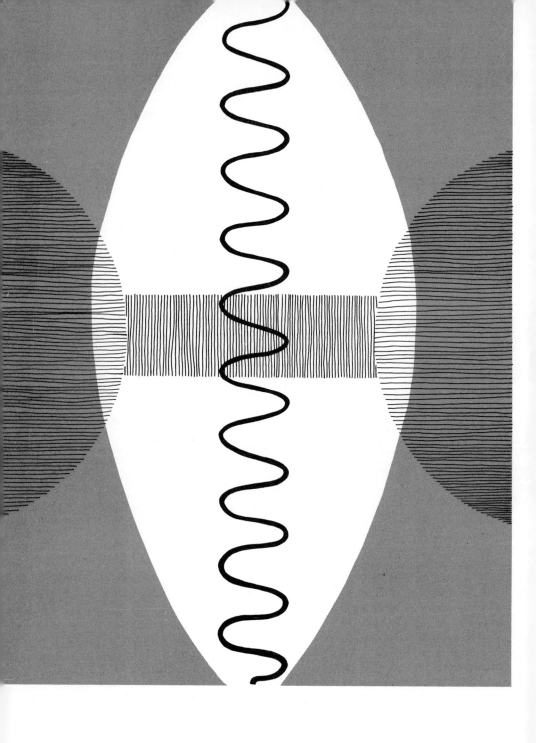

7 STRENGTH

Billy says, "I'm the strongest kid in my grade at school." What he means is that his muscular strength is sufficient to overcome others in feats of strength such as lifting weights, tug-of-war games, hand wrestling, and other combative activities. Lack of strength may be a limiting factor in effective human movement. The understandings related to the acquisition of strength are important for the elementary teacher.

Definition of Strength

Strength is the ability of the organism to mobilize force in an effort to overcome resistance. Muscles tend to increase in size as they are used. Morehouse and Miller state that, all other things being equal, the strength of a muscle is roughly proportionate to its circumference.[1] Muscles that are not used become weak and flabby, contract with difficulty, and produce very little power.

[1] Laurence E. Morehouse and A. T. Miller, *Physiology of Exercise* (St. Louis: The C. V. Mosby Co., 1959), p. 193.

Importance and Need

Each person needs the muscular strength to: (1) meet the requirements of daily activity without undue fatigue or loss of physiologic efficiency, (2) move effectively for prolonged periods in emergency situations, (3) enjoy many different kinds of movement experiences, and (4) successfully perform new movement tasks with confidence.

The individual with insufficient muscular strength may have difficulty in managing his environment. For the child, this may consist of the strength needed for running, jumping, kicking, throwing, climbing, and other skill combinations of the basic flexing, extending, and rotating capability of the organism. The mobilization of force to be fastest, or cleverest, becomes acutely important to the individual in the development of a sense of adequacy, a feeling of worth.

Growth and Development

Strength is developmental, and increases with age from birth to maturity. Earlier maturing girls generally attain adult strength levels before boys, consistent with earlier average maturing of girls in other physiologic aspects. Strength increases rapidly during the elementary school years for both boys and girls, although there is a wide range of individual variability both within and between the sexes. Preadolescent girls, it would seem, would have greater strength than preadolescent boys, because of the maturational advantage. Boys, however, are generally superior to girls in strength at all ages, and significantly so during and after adolescence.

For elementary-age children, the boys' superiority is probably caused by cultural demands. Boys' games traditionally require greater physical exertion than do girls' games, and boys who cannot meet the cultural expectations are frequently made to feel inferior. Parents are concerned about developing superior muscle strength in their sons, but they tend to shield their daughters from activities demanding exertion or stamina.

Some elementary schools separate boys and girls in physical education activities as early as the second grade, although there is no justification for this procedure on the basis of strength differences.

Strength should be acquired in a manner that will lead to the symmetrical and continuous growth of bones. Muscles that operate to generate force are pulling on bones. This pulling action is recognized as a major stimulus for bone growth. Wolff's law states that bones in their external and internal architecture conform with the intensity and direction of the stresses to which they are habitually subjected. This fact, stated here in somewhat simplified form, has an obvious place in any consideration of appropriate activities for the growing, developing child. Activities that would lead to symmetrical growth and development would be those placing stress upon the bones in a balanced relationship. Such activities are hanging, swinging, climbing, and others of a developmental nature.

Scooters and skate-boards may cause asymmetrical development if the child constantly uses one foot to push off from the ground. Alternating feet will correct this tendency.

Care should be taken to insure that activities are planned with the general concepts of uniform bilateral development in mind.

Overload Principle and Strength Attainment

Strength may be developed only if the muscle is overloaded, or made to do more work in each succeeding period of exercise. Overloading can be accomplished in three ways.

First, one can overload by increasing the *intensity* of the exercise, which usually means adding a heavier work load. For example, the child may perform sit-ups by lying on the floor, legs extended, and arms extended over his head. Then he sits up by raising his arms and rolling forward to touch his toes. He might be able to do ten or fifteen sit-ups in this way. He might then increase the intensity of the exercise by placing both hands at the base of the neck, by bending his knees while performing the sit-ups, or by doing sit-ups using both these positions. Later, additional weight may be added in the form of books, bags of sand, and the like. This method of overload is well suited to a school that has gymnasium facilities where the appropriate stations can be set up and maintained.

A second method for overloading is to increase the *duration* of the exercise, adding cycles of repetitions at the rate of one to two repetitions during successive activity periods. This method of overloading is effective, but ultimately results in taking up more and more time; this may be a disadvantage, unless the primary goal for the entire period is the acquisition of strength, the performance of other activities being incidental.

The third method of overloading is accomplished by increasing the *rate* at which an individual exercises. In this method, the individual takes a predetermined battery of exercises, such as ten sit-ups, ten push-ups, or ten squat-thrusts, and is timed on how long it takes him to accomplish this work. During successive activity periods, he attempts to reduce the time involved in accomplishing the battery of exercises. This method has the obvious advantage of reducing the amount of time involved in performing the intensive exercises.

The fact that strength can be improved in this straightforward fashion makes it possible for the teacher to incorporate the principles of overloading in a variety of movement activities that may be primarily designed for other purposes. The teacher should help the child recognize that the application of the overload principle to any movement experience may help him become progressively stronger in the muscles utilized.

Circuit Training

Circuit training is a technique whereby each individual works at his own pace against an individual work load. This is particularly important when working with elementary school children, who exhibit a wide range of variability in strength increments. A simple example will provide an understanding of the technique, which can be modified in any number of ways.

Let us assume that we wish to provide a general conditioning program with emphasis upon the shoulder girdle, trunk flexors and extensors, hip and knee extensors, and the circulatory and respiratory systems. We should select several exercises that would utilize the desired muscle groups. These might include push-ups, sit-ups, squat-thrusts, wood choppers, dorsal arches, and hopping on one leg then the other leg, then running.

We first find out how many of each exercise can be accomplished by each child in 30 seconds. Let us assume that Ted's score is as follows:

Exercise	Score	Time (sec.)
Push-up	7	30
Sit-up	11	30
Squat-thrust	6	30
Wood Chopper	16	30
Dorsal Arch	12	30

To set up the circuit for Ted, we take half the load for each exercise plus the hopping and running. Thus, the following day Ted would first do several stretching activities using muscles of the shoulder girdle, trunk flexors and extensors, and hip and knee extensors; then, at a starting signal, he would do four push-ups, six sit-ups, three squat-thrusts, eight wood choppers, six dorsal arches, hop 20 yards on the left leg, hop 20 yards on the right leg, race back to the start, and repeat the entire performance. The entire double circuit is timed to the nearest second. Each day the circuits are repeated and the times are recorded, so that each student can follow his own progress. Every four weeks new loadings can be established or the exercises can be changed.

In administering the double circuit to an entire class, the teacher can start all children together and by calling out the seconds, each child can record his own time after he completes his own double circuit. It should be recognized that the circuit training method can be applied to any combination of exercise activities and, as the time is reduced, additional units of exercises can be introduced, bringing about overload in intensity as well as in rate. Any series of appropriate developmental activities could be put into the circuit and carried on effectively. A variety of exercises and activities for the development of strength, endurance, and flexibility (stretching) may be found in Chapter 16, *Stunts and Tests*.

It is possible to incorporate various basic movement patterns such as running, jumping, and kicking into the circuits. The primary advantage of the circuit is gaining an intensive circulo-respiratory stimulation during a short time period. Special emphasis should be placed on correct performance of the exercise patterns that constitute the circuit, in order to gain maximum benefits from these exercises.

Each child should understand that the goals he is working on were established for *him*. The aim is to improve his own score, not to outdo everyone else in the class. When using circuit training, one occasionally finds a plateauing of times that would seem to indicate no further improvement. These plateaus are to be expected. Unless they persist for extended periods, they should be disregarded—minor ailments or overtiring could be the cause.

In summary, strength may be developed only if the muscle is overloaded, and overloading may be accomplished by increasing the intensity, the duration, the rate of exercise, or all three factors.

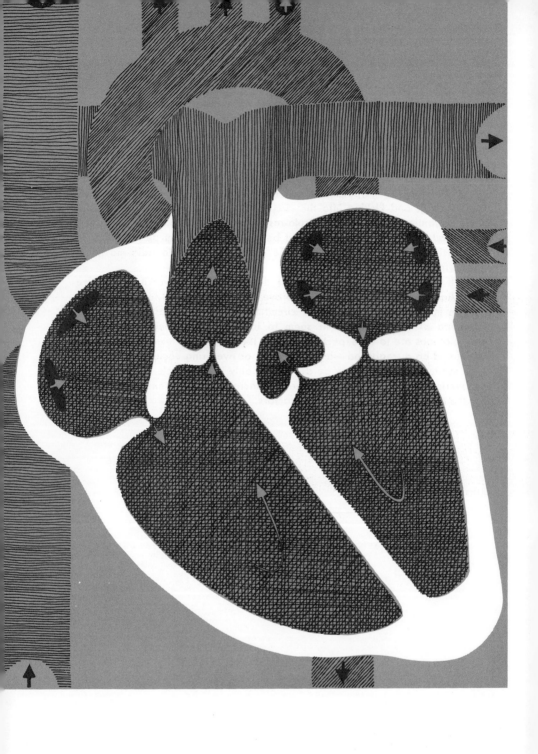

8   ENDURANCE

Barbara says, "I can jump rope longer than anyone else in the third grade." Barbara means that she is able to withstand the onset of fatigue produced by the muscular action of jumping a rope for a longer period of time than others in the third grade. She may have added that she can jump rope for a longer period of time now than when she first started to jump rope. She is developing endurance in rope jumping.

Definition of Endurance

Endurance is the capacity to withstand the cumulative effects of stress accompanying muscular work. Stress as defined by Morehouse and Miller consists of "bodily changes produced by physiologic or psychologic conditions which tend to upset the homeostatic balance."[1] Individuals react to stress differently in their attempts to regain homeostasis; some adapt more readily than others to stressful conditions.

[1] Laurence E. Morehouse and A. T. Miller, *Physiology of Exercise* (St. Louis: The C. V. Mosby Co., 1959), p. 205.

Importance and Need

An individual is likely to have enough endurance to perform his daily tasks without undue fatigue. In addition, one should be able to meet the demands of emergencies, but unless he is pushed beyond his usual output, he is not aware of having endurance problems. The person who tires easily is unable to participate in many enjoyable movement experiences that might enrich his life and add to the zest of living. Thus, one needs endurance as much as strength to participate in life activities with satisfaction and enjoyment. The amount of endurance needed is determined by individual biologic and environmental demands.

Growth and Development

Endurance, like strength, is developmental in that the maturation of muscular, respiratory, and circulatory systems from infancy through adolescence affects muscular and organic efficiency. The slowest period of growth of the circulatory system is between the fourth and tenth years. During this period of growth, the heart is smaller in proportion to body size than at any other stage of development. This would mean that a relatively small heart must maintain adequate circulation for the growing child. In the past many people have believed that sustained periods of strenuous activity should be curtailed during this time in the child's life in order to avoid serious heart damage. There is no scientific evidence, however, to support this view, and for the healthy child the dangers appear to be minimal and vigorous activities should be encouraged in the best interests of optimal development.

Maturation is a factor in the development of both strength and endurance. Consequently, it is preferable to emphasize individual attainment rather than group standards and norms.

Attainment of Endurance

Conditions that affect endurance are muscular, circulo-respiratory, psychologic, and mechanical, assuming that all conditions for healthy growth and development are present.

Muscular. The muscular aspects of endurance are twofold. (1) Muscles with the greatest strength have the greatest endurance, and the amount of work required to induce muscular exhaustion is dependent upon the strength of the muscles involved;[2] (2) stronger muscles utilize fewer fibers for a given amount of work than do weaker muscles. Thus, the development and maintenance of muscular strength is an important factor in the development and maintenance of endurance.

The heart is composed of specialized muscles and, like other muscles, it responds to training. Regular exercise brings about a larger, stronger heart, capable of pumping more blood. This enables the heart to work at a slower rate while pumping adequate supplies of blood through the circulatory network. A large, strong heart can also respond to increased demands faster, and has the capability for faster recovery after periods of heavy exercise.

Skeletal muscle increases in size and strength as a result of increased exercise. It also has the capability of carrying greater energy reserves which, in turn, result in improved work potential. In addition, an increase in capillarization in the tissue results in improved circulatory capability.

Circulo-respiratory. The circulo-respiratory aspect of endurance reflects the ability of the organism to extract and utilize oxygen; it can be developed by a progressive increase in levels of activity, with a concomitant increased demand upon the circulatory and respiratory systems. The effects of exercise on respiration can be generally identified as increased efficiency in pulmonary ventilation, and the exchange of gases resulting in increased oxygen uptake from inspired air. There is also a noticeable decline in the rate and depth of breathing at rest, and an increase in the vital capacity of the individual.

The child runs rapidly for as long as possible; he breathes deeper to obtain the needed oxygen; his heart pumps greater quantities of blood to the tissues, and begins to develop into a larger, stronger muscle. As the intensity of endurance-type activities progressively increases over a period of years, the organism steadily improves in its ability to withstand the cumulative stresses of prolonged work.

Psychologic. The psychologic aspect of endurance is related to the individual's willingness to accept the discomfort of strenuous effort. The discomfort arises from several sources, including increased breathing rate, a build-up of carbon dioxide in the system, increased muscular effort, and inadequate removal of metabolites from the tissue.

Unfortunately, training without exercise vigorous enough to bring about these circumstances will not go far toward improving endurance. The individual, then, must be sufficiently motivated to be able to ignore the discomfort accompanying the increased work loads. This acceptance level can and does improve with training. A person learns that the discomfort quickly dissipates during recovery from the effort, and that there is no injury to the

---

[2] Harrison H. Clark, "Muscular Strength-Endurance Relationships," *Archives of Physical Medicine and Rehabilitation,* XXXVIII (September, 1957), 584–6.

organism. This in turn leads to the development of confidence in one's ability to sustain hard work. Such confidence is as important to the individual as any other aspect of endurance.

Mechanical. Because the mechanical aspect of endurance is often misunderstood, frustration may result. Improved movement efficiency will bring about an improved level of skill performance; and the smaller number of extraneous movements in the performance of an activity will reduce the energy demands, thus permitting the individual to endure for a longer period of time for the same energy cost. However, an individual who improves in the movement skill aspect with a resultant performance that is equal to or better than before, may find, at the same time, that he has declined in one or more of the other aspects of endurance. This means that the individual is operating at a level considerably below that of his immediate potential.

The development of movement skill may be accomplished by understanding and applying the principles of human movement (See Chapters 2, 3, and 4). The application of the principles will result in the reduction or elimination of unnecessary muscular contractions, and the efficiency of the movements will increase.

To summarize, the individual who has developed higher levels of endurance might then be expected to possess: (1) larger, stronger musculature; (2) increased efficiency of movement; (3) a larger, more powerful heart, which will beat more slowly at rest, will pump greater quantities of blood to the tissue during exercise, and will increase the stroke volume (resulting in less drastic heart rate changes) during exercise; (4) increased ability to extract oxygen from the air and transport it to the tissue; (5) lower systolic blood pressure during work; (6) increased depth rather than rate of breathing during work or rest; and (7) higher level of personal confidence in the ability to sustain work.

A gross evaluation of working capacity can be carried out on an individual basis with little equipment and in a short time. We have known for some time that oxygen uptake changes during exercise are directly proportional to intensity of work load within submaximal ranges.[3] It has also been demonstrated that pulse rate changes have an almost linear relation to work intensity. We can, therefore, assume a linear relation between pulse rate and oxygen uptake for submaximal work. This concept becomes important to us because it enables us to use a standard work task that is sufficiently difficult to raise the pulse rate to 140–170 beats per minute as a gross index of working capacity. Individuals with higher working capacities should demonstrate a smaller degree of change during work and should also recover at a faster rate than the person with a reduced working capacity.

One of the simpler techniques is as follows. A wooden step 8 to 9 inches high is used to provide the work load. First, the resting pulse rate is taken.

[3] A. V. Hill, *Muscular Activity* (Baltimore: The Williams and Wilkins Co., 1926).

Then the individual faces the step and, at a signal, steps up and down at the rate of 25 steps per minute. The individual continues this exercise for three minutes and stops. Pulse rate is taken at the end of the first and second minutes of recovery. The person with a higher working capacity will exhibit lower pulse rates in general and will recover the resting pulse rate by the end of the second minute.

This procedure can be useful in identifying changes brought about by a conditioning program. If the children can be taught to take their own pulses with some degree of reliability, the test can be conducted with larger numbers of individuals. The perception of pulse rate can be learned. The individual is shown the location of the two easiest pulse pick-up points—one is on the palm side of the wrist, approximately one inch above the base of the thumb, and near the junction of the radius and the small bones of the wrist; the other is on the throat, generally on a line from the ear to the sternum just below the chin.

Since maturation is a factor in the development of endurance, individual rather than group goals should be encouraged. The key to the satisfactory development of endurance lies in planning programs that stimulate vigorous activity at frequent and regular intervals, such as two or three times weekly throughout the year. During these periods, the child should be encouraged to work at levels in which heavy breathing, rapid pulse and perspiration are accepted as signs of strenuous effort. The healthy child will respond with progressive improvement and increased capacity for endurance.

Many of the running games played by children in the elementary school help with the development of endurance if all children can participate vigorously during most of the physical education period. Many of the activities included in Chapters 15, 16, and 17 contribute to the development and maintenance of endurance.

9 FLEXIBILITY

We are amazed by the supple, resilient movement of the acrobat as he bends and twists in the performance of his stunts. Some of us assume that he must indeed be "double-jointed" to be able to place himself in such contorted positions.

We watch the baby chew contentedly on his great toe, or the small child bend himself double as he studies an ant crawling on the ground, and we nostalgically recall the days of our childhood when we too were limber and agile in the performance of a great range of movements. What is flexibility in human movement? How may it be attained? And why do we tend to lose it in adulthood?

Definition of Flexibility

The term *flexibility* as related to human movement describes the range of motion in the various joints of the body. Flexibility can be specifically identified in a single joint, or collectively related to the total limits of movement in more complex relationships such as bending, twisting, and stretching.

Importance and Need

The degree of flexibility needed by an individual is dependent upon the demands that are habitually placed upon the joints. Certainly, each individual should be able to exert force through a full range of motion for a given joint.

Skeletal joints are generally classified as: (1) immovable, (2) slightly movable, and (3) freely movable. The sutures of the skull represent an example of an immovable joint. The structure of this joint is such that growth is permitted, but stability exists for protection against injury.

Slightly movable joints, such as the articulations between the clavicle and the sternum, or the ribs and the sternum, provide stability for structures that must retain their relative shapes under conditions that necessitate some movement. The freely movable joints provide lubricated articulations that have low-friction surfaces and freedom to move in a number of roles. Freely movable joints, such as the hips, shoulders, elbows, and knees, are remarkably suited to permit complex movements to occur without damage to the bones.

Growth and Development

Skeletal development begins with the osseous tissue replacing the cartilaginous tissue in the bones resulting from deposits of calcium salts. The increase of calcium is accompanied by a decrease of water and cartilage resulting in harder, less pliable bones. Ossification follows the cephalo-caudal developmental pattern, proceeding from the head to the extremities and starting with the bones in the skull, although one of the last areas to solidify is the center of the skull. By the end of childhood, ossification is complete, except for a strip of cartilage at the joints where all further longitudinal growth takes place.

Since the stage of ossification of the hand and wrist is indicative of growth of other skeletal parts, skeletal maturity is frequently determined by examining this area. Girls generally mature before boys in skeletal development, and this difference between the sexes increases with age.

Because of the softness of the bones during the early years, children may sustain hard falls without severe injury. This condition, plus other factors, particularly the significant role in joint flexibility played by the musculature, tends to give children a wider range of motion than that typical of adults.

Attainment of Flexibility

Not all skeletal joints are constructed to move in all ways.   Each joint has limits placed upon it by a number of factors, such as joint structure, the condition of the ligaments, muscle adaptation, and injury.

The role of joint structure as a limiting factor in the range of motion is readily apparent if we consider the elbow joint as an example.   The articulation is between the ulna and the humerus.   As the elbow is extended, the tip of the ulna moves into a pocket in the humerus until it can go no farther.   It is obvious that the limit has been reached, and that further extension will result in pain or injury.

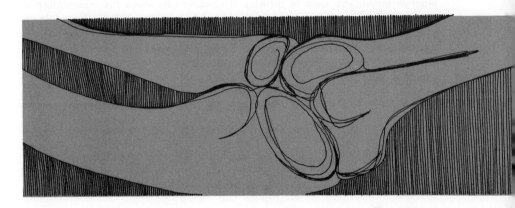

Structural limitations are quite permanent, and care should be taken to prevent strong movements that "jam" the bones together.   Slow, volitional movements can be used to exercise through the full range of motion of these joints with little danger.   Exercises that involve the development of momentum, which is then arrested by the jamming of two or more bones, should be avoided.   For example, one could safely use a weight to develop strength in elbow flexors while *slowly* raising and lowering the weight through the range of motion.   One would not, however, attempt to extend the arm forcibly by swinging it rapidly downward, since the momentum could cause the shock of stopping to be taken by the juncture of the two bones.

Ligaments are specialized tissue for joining bone to bone, and as such, they play an important role in flexibility.   If the ligaments are very tight, joint mobility is lost; if very loose, the joint becomes unstable.   An example of the nature of ligament limitation of movement may be found in the knee joint, where the cruciate ligaments permit flexion and extension of the knee but resist anterior-posterior displacement.   Excessive tightness or looseness of these ligaments would result in significant differences in joint mobility. The ankle joint provides another example of ligament function. When the ankle is "turned" or twisted, the ligaments may tear while an attempt is made to hold the joint in its proper position. This may result in pain, swelling, and discoloration for a few days.

If strain has been sufficient to separate two bones, dislocation may occur at a joint. The lower jaw, for example, may become dislocated and require pushing back into place; the same thing may happen to the shoulder joint if the arms are used to receive the impetus of a hard fall.

The role of musculature in joint flexibility has to do with the ability of muscle tissue to adapt to habitually lengthened or shortened positions. An example of this limitation may be found in most sedentary individuals, and is associated with much of the lower back pain in middle age. Generally, inactive individuals tend to develop a condition in which the musculature of the abdomen becomes weakened because of lack of exercise. The muscula-ture of the back, on the other hand, continues to support the trunk and thereby maintains higher levels of strength. Since all muscles exert force by pulling, the stronger back muscles pull up on the rear of the pelvic girdle, tilting the structure down in the front. The weakened abdominal muscles respond by lengthening as the hip and back extensors shorten. This vicious circle can continue until the adaptive shortening causes pressure on the vertebrae of the lower back, which often results in extreme pain. The resolution of this problem is to shorten the abdominals and lengthen the back extensors, bring-ing the pelvis and the intervertebral joints back into anatomical alignment.

If one recognizes the need for a balance of strength in the musculature on opposite sides of a joint, the importance of exercise programs that develop strength in opposing muscle groups can be appreciated. An overemphasis on strenuous activity that utilizes the musculature on one side of a joint can result in changes in the flexibility of that joint. Consistent changes involving a number of joints can produce changed postures and, possibly, movement difficulties. *Injuries* can bring about similar circumstances, for an injury often involves joint structure, changes in bone structure, and weakened musculature.

Since the structure of the joint is permanent, flexibility increases are gained by altering the range of motion by forced stretching of the musculature that is limiting the movement. The stretching should be executed in a slow, controlled manner, without developing momentum. Slow stretching appears to be as effective in increasing range of motion as fast stretching, and does not result in the residual pain that often accompanies fast stretching.[1] There is also evidence that stretching exercises prior to strenuous activity lead to a reduction of "pulled" muscles, and discomfort.

The development of flexibility in children is not considered a serious prob-lem. The promotion of programs that induce the habits necessary to *retain*

---

[1] Gene A. Logan and G. H. Egstrom, "The Effects of Slow and Fast Stretching on the Sacro-Femoral Angle," *Journal of the Association for Physical and Mental Rehabilitation*, XV, No. 3 (May–June, 1961), 85–89.

flexible bodies is, however, of extreme importance. Diversified activities that call for bending, twisting, and stretching to the limits of the range of motion include tumbling, hanging, swinging, climbing, and various stunts and exercises. Many of the methods for exploring movement in games and dance activities are also useful in developing good habits. It is important to remember that the activity should provide equal emphasis for opposing muscle groups.

10   RELAXATION

To many adults, harassed by the problems of making a living, keeping up with the Joneses, and struggling toward fulfillment of personal hopes and aspirations, the child's world in retrospect seems to be one of euphoria and relaxation. The child's "work" is mostly "play," his problems and worries so minimal that they are quickly resolved by the adults in his life, and the only demands made upon him are that he laugh and play all day and grow up to be a credit to his parents.

The conflicts that cause anxiety and tension in adults, however, also give children anxieties and tensions. Some psychologists believe that the origins of anxiety begin with the infant's attempts to cope with his environments, and his helplessness and frustration in conforming to adult expectations. Horney contends that anxiety stems from cultural experiences in childhood, usually in relation to his parents.[1] She indicates that the individual strives to cope with his environment by using aggression, withdrawal, or compliance. These forms of behavior may be expressed in many ways, and the same person may use one or all of them.

Fromm suggests that the child loses security as he develops independence from adults, which results in fear and loneliness.[2] Sullivan believes that anxiety arises from the disapproval of people who surround the child, and is, in turn, reflected in his appraisal of himself.[3]

---

[1] Karen Horney, *The Neurotic Personality of Our Time* (New York: W. W. Norton & Company, Inc., 1937).

[2] Erich Fromm, *Escape From Freedom* (New York: Rinehart, 1941).

[3] Harry Stack Sullivan, *The Meaning of Anxiety in Psychiatry and in Life* (New York: W. A. White Institute of Psychiatry, 1948).

During the elementary school years, children's anxieties may be instigated by expectations of parents and teachers, unsatisfactory peer relationships, personal failures and inadequacies in achieving school goals, rejections and reprisals from adult status figures.

Children's tensions may be reflected in their postures and movement. Davies describes signs of tensions in children such as legs wrapped tightly around chair legs, hands tightly clasped, hands clutching chairs or other objects, clenched fists, head held tensely to one side, continual movement of feet and hands, uncoordinated movement, jerky gait, and inability to keep from stumbling, bumping into things, or falling.[4] Other tension-reducing devices are biting lips or nails, clenching jaws, hunching shoulders, chewing pencils and other objects, pulling ear-lobes, twisting hair around fingers, and the like.

Definition of Relaxation

Relaxation is the abatement or release of tension in the muscles. Any nervous stimulation of a muscle causes contraction of that muscle and results in muscle tension. Normal, healthy muscles are always in a state of slight contraction, described as *muscle tonus*. Tonus allows easy, uniform movement when the muscle is stimulated, and the response is quicker than in a limp muscle. Scott uses an interesting simile in her description of tonus, comparing it to a car towing another behind it.[5] A towing rope that is taut before movement starts eliminates the jerk, and the towed car moves at once. Consequently, a mild amount of tension in the muscle is desirable at all times.

When excessive stimulation, resulting in hypertension, is produced by emotional conditions, fatigue and lack of sleep, poor nutrition, postural problems, and other causes, the need for relaxation therapy of some nature is definitely indicated. Children frequently use activity for this purpose. When muscular tension occurs in the absence of movement, the result is loss of efficiency because of unnecessary fatigue. Movement helps to dissipate the energy produced when the muscle is stimulated.

Tests of relaxation are in reality tests of muscle tension. The "knee jerk" test used by medical doctors is a test of tension in which the jerk becomes less pronounced as the muscles are more relaxed. Rathbone describes a test in which the person lies on his back, and the test administrator lifts various body parts to determine whether hypertonus is present.[6] Some indications

---

[4] Evelyn A. Davies, *The Elementary School Child and His Posture Patterns* (New York: Appleton-Century-Crofts, Inc., 1958), pp. 26–7.

[5] M. Gladys Scott, *Analysis of Human Motion* (New York: F. S. Crofts & Co., 1947), p. 76.

[6] Josephine L. Rathbone, *Corrective Physical Education* (Philadelphia: W. B. Saunders Co., 1944), p. 122.

of hypertension are: (1) the person continues the motion started by the test administrator, (2) the person assists or resists the motion, and (3) the person holds the position in which the body part is placed by the test administrator.

Importance and Need

An individual needs relaxation to live happily in the world around him. The person who is strained, tense, or irritable is a miserable human being, unhappy with himself and avoided by many others. He is constantly fatigued because he uses excessive amounts of energy in carrying out his daily tasks. His nutrition is poor because he gulps his food, or is too tense to eat properly; and he worries when he should be sleeping. Be he child or adult, he needs more relaxation. If his tension springs from boredom, he needs new activities that are stimulating and refreshing to him. If his health is poor, he needs a medical checkup and appropriate treatment. If his work is too confining and demanding, he needs new vocational goals, a change of jobs. If guilt or neuroses are overpowering him, he needs psychological counseling. If his peer relationships are distressing him, he needs a new social group. Whatever the cause of tension, he needs help in problem-solving to reduce his tensions.

An individual needs relaxation for skillful performance of movement activities. Wells describes this as "differential relaxation," or the ability to relax unneeded muscles in performance of a skill to obtain efficient movement.[7] When a particular group of muscles is stimulated to act, the muscles that act in opposition to them, the "antagonists," are usually allowed to relax. Scott states that relaxation is not only a factor in improvement of coordination but also contributes to rest and endurance.[8] Relaxation is particularly important in learning new movement patterns. Bunn points out that the effect of tension may be clearly demonstrated in most beginning swimmers; usually it is caused by fear of the water.[9] He agrees that " 'the individual who has implicit confidence in his instructor so that he has no fear and can relax can be taught to swim in fifteen minutes,' " and observes that the individual should aim toward learning to relax in all situations.

[7] Katharine F. Wells, Kinesiology, 3rd ed. (Philadelphia: W. B. Saunders Co., 1960), pp. 327–28.

[8] M. Gladys Scott, op. cit., p. 325.

[9] John W. Bunn, Scientific Principles of Coaching (Englewood Cliffs, N.J.: Prentice-Hall, Inc., 1955), pp. 83–84.

Attainment of Relaxation

Relaxation is an individual matter. Techniques that may help one person learn to relax may have no effect upon another. For all tense individuals, the first consideration is to determine the origin or cause of the tension; then positive measures toward solving the problems can be taken. Problems may be medical, such as hearing difficulties or hyperthyroidism, or they may be due to unresolved worries or fears. Some tensions may be produced by lack of sufficient exercise during the school day, or by enforced sedentary positions for long periods. Whatever the cause, the teacher should use all the means at his command to help the child rid himself of the tension-producing factors.

Relaxation may be learned but like other learning the individual must be motivated to want to do something about it, and must understand the meaning and control of tension. Jacobson, in his work on progressive relaxation indicates that relaxation can be taught if the individual is first made aware of tension.[10] His technique employs the development of tension in large muscles or groups of muscles, and a subsequent release of the tension. The releasing pattern can be learned for each of the large muscles or groups of muscles; and a conscious pattern for relaxation can also be learned. In one pattern, a reclining individual tenses the muscles of the body and gradually releases the tension until no further tension can be felt. The more sensitive the individual becomes to the feeling of tension, the more he should be able to relax.

Some activities that may help the elementary school child develop sensitivity for the feeling of tension are: (1) swinging-swaying exercises, rhythmically performed; (2) tension-relaxation exercises where the child recognizes the difference between stiffness and looseness; (3) stretching-bending exercises, performed rhythmically; (4) deep-breathing exercises performed rhythmically, increasing the exhalation phase of breathing; (5) sustained, controlled motion of body parts; (6) use of imagery, such as imagining oneself to be a leaf floating to the ground, a furry kitten sleeping on a pillow, a fluffy cloud floating in the sky; (7) play activities using the large muscles, and done recreationally, or activities pleasurable to the doer and a change from work activities, such as reading, listening to music, painting, and talking to friends.

[10] Edmund Jacobson, *You Must Relax* (New York: McGraw-Hill Book Company, Inc., 1934), p. 70; *Progressive Relaxation* (Chicago: University of Chicago Press, 1938).

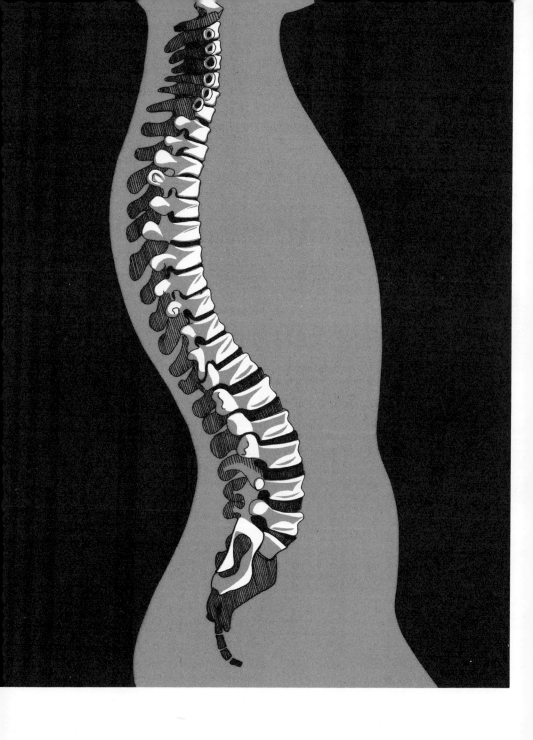

11 POSTURES

The individual's postures are the result of his unique structure, and of his environments.

Structurally, the spine supports the trunk, upper extremities, and head, and acts as a shock absorber for movement such as jumping, hopping, and running. It serves also as a stable structure for muscle attachment; yet it is flexible enough to allow movement of trunk and head in many directions, and it encloses and protects the fragile spinal cord.

The spine consists of seven cervical, twelve thoracic, and five lumbar vertebrae, the sacrum, and the coccyx. The cervical vertebrae are at the top of the column and form the neck of the individual, followed by the thoracic vertebrae to which the ribs of the chest cavity are attached. The lumbar vertebrae follow the thoracic and are in the lower part of the spine. When the lumbar curve is exaggerated, lordosis or "sway-back" results. Kyphosis is an exaggerated curve in the thoracic region. When the spine curves sideward, the deviation is referred to as scoliosis.

The sacrum, attached to the fifth lumbar vertebra, is composed of five vertebrae that have fused into a single bone, forming the rear wall of the pelvis. The coccyx consists of four fused rudimentary vertebrae, and is at the tail of the spinal column.

When viewing an individual from the side, the cervical and lumbar regions are seen to curve inward toward the front of the body (convex forward), and the thoracic and sacrococcygeal regions are seen to curve in the opposite direction (convex to the rear). The latter two curves are developed before birth, and the cervical and lumbar curves develop during infancy and early childhood.

Many of the postural problems of adulthood begin during infancy and childhood, and even before birth.   The mother's nutritional status during pregnancy may affect the baby's structural development.

Inadequate sleep, lack of activity, low-grade infections and disease, and poor nutrition are environmental factors that may be detrimental to good postures.   A child who is fatigued and operating at a low level of vitality is likely to slump, drag his feet when he walks, and lean against available supports when standing or sitting.

Self-concepts are also reflected in postures.   The child who feels inadequate and unworthy may move in a way that expresses his feelings of anxiety, fear of ridicule, and lack of self-confidence; or belligerence and hostility may be responsible for tense and rigid postures.

Overemphasis of particular activities may cause asymmetrical development.   The classic example of this is the child with the scooter—overuse of one foot results in overdevelopment of one side and shortening of the opposite leg.   Another example is that of the child who carries all his books on one side, causing one shoulder to be higher than the other, with an accompanying curve in the spinal column to compensate for the uneven distribution of weight.

Definition of Postures

Human posture refers to the arrangement of the body parts in relation to each other.   Since the human body assumes many positions in walking, sitting, running, standing, and other movement activities, an individual has not one but many postures.   Because each individual is unique, his postures are also a unique reflection of his "self," his genes, his environments or experiences, his motives, feelings, and aspirations.

Growth and Development

At birth, the baby has little control over his head and spine.   As the muscles of head and neck become stronger, he is able to hold his head up for short periods.   By the end of the third month, he can turn his head to either side and push up his head and chest with hands and arms while lying on his stomach.   As back and shoulder muscles become stronger, he can sit up with support, sometimes around the fourth or fifth month; and by the sixth to eighth month he can sit up by himself.

By the tenth or eleventh month, the baby can move independently from lying to sitting position and from sitting to lying.   He may also crawl and creep and pull himself to a standing position by holding on the furniture or playpen.   Lowman and Young believe that it is advantageous for the baby to crawl for several months before walking because such activity strengthens the pelvic and trunk muscles, and this tends to give him a straighter spine and better balance when he begins to walk.[1]   They warn that arriving at the standing position before adequate muscle strength is developed may contribute to faulty leg alignment, and foot problems.

When the infant is between twelve and fifteen months old, he is usually able to stand alone, walk with support, and walk independently.   By the time he is five years old, postural control and balance are well-developed.

Although the upright position is one of man's greater assets over four-footed animals, it is also responsible for many aches and pains when poor body alignment causes unnecessary strain on joints and ligaments.   Some of the deviations leading to poor body alignment that should be corrected during childhood include: (1) toeing out or toeing in, (2) bowlegs or knock knees, (3) atypical thoracic or lumbar curves, (4) protruding abdomen, (5) hyperextended knees, (6) faulty leg alignment, (7) pronated ankles, and (8) sensory defects, such as blindness or deafness.   Some of these problems may be present at birth, or they may be caused by environmental factors such as poor sleeping positions while the child is an infant, poorly constructed shoes, ill-fitting clothing, and the like.

Attainment of "Good" Postures

Postures are fluid rather than static.   The individual assumes many postures as he moves from one position to another.   Some last for a brief interval; he may maintain others for a longer period when he is sitting or standing.

There are many definitions for "good" postures, with very little scientific evidence to justify them.   Some writers maintain that an analysis of the individual's standing posture is useful if it represents his other postures. Good alignment is frequently described as a vertical line extending from the lobe of the ear through the point of the shoulder, the hip joint, the rear of the patella (kneecap), slightly in front of the ankle and halfway between the heel and ball of the foot of a standing individual viewed from the side. From the back view, the line should bisect the body from the head through the ankles, with shoulders and hips level, and weight evenly distributed on both feet.

Other writers indicate that good posture is that which requires minimal energy expenditure; they assume that good alignment requires less mus-

[1] C. L. Lowman and C. H. Young, *Postural Fitness* (Philadelphia: Lea & Febiger, 1960).

cular effort than poor alignment. This is certainly open to question when one considers the characteristic "fatigue slump" of individuals with diminished vitality.

Because of the lack of scientific evidence and the conflicting opinions of authorities, Wells has suggested some "postural principles" based upon the best available knowledge;[2] and Rasch and Burke have formulated a list of "postural implications" based upon biologic, mechanical, and physiologic data.[3]

Stated simply, these principles and implications indicate the following postural guidelines:

1. Standing positions should be easy extensions of the weight-bearing joints, with the center of gravity of body parts vertical to the center of the base of support. Body position should be frequently shifted to avoid stress and strain.

2. Proper supporting devices, such as chairs, seats, and mattresses, should be provided for sitting or lying positions to allow the specific muscle groups appropriate relaxation.

3. The bones, tendons, and muscles should be strong enough to maintain, and flexible enough to permit, good alignment without excessive effort or strain.

4. Spinal curves should be minimal during strong, forceful movements, thus allowing for spinal flexion to absorb the shock of impact.

5. Good posture for any individual is that which meets the demands made upon it with efficient and economical expenditure of energy, and minimum wear and tear on joints and ligaments.

Home and school should have equal responsibility in helping children to improve their postures. Parents should provide the child with proper nutrition, adequate rest and relaxation, freedom from poisons and focal infections, adequate medical and dental care, sight and hearing corrections when needed, and properly constructed shoes and clothing. Lowman and Young[4] emphasize the importance of well-fitting clothing, with clothing weight supported at the base of the neck rather than on the tip of the shoulders to avoid forward sag in the shoulder girdle.

Both school and home should provide many opportunities for a variety of movement experiences, and should help each child toward the development of healthy self-concepts.

---

[2] Katharine F. Wells, *Kinesiology*, 3rd ed. (Philadelphia: W. B. Saunders Co., 1960), pp. 365–67.

[3] P. Rasch and R. Burke, *Kinesiology and Applied Anatomy*, 2d ed. (Philadelphia: Lea and Febiger, 1963), pp. 373–4.

[4] *Op. cit.*

Because of the wide range of individual variability in structure, and the variety of individual postural problems, selection of activities should be determined by individual need. Children with marked divergencies need help from specialists, and the teacher should follow the recommendations of medical personnel in choosing movement experiences for these children. Activities that improve strength, endurance, flexibility, relaxation, coordination, and balance will also meet postural goals if they are performed correctly from a body mechanics standpoint, following postural principles.

The school should provide equipment for crawling, climbing, hanging, stretching, and swinging, and should have adequate space and proper surface for running, jumping, leaping, kicking, sliding, hopping, and the like. In the classroom, each child should have chairs, tables, and desks of a height that allows a comfortable position of back and shoulders when the feet are flat on the floor.

The responsibilities of the elementary school teacher, therefore, include: (1) observing and referring to a specialist any child with postural divergencies; (2) understanding and following the latter's recommendations; and (3) helping children to select and perform correctly the activities that help them to meet their postural needs. Some of these activities may be to develop strength in antigravity muscles, others may be to improve flexibility, and others may be for coordination. Although most children need all these types of activities to some degree, some children need more of one kind than another.

12 MOVEMENT AND THE BIOLOGIC CONDITION

As an individual grows and matures he is in a continuing struggle to cope with his environments, and the improvement of his movement performance levels may help him to achieve some control. Improved levels of performance lead to a more effective adaptation to the demands of the environments that surround and limit him. Frequently, however, he may become confused about the nature of the adaptation, accepting a tolerable but less than adequate adaptation, rationalizing, "Well, that's the best I can do."

A more successful adaptation is one in which an individual is able to bridge the gap between his accepted level of performance and his potential for improved performance. This gap holds barriers that can be surmounted with varying degrees of success, depending upon one's ability to identify his baseline performance and gain insight into improvement.

Anatomic Barriers to Performance

The first category of barriers to performance can be identified as anatomic barriers. It is well-known that the human skeletal system is composed of bones whose length and strength vary according to their intended use. It is also well-known that muscles that have tendinous attachments that cross the junctures of two bones provide the motors that move the levers of the body. It is less well-known, however, that the tendinous attachments of muscle to bone vary significantly, and create levers with greater or lesser mechanical advantage.

For example, one of the attachments of the biceps muscle of the upper arm is near the elbow joint.   Since this attachment provides for the application of force to the ulna, it can be recognized that the farther from the elbow joint the attachment is located, the greater the mechanical advantage of the lever, or the longer the force arm of the lever.   Individual variation in the location of this attachment is significant, and accounts for a wide range of strength scores in individuals whose muscles and arm lengths appear to be very similar.

This concept of "better" or "poorer" levers can be applied to most if not all the joints of the body.   Understanding the net effect of this hereditary difference enables us to appreciate the apparent incongruities between the performances of a very muscular child with relatively poor levers and his leaner or fatter counterpart who has inherited more efficient levers.   It is conceivable that the more muscular child has developed the heavier musculature to overcome the limitations imposed by the poorer lever system.   This anatomic barrier can be identified in part by the use of objective tests of strength.   The usual superficial observation, "He certainly looks strong," is clearly unreliable.

The length of limbs is another anatomic barrier that can limit performance.   As the child grows, there is the tendency for skeletal growth to outdistance muscular development.   This creates an imbalance between the systems that can result in awkward movements and severe coordination problems.   It is necessary to provide activities that will develop strength not only to handle the levers, but also to aid in the development and refinement of the many movement patterns—running, jumping, throwing, and the like.

Physiologic Barriers to Performance

Physiologic barriers are reflected in the processes and activities of living organs and the systems they comprise.   Generally, the physiology of the child during activity is a limiting element, due to the function of two basic systems, circulatory and respiratory.   The circulo-respiratory function depends largely upon the ability to extract oxygen from the inspired air and transport it to the muscle tissue where it is utilized, then to carry off the byproducts of metabolism, principally carbon dioxide.

The circulatory system provides an internal circulating bath that supplies oxygen and other nutritive materials to the body tissues and later transports the carbon dioxide and other waste products either to organs such as the gastrointestinal tract and kidneys where they are excreted, or to the lungs where they diffuse into the expired air.

Let us for a moment study the blood circulatory system, composed of a double pump, the heart, and a double network for circulation. Blood is driven from the right side of the heart into the blood vessels of the lung, where oxygen is taken up by the blood through a diffusion process. The oxygenated blood is then forced into the left side of the heart, from which point it is forced into the arterial network. Arterial blood carrying oxygen and nutrients is pumped to the tissues, where it is used in tissue metabolism. The oxygen is removed, and carbon dioxide and other byproducts of metabolism move across the capillary bed into the venous system. The venous blood is then drawn into the right side of the heart, and pumped once again into the lungs. The complexity of this network can be appreciated if we recognize that, in a male of average size, the area of the capillary bed across which the blood moves at the tissue level has been estimated to be almost two acres.

During exercise, the need for additional oxygen and the increased carbon dioxide output increase markedly. This demand gives rise to an increased circulation of blood between the lungs and the tissue as a result of increased pulse rate and respiratory rate.

Respiration itself is the result of a rhythmic relaxation and contraction of the musculature surrounding the rib cage, which encloses the chest cavity. This cavity contains the lungs, a spongy mass connected to the ambient air through a series of air passages from the bronchi, the trachea, and the upper respiratory passages.

Movements of the chest wall and related musculature cause slight increases or decreases in the volume of the chest cavity. Corresponding changes in the pressure of the air in the lungs then result in the flow of air in and out of the lungs, through the air passages, until the pressure inside the lung is equal to the external pressure. This interchange occurs at the rate of 18 to 22 times per minute in children, and 12 to 16 times per minute in adults at rest. These figures are approximations since the rate is specifically regulated by the nervous system, which responds to changes in blood oxygen and carbon dioxide levels. Low blood oxygen and high blood carbon dioxide will result in exchanges at double and even triple the resting rate. This increased respiratory rate is accompanied by an increased heart rate, which can also double or triple under heavy exercise. Increased demands are met much more easily if the individual is stimulated to these higher work loads at regular intervals.

The air that is drawn into the lung is composed of approximately 21 per cent oxygen and 79 per cent nitrogen. This mixture is distributed in the lungs until it reaches the alveolar wall, composed of tiny thin-walled air sacs containing the very fine pulmonary capillaries that carry blood from the right side of the heart. This blood has perhaps 18 per cent oxygen, 3 per cent carbon dioxide, and the remainder nitrogen. Since the air in the alveoli contains 21 per cent oxygen and no carbon dioxide, the gases seek equilibrium by diffusing through the membrane. The enormous surface area permits a rapid exchange until the blood oxygen rises and blood carbon dioxide drops. A corresponding drop in respiratory oxygen levels, and rise in carbon dioxide, occur. During the next exchange, the respiratory gases are replaced by ambient air, and are prepared for the diffusion with the next increment of blood that has been forced into the alveolar capillary bed.

During prolonged muscular work, the increased muscular activity results in the utilization of available oxygen in the tissue, accompanied by an increase in carbon dioxide and metabolites. In order to satisfy the demand for additional oxygen, and to remove the carbon dioxide and metabolites, a series of reflexes is stimulated. The response that follows the stimulation results in an increased pulse rate and an increased stroke volume, which in turn results in a greater flow of blood through the tissue. At the same time, the respiratory mechanism is stimulated, resulting in increased rate and depth of breathing called *hyperventilation*. The increased functioning of the circulo-respiratory system results in an increased supply of oxygen and nutrients to the tissue. Finally, when the demands for additional oxygen are met, the system becomes balanced and remains so until there are demands for additional adjustments.

It is apparent, therefore, that the ability of an individual's circulatory and respiratory systems to extract and transport oxygen becomes the critical factor for endurance. The type of biologic efficiency that is necessary for prolonged muscular exertion is strongly related to the individual's oxygen uptake capacity; and many researchers feel that this oxygen capability is the best currently available index of working capacity.[1]

This extraction capability is improved when the organism is subjected to work loads greater than those normally attained. This means that the regular exercise periods must be of sufficient intensity and duration to promote a rapid heart beat rate and respiratory rate. It also means that prolonged periods of exercise levels so low that they do not tax the system will result in reduced levels of working capacity.

The physiologic barriers permit us to operate effectively only as long as the energy demands are met. Failure to meet the demand for sufficient oxygen results in failure of the muscle tissue to contract in order to move the body levers, thus effecting movement. These barriers can be pushed back gradually by following the overload technique. Overloading is simply doing more work this time than you did last time; it can be accomplished by increasing the intensity, duration, or rate at which work is accomplished. It is recommended that the intensive work period be preceded by a preliminary period of stretching activities. Other suggestions for intensive work are presented in Chapters 6 and 7.

Psychologic Barriers to Performance

When a child is asked to catch a ball, it is important to know whether he has ever successfully caught a ball. If he has not been successful, he may

[1] Irma Astrand, "Aerobic Work Capacity in Men and Women," *Acta Physiologica Scandinavia*, IL, Supplementum 169, 1960.

only be aware that an object traveling at high speed is about to hit him in the hands. His fears about the subsequent "sting" may result in repeated failures, simply because he cannot recognize that proper catching technique will permit him to gradually absorb the shock of impact without experiencing stinging.

A more pointed example occurs when a child is asked to jump from the one-meter diving board into the water. He will usually walk gingerly out to the end of this unstable board and wait until he can summon enough courage to jump. Once he has done it without undue calamity, he finds it is pleasant and often jumps repeatedly without further urging. The removal of the mystery concerning what will happen removes the barrier. As Aristotle is reputed to have said, "Half the strength of a giant lies in knowing that he is a giant."

By the same token, if an individual believes that he cannot perform a particular activity, it is almost a certainty that he will not be able to do so. With this in mind, it becomes important to expose the child to gradually increasing challenges. The sequential presentation of these challenges will reduce the effect of psychologic barriers. It has ben estimated that the average person operates at approximately 20 per cent of his anatomic and physiologic capability. He does so largely because he is restricted by previously learned psychologic barriers.

Psychologic barriers to performance are the least understood, and the most difficult to identify and modify. They can be recognized more easily after they have been changed. For example, several generations of mile runners felt that the four-minute mile was an almost impossible feat. An English medical student, Roger Bannister, studied the problem carefully and decided that he could break the barrier. A strenuous training program, plus careful calculations on energy expenditure, ultimately led to success. How strange that since the barrier was broken a "good" mile runner is now expected to run under four minutes. Obviously, the *potential* for the achievement was present; the security of the knowledge that it could be done was missing.

This phenomenon is present to a degree whenever an individual learns a new activity. The mystery or uncertainty that accompanies a new experience can create a severe problem in learning.

Methodologic Barriers to Performance

Methodologic barriers to performance may cause an individual to become stifled because he is utilizing poor mechanics of movement. Let us assume that a child wishes to learn to throw a ball. Several critical steps, if overlooked, can result in an ineffective performance. A right-handed child, for example, must learn to step out with his *left* foot as he prepares to throw. This step permits him to stretch the musculature links that run from the lower

left side of the body to the upper right side.   This stretching, in turn, permits a strong powerful contraction of the muscles involved, and they are
able to contribute to the throw.   A common fault in throwing is to step out
with the incorrect foot thus negating the contribution that could have resulted
from these powerfully contracting muscles.

A second methodologic barrier in throwing occurs when the thrower
extends or straightens his arm too soon.   An effective thrower swings his
arm so that the elbow precedes the ball as it passes the head.   This enables
the ball to be pulled rather than pushed, and the shortened radius permits a
faster movement.

The ability to overcome methodologic barriers is based on the study of
the analysis of movement as an art and a science.   Chapters 3 and 4 present
information to help the elementary teacher understand many of the general
principles for good performance of numerous movement patterns.

In summary, barriers to performance of movement activities may be anatomic, physiologic, psychologic, and methodologic.   The individual's success in
surmounting these barriers depends upon his ability to identify his baseline
performance, and to gain insight into ways and means of improving his
movement performance levels.

Suggested Readings: The Science of Human Movement

Study of Human Movement

Broer, Marion, *Efficiency of Human Movement*.   Philadelphia: W. B. Saunders
Co., 1960.

Brown, Camille, and Rosalind Cassidy, *Theory in Physical Education*.   Philadelphia: Lea & Febiger, 1963.

Bunn, John W., *Scientific Principles of Coaching*.   Englewood Cliffs, N.J.:
Prentice-Hall, Inc., 1955.

Duvall, Ellen N., *Kinesiology: The Anatomy of Motion*.   Englewood Cliffs,
N.J.: Prentice-Hall, Inc., 1959.

Karpovich, Peter, *Physiology of Muscular Activity*.   Philadelphia: W. B.
Saunders Co., 1959.

Morehouse, Laurence E., and Augustus Miller, *Physiology of Exercise*.   St.
Louis: The C. V. Mosby Co., 1959.

Scott, M. Gladys, *Analysis of Human Motion*.   New York: F. S. Crofts & Co.,
1947.

Wells, Katharine F., *Kinesiology* (3rd ed.).   Philadelphia: W. B. Saunders Co., 1955.

Growth and Development

Ausubel, David P., *Theory and Problems of Child Development.*   New York: Grune & Stratton, Inc., 1958.

Dennis, Wayne, ed., *Readings in Child Psychology* (2nd ed.).   Englewood Cliffs, N.J.: Prentice-Hall, Inc., 1963.

Gordon, Ira J., *Human Development from Birth Through Adolescence.*   New York: Harper & Row, Publishers, 1962.

McCandless, Boyd R., *Children and Adolescents.*   New York: Holt, Rinehart & Winston, 1961.

Merry, Frieda K., and Ralph V. Merry, *The First Two Decades of Life.*   New York: Harper & Row, Publishers, 1950.

Postures and Relaxation

Davies, Evelyn A., *The Elementary School Child and His Posture Patterns.*   New York: Appleton-Century-Crofts, Inc., 1958.

Jacobson, E., *Progressive Relaxation.*   Chicago: University of Chicago Press, 1938.

Logan, Gene A., *Adaptations of Muscular Activity.*   Belmont, Calif.: Wadsworth Publishing Co., Inc., 1964.

Lowman, C. L., and Carl H. Young, *Postural Fitness.*   Philadelphia: Lea & Febiger, 1960.

Metheny, Eleanor, *Body Dynamics.*   New York: McGraw-Hill Book Company, Inc., 1952.

Rasch, P., and R. Burke, *Kinesiology and Applied Anatomy* (2nd ed.).   Philadelphia: Lea & Febiger, 1963.

Rathbone, J. L., *Corrective Physical Education.*   Philadelphia: W. B. Saunders Co., 1944.

Expression

Allport, Gordon W., *Pattern and Growth in Personality.*   New York: Holt, Rinehart and Winston, 1961.

Anderson, Harold H., ed., *Creativity and Its Cultivation*. New York: Harper & Row, Publishers, 1959.

Ausubel, David P., *Theory and Problems of Child Development*. New York: Grune & Stratton, Inc., 1958.

Torrance, E. Paul, *Guiding Creative Talent*. Englewood Cliffs, N.J.: Prentice-Hall, Inc., 1962.

Sensation and Perception

Hebb, D. O., *A Textbook of Psychology*. Philadelphia: W. B. Saunders Co., 1958.

Krech, David, and R. S. Crutchfield, *Elements of Psychology*. New York: Alfred A. Knopf, Inc., 1959.

McGraw, M. B., "Neural Maturation as Exemplified in the Reaching-Prehensile Behavior of the Human Infant," *Journal of Psychology*, XI (1941), 127–41.

Milne, Lorus J., and Margery Milne, *The Senses of Animals and Men*. New York: Atheneum Publishers, 1962.

Sherman, M., and I. S. Sherman, "Sensori-motor Responses in Infants," *Journal of Comparative Psychology*, V (1952), 53–68.

Solley, Charles M., and Gardner Murphy, *Development of the Perceptual World*. New York: Basic Books, Inc., Publishers, 1960.

Other Sources for Further Study

Association for Supervision and Curriculum Development, *Perceiving, Behaving, Becoming—A New Focus*. Washington, D.C.: The Association, 1962.

Combs, A. W., and Donald Snygg, *Individual Behavior* (2nd ed.). New York: Harper & Row, Publishers, 1959.

de Grazia, Sebastian, *Of Time, Work and Leisure*. New York: The Twentieth Century Fund, Inc., 1962.

French, Will, *Behavioral Goals of General Education*. New York: Russell Sage Foundation, 1957.

Hefferman, Helen, ed., *Guiding the Young Child: Kindergarten to Grade Three*. Boston: D. C. Heath & Company, 1959.

Latchaw, Marjorie, and Camille Brown, *The Evaluation Process in Health, Physical Education and Recreation.* Englewood Cliffs, N.J.: Prentice-Hall, Inc., 1962.

Metheny, Eleanor, "The Unique Meaning Inherent in Human Movement," *The Physical Educator,* March, 1961.

Smith, Paul, ed., *Creativity: An Examination of the Creative Process.* New York: Hastings House Publishers, Inc., 1959.

Stein, Maurice I., and Shirley J. Heinze, *Creativity and the Individual.* Glencoe, Ill.: The Free Press, 1960.

PART TWO

MOVEMENT ACTIVITIES
FOR CHILDREN

13 MOVEMENT EXPLORATION

The materials in this chapter provide specific suggestions for stimulating experimental movement for experimental development of the child. Children should be encouraged to move freely and independently, to explore new ways of moving.

For the elementary-age child, most movement experiences are exploratory in nature. When he is in the process of learning to kick, to jump on the trampoline, or to climb a rope, he is exploring movement possibilities for coping with the environment. When he is hopping sideways, forward, backward, high and low, fast and slow, in rhythm to a sound he hears or to a tune he whistles, he is exploring movement. When he is playing a game with others, finding ways to overtake and capture another, or to avoid being captured by another, he is investigating movement possibilities.

Movement exploration, therefore, is a broad term relating to a process for developing many movement patterns, skills, and activities learned in many and varied situations. Activities for exploring movement problems related to coping with the environment are presented in the remaining six chapters of this book. The material includes exploration of: (1) media of land, air, water; (2) objects of location, such as balls, bats, apparatus, human relationships; (3) time and space factors, such as varying speeds and directions of movement. For example, a game of tag may present problems in moving on a particular surface, in different directions, at various rates of speed, and in relation to other moving children.

Exploratory movement for coping with the environment differs in its objective from exploratory movement for experimental development, and from exploratory movement for expressive form. Brown and Cassidy stress the need for "creative experimentalism" in the new world. They state that for the attainment of this objective, evaluation must be internal, with each participant setting his own ideal state of affairs.[1] Any attempt on the part of the teacher or other outsiders to describe a performance as creative or noncreative, good or bad, or to compare one child with another prevents the fulfillment of the objective. They further describe "expressive form" as movement that expresses "ideas of feelings." When referring to movement with expressive form as the objective, the terms dance, modern dance, choreography, and the like, are frequently used.

Social and folk dances are cultural forms that have prescribed movement patterns and structures. These dances are useful in helping the child to understand the movement of the cultures from which they were produced.

The ideas presented in this chapter are examples of problems that may be used to help children experiment with many movement possibilities. Experimentation is the primary goal. Learning in skill and other areas is incidental, and should not interfere with the child's experimental development. Each activity presented here is followed by suggestions for further exploration, and each may be repeated in many different ways as ideas are expanded and developed. Each problem may be adapted to the maturation level of the particular group of children.

Children may wish to use some of their new ways of moving to express an idea of feelings. They may wish to recapture and repeat the movements and develop them into a dance composition. They may wish to experiment with various kinds of accompaniment, using percussion, words and sounds, songs and music. Some dances may be performed in groups and others may be performed individually.

Exploring Movement Patterns

Brown and Cassidy suggest a unique method of movement experimentation, varying environmental variables in the performance of a given movement pattern. The following chart includes some of the factors used for movement problems of this nature.[2]

[1] Camille Brown and Rosalind Cassidy, *Theory in Physical Education* (Philadelphia: Lea & Febiger, 1963), pp. 136–42, and Chapter 7.
[2] *Ibid.*, pp. 138–40.

Movement patterns	Some environmental variables*				
	Media	Speed	Direction	Force	Relationships
Walk	Water	Fast	Far	Heavy	Alone
Run	Air	Slow	Close	Light	Partner
Leap	Land	Medium	Up	Jerky	Team
Jump	Sand	Others	Down	Hard	Others
Skip	Cement		Forward	Soft	
Slide	Grass		Backward	Rhythmic	
Hop	Wood		Sideward	Controlled	
Throw	Gravel		High	Others	
Kick	Ice		Low		
Pull	Mud		Level		
Push	Others		Others		
Others					

* Brown and Cassidy include the environmental variables of "Objects and Obstacles," which have been intentionally omitted from this list, since they are presented in the remaining six chapters of this book.

WAYS OF WALKING

Behavioral goal: To find many different ways of walking.
Concept: Movement expression and creativity.
Biologic efficiency: Coordination; agility.
Movement skill: Walking.

Children are asked to perform the following movement: Walk on the grass with medium speed, in a forward direction, lightly, and alone.

They are asked to experiment with walking by:

(1) Varying the speed from medium to fast and slow;

(2) Varying direction from forward to backward, sideward, high on tiptoes, low with bent knees;

(3) Varying force from walking lightly to walking heavily, stamping feet, walking rhythmically, walking with jerky movement;

(4) Varying relationships from walking alone to walking with a partner, in threes, fours, fives, in a file line, in a circle;

(5) Varying media from walking on the grass to walking on blacktop, on the sidewalk, on dirt, on sand or gravel, on wood, on leaves, on any other available media.

RUN HIGH, RUN LOW

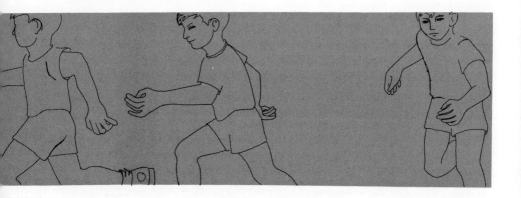

Behavioral goal: To experiment with different ways of running.
Concept: Movement expression and creativity.
Biologic efficiency: Coordination; agility; endurance.
Movement skill: Running.

Children are asked to run high on tiptoes, knees raised, then run low with body close to ground, on blacktop with medium speed, in a forward direction, lightly, and alone.

Children experiment with running in many different ways by varying the environmental factors, as described in "Ways of Walking."

RUN AND LEAP

Behavioral goal: To find many different ways of leaping.
Concept: Movement expression and creativity.
Biologic efficiency: Coordination; strength; endurance.
Movement skill: Running and leaping.

Children are asked to perform the following movements: run several steps and leap in a forward direction, landing lightly, and moving alone.

They are asked to experiment with run and leap by:

(1) Varying the speed from medium to fast to slow;
(2) Varying direction as follows:
    (a) Pretend you are running and leaping over a high tree
    (b) Pretend you are running and leaping over a low wall
    (c) Pretend you are running and leaping sideward over a high bar
    (d) Run and leap over a line on the ground
    (e) Run and leap over two widely spaced lines on the ground
    (f) Pretend you are running and leaping over a wide river
    (g) Run and leap as high as you can
    (h) Run and leap as low as you can;
(3) Varying force from a high leap landing lightly to a very low leap landing heavily;
(4) Varying relationships from moving alone to moving with others;
(5) Varying media from moving on grass to moving on wood, sand, in water; avoid media such as loose gravel, concrete, and slippery surfaces, which may cause injury from falling.

EXPLORING THE JUMP AND HOP

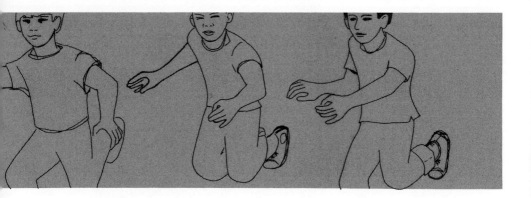

Behavioral goal: To find many different ways of jumping and hopping.
Concept: Movement expression and creativity.
Biologic efficiency: Coordination; strength; endurance.
Movement skill: Jumping; hopping.

Children experiment with jumping and hopping in many different ways by varying environmental factors, as described in "Run and Leap."

WAYS OF SKIPPING

Behavioral goal: To find many different ways of skipping.
Concept: Movement expression and creativity.

Biologic efficiency: Coordination.
Movement skill: Skipping.

Children are asked to skip alone, on blacktop, forward in a circle, landing lightly.

They are asked to experiment with other ways of skipping by:

(1) Varying the speed from medium to fast to slow;

(2) Varying direction from forward to backward, from high to low;

(3) Varying force from light to heavy, from rhythmic to jerky;

(4) Varying relationships from alone to a partner, to a group;

(5) Varying media from blacktop to grass, dirt, sand, gravel, wood, shallow water, and any other available media.

WAYS OF SLIDING AND GALLOPING

Behavioral goal: To find many different ways of sliding and galloping.
Concept: Movement expression and creativity.
Biologic efficiency: Coordination.
Movement skill: Sliding; galloping.

Children experiment with sliding and galloping in many different ways by varying environmental factors, as described in "Ways of Skipping."

THROW AND CATCH

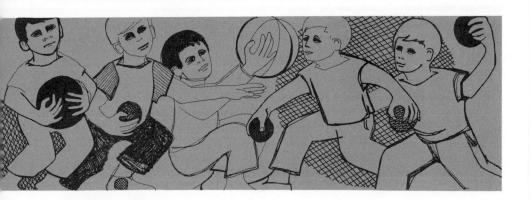

Behavioral goal: To find many different ways of throwing and catching.
Concept: Movement expression and creativity.
Biologic efficiency: Coordination.
Movement skill: Throwing; catching.

    Children may be given an object to throw and catch, or they may pretend that they have an object. They experiment with throwing and catching by varying the environmental factors of media, speed, direction, force, and relationships.

EXPLORING OTHER MOVEMENT PATTERNS

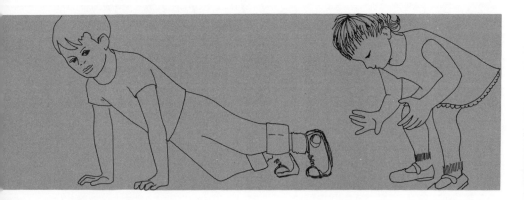

Behavioral goal: To find many ways of performing a particular movement pattern, such as pulling, pushing, kicking, striking, crawling, and others.

Concept: Movement expression; creative experimentalism.
Biologic efficiency: Coordination; agility; strength; endurance; flexibility.
Movement skill: Specific pattern being performed.

Children should be free to explore in a rich and varied environment, without fear of censure or labeling.   Experimentation is the primary goal, with learnings in the areas of biologic efficiency and movement skill necessarily concomitant.

Children experiment with the particular movement patterns by varying the environmental factors:

(1) Media, including any surfaces available;
(2) Speed, varying from slow to fast;
(3) Direction, including distances from close to far, up to down, high to low, and directions of forward, backward, sideward, circular, linear;
(4) Force from heavy to light, jerky to rhythmical;
(5) Relationships, from alone to a partner, threes, fours, and so on.

Exploring Sensory Stimuli[3]

Sensory stimulation (vision, hearing, taste and smell, touch, pressure, pain, temperature, kinesthesis) may result in movement.   Experimentation with movement, using sensory stimuli as the movement sources, is described in the following examples.   These examples may be adapted to any grade level and to the interests and needs of any group of children.   The teacher may provide many other movement opportunities using varied sensory stimuli in many ways.

[3] Materials in this section are modified from Marjorie Latchaw and Jean Pyatt, *A Pocket Guide of Dance Activities* (Englewood Cliffs, N.J.: Prentice-Hall, Inc., 1958).

TASTE AND SMELL

Behavioral goal: To move in ways that various tastes and smells make one feel.

Concept: Sensation and movement.

Biologic efficiency: Coordination; agility; flexibility.

Movement skill: Locomotion and nonlocomotion.

Teacher and children discuss various tastes and smells, describing them and telling how they would feel in movement. Some responses may be:

(1) The taste of lemon makes me feel all scrunched together and shivery;

(2) My mother's perfume makes me feel like closing my eyes and floating like a cloud;

(3) Chocolate candy tastes like jumping up and down;

(4) When I smell a carnation, I feel like turning round and round and waving my arms;

(5) The smell of a cake baking makes me hug myself and sway back and forth.

Children choose a favorite taste or smell. They show how it makes them feel in nonlocomotion, such as sitting, kneeling, or standing, and in locomotion or traveling across the room. For example, a child may decide that a lemon makes him feel small, wrinkled, and shivery when he tastes it. He may sit on the floor, hunching his shoulders, bringing his head to his knees, clenching his fists, and moving from side to side. He may repeat the movement, rising to his knees, then to his feet, and traveling through space with some form of locomotion.

Children may group together and choose a taste or smell. Each child in the group may move as the taste or smell makes him feel. Some children may sit on the floor, others may kneel, others may stand. Some children may move among those who are stationary.

I AM A SOUND

Behavioral goal: To move in ways that show how various sounds make one feel.

Concept: Sensation and movement.

Biologic efficiency: Coordination; agility; flexibility.

Movement skill: Locomotion and nonlocomotion.

A variety of sound-producing objects is used, such as whistles, pots and pans, toy snappers, baby rattles, wooden blocks, triangles, music box, electric razor or motor, bird whistle, and so on. Teacher produces a sound from an object and children show through movement how the sound makes them feel. Teacher may or may not let children see object.

For example, a sharp whistle may make a child think of a series of circles moving rapidly through space. He might make small circles with his head and body, allowing them to get larger and larger as he moves in a circular path of ever-increasing size. Crackling paper might make a child think of sharp, jagged lines, which he may show by jabbing his hands, head, knees, or body through space as he hops or jumps.

I AM A COLOR

Behavioral goal: To move in ways that a color makes one feel.
Concept: Sensation and movement.
Biologic efficiency: Coordination; agility; flexibility.
Movement skill: Locomotion and nonlocomotion.

Objects of many different colors are made available—scarves, hats, boxes, construction paper, tissue paper, and the like. Teacher holds up a colored object and all discuss how the color makes them feel. If the shape of the object appears to influence the feeling, use only colored paper.
Teacher might ask:

(1) What do you think of when you see blue?
(2) Does blue make you feel like moving fast or slow?
(3) Does blue make you feel open or closed?
(4) Does blue make you feel happy? Shivery? Angry? Sunny? Hot?

HOT OR COLD

Behavioral goal: To move in ways that show how temperatures make one feel.

Concept: Sensation and movement.
Biologic efficiency: Coordination; agility; flexibility.
Movement skill: Locomotor and nonlocomotor movements.

Teacher discusses temperature perception with children.   They discuss how hot and cold things make them feel.   Teacher may ask:

(1) How do you feel when you are lying in a tub of warm water?
(2) How do you feel when you jump into a cold swimming pool?
(3) How do you feel when you touch a hot match?
(4) How do you feel when a cold ice cube is in your mouth?
(5) How do you feel when hot air is blowing in your face?   When a cool breeze blows through your hair?   When a freezing winter wind blows against your face?

Children choose something hot and something cold and move in the way these contrasting objects make them feel, using nonlocomotion and locomotion.

ROUGH OR SMOOTH

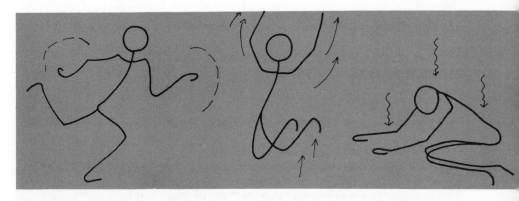

Behavioral goal: To move in ways that tactile perception makes one feel.
Concept: Sensation and movement.
Biologic efficiency: Coordination; agility; flexibility.
Movement skill: Locomotion and nonlocomotion.

Teacher discusses tactile sensitivity with children.   Objects of varying textures are made available, such as silk cloth, burlap, feathers, rope, seashells, mirrors, balls, driftwood, beads, furry slippers, and so on.

Children form small groups and each group receives an object.   Each child shows how the object makes him feel.   For example, a feather may make him feel soft, smooth, and light. He may stand in a straight line with arms and legs extended, then move softly with arms waving gently from side to side.

WORDS AND SOUNDS

Boom   Tweet   Dum – de   Da – de – da

Behavioral goal: To move in ways that sounds may make one feel.
Concept: Sensation and movement.
Biologic efficiency: Coordination; agility; flexibility.
Movement skill: Locomotion.

Children say, "Boom! Boom! Boom!" Then they walk in any direction, stepping on each "Boom!" Children say, "Tweet! Tweet!" They continue walking, stepping on tiptoe on each "Tweet!" Children say, "Da-da-da-da!" They continue moving, running on each "Da!"

Teacher suggests a sentence of nonsense syllables, such as, "Dum de, dum de, dum de, ho, ho, ho, boom!" Children move to the sounds. For example, they may skip on "dum de," run on "ho" and jump on "boom!"

Children make up their own nonsense syllables and move to them.

Other sounds may be words, such as a child's name. Sounds such as gasps, sighs, groans, or hisses, or chanted, rhythmic poems are also appropriate.

ECHO

Behavioral goal: To echo a sound by moving in different ways.
Concept: Sensation and movement.
Biologic efficiency: Coordination; agility; flexibility.
Movement skill: Locomotion and nonlocomotion.

Teacher beats a rhythm pattern, using a percussion instrument or clapping with her hands. Children echo the rhythm pattern by moving their bodies in the pattern. Teacher may suggest a movement—walk, hop, swing, sway, push and pull—or children may choose movements.

Children may get in small groups and take turns beating a rhythm pattern for others to echo. Examples of rhythm patterns:

(1)

(2)

(3)

ROUNDS

Behavioral goal: To move to a song, alone and with others.

Concept: Sensation and movement.

Biologic efficiency: Coordination; flexibility; agility.

Movement skill: Locomotion and nonlocomotion.

Teacher and children select a familiar round tune and sing it several times, in unison and in round form. Examples of rounds are *Little Tom Tinker*, *Three Blind Mice*, and *Coral Bells*.

Each child plans a movement pattern for each line of the round. Children get into groups of fours and decide on a movement for each line; then they move together until they are familiar with the planned movement patterns. Children use round form, with one child singing and moving to first line followed by other children in succession, until song is completed.

Entire class may divide into four groups and sing and dance the selected movement patterns.

MOVING TO MUSIC

Behavioral goal: To experiment with many ways of moving to music, moving as it makes one feel.

Concept: Sensation and movement.
Biologic efficiency: Coordination; flexibility; agility.
Movement skill: Locomotion and nonlocomotion.

Children listen to music played from records or piano. They sit on the floor in a circle, backs to the center, eyes closed. As music is played, they experiment with different ways of moving to the music without leaving their sitting positions.

Music should be varied to stimulate different responses. Slow, rhythmic music may produce swinging movements of head, arms, torso; fast music may bring a response of very small, rapid movements.

Similar explorations may be done at different levels, such as kneeling, standing, or lying. Children may also choose to travel to the music, using varied movement patterns, speeds, directions, forces, and relationships.

Exploring Ideas and Imagery[4]

Movement ideas may be found in many experiences common to children. Familiar games, stories, holidays, occupations of fathers, and pets are appropriate sources of ideas. Movement might take the form of role-playing or pantomime, or it might move into the realm of abstraction by capturing qualities of speed, force, shape and direction, or range. Imagery is useful in helping children to explore movement qualities. Children find pleasure in experimenting with movement, using varied qualities in juxtaposition, such as swinging and then collapsing.

[4] Modified from Latchaw and Pyatt, op. cit.

COLLAPSING PUPPETS

Behavioral goal: To experiment with ways of collapsing.
Concept: Movement expression and creativity.
Biologic efficiency: Relaxation; flexibility; coordination.
Movement skill: Collapsing.

Children lie on floor with eyes closed. Teacher slowly and quietly tells them that they are sawdust dolls with a hole in the toe, and the sawdust is slowly running out of each part of the body, starting with the toe, foot, legs, and torso, ending with the arms, hands, fingertips and head. Ultimately the children are collapsed (relaxed) on the floor.

Teacher tells children they are puppets, and the puppet master is pulling the strings to lift them from the floor. The puppet master stretches them tall and high, then collapses the wrists, the arms, the head, the shoulders, the torso, the legs until the children are again stretched on the floor.

Children experiment with collapsing, varying speed, force, and direction:

(1) Starting from sitting position, collapse fast, then collapse slow. Repeat from kneeling and standing positions;
(2) Collapse gradually, like a tire deflating because of a slow leak;
(3) Collapse jerkily, one part at a time;
(4) Collapse slowly, as though gradually tiring, then suddenly becoming exhausted.

HOLIDAY IDEAS

Behavioral goal: To show an idea in movement.
Concept: Movement expression and creativity.
Biologic efficiency: Relaxation; flexibility; agility.
Movement skill: Locomotion and nonlocomotion.

Children and teacher select a holiday, and make a list of objects and a list of feelings that describe the holiday.

Objects related to Halloween may include black cats arching their backs and hissing, witches riding on broomsticks or stirring cauldrons, owls hooting in trees, a smiling full moon, bats flying through the sky, and children dressed in costumes for trick-or-treat. Feelings may be merry, spooky, stealthy, scary, excited, happy.

Each child chooses a favorite object (or objects) and shows what it looks like in movement, and how it feels. Children might move in the shape of the object; they might draw the object in space, using different parts of the body as the pencil. They might move in the quality of the object, pretending to be bats sailing and darting through space, or black cats stealthily slinking through space, then collapsing in exhaustion.

Groups of children having related objects may devise dances for the others in the class, accompanying themselves with percussion instruments, records, songs, or voice sounds.

THE PLAYGROUND

Behavioral goals: To show a playground activity in movement.
Concept: Movement expression and creativity.
Biologic efficiency: Relaxation; flexibility; agility.
Movement skill: Locomotion and nonlocomotion.

Children and teacher list playground activities on the chalkboard, such as kickball, softball, Jungle Gym, see-saw, slides, and so on. Each child selects a favorite activity and pantomimes how it is played. Then he pretends to be a piece of equipment used in the activity, and shows in movement how the equipment looks and moves. For example, a ball might roll on the floor, or it might stand up and spin about as it travels forward.

Children accompany themselves with sounds; for example, "whish, whish" for rope jumping.

INANIMATE OBJECTS

Behavioral goals: To show with the body the shapes of objects, and how they move.

Concept: Movement expression and creativity.
Biologic efficiency: Coordination; agility; flexibility.
Movement skill: Locomotion and nonlocomotion.

Children and teacher list inanimate objects on the board. Children show with their bodies the shapes of the various objects. If the object is moved by an external force, they show with their bodies how the object would be moved. For instance:

An orange being peeled;
A standing lamp being carried across the room;
A wall with a vine growing over it;
A paper clip being inserted on paper;
An ice cube melting;
A balloon with air coming out of it;
A cloud drifting through the sky, slowly changing shapes;
Smoke coming out of a chimney;
A twisted pin being thrust into paper;
A rubber ball bouncing along the ground;
A boat being tossed by the waves;
An arrow being shot through the air.

ANIMALS

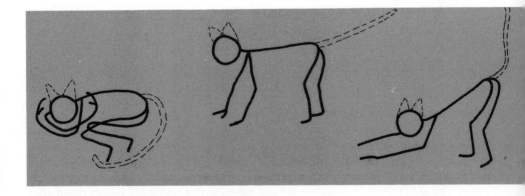

Behavioral goal: To move like an animal.
Concept: Movement expression and creativity.
Biologic efficiency: Coordination; agility; flexibility.
Movement skill: Locomotion and nonlocomotion.

Teacher and children select an animal and decide on the physical characteristics that are related to its movement. For example, a cat's soft fur stands up when the cat is frightened; it can wrap its long tail around itself; it is quick, and leaps and jumps very high; it is very flexible, and can curl into a small ball or stretch out very long.

Children explore movements characterizing the animal.

Each child chooses a favorite animal and shows others how the animal moves.

UNWINDING

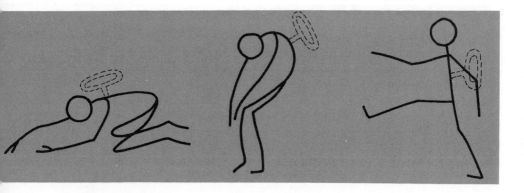

Behavioral goal: To move like a wind-up toy and collapse.
Concept: Movement expression and creativity.
Biologic efficiency: Coordination; agility; flexibility.
Movement skill: Locomotion and nonlocomotion.

Children pretend to be wind-up toys (dolls, dogs, monkeys, rabbits, clowns). Teacher winds up the toys and the children begin moving at a brisk pace, then slower and slower, until they are completely "run down" and topple or collapse to the floor. Teacher or child rewinds the toys, and the sequence is repeated.

Children explore moving in the manner of many kinds of wind-up toys, using both locomotor and nonlocomotor movement. For example, a child may be a toy monkey, hopping up and down and clapping his hands together, a toy bear beating a toy drum, or a toy duck, waddling and quacking. Children might bring their wind-up toys to school to stimulate other ideas.

MY HEAD IS A SWING

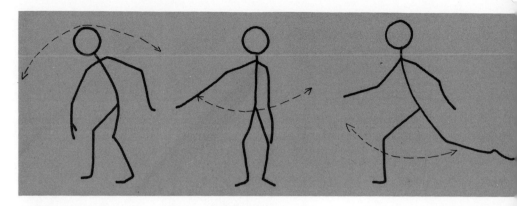

Behavioral goal: To move head and body like a swing.
Concept: Movement expression and creativity.
Biologic efficiency: Coordination; agility; flexibility.
Movement skill: Locomotion and nonlocomotion.

Children and teacher chant, "My head is a swing and it swings and swings and swings . . . ," each swinging his head up and down, side to side, around and around, allowing the head to fall as far as possible each time.

Then they chant, "My arm is a swing . . . ," swinging one arm, then the other, then both together. They continue chanting and swinging the trunk, each leg in many different directions.

I AM A RIVET MACHINE

Behavioral goal: To vibrate like a rivet machine.

Concept: Movement expression and creativity.
Biologic efficiency: Coordination.
Movement skill: Locomotion and nonlocomotion.

Children vibrate their bodies as though they were holding a rivet machine. They try to vibrate isolated parts of the body, then see how many body parts they can vibrate together.

Children try traveling as they vibrate body parts, shaking their hands, head, torso, feet, and legs.

Children select an idea using vibratory movement, such as shaking water off one's body like a dog, riding on a bumpy road, taking off in a rocket, or shaking with cold, and explore moving in this way.

I AM A HAMMER

Behavioral goal: To move with a percussive quality.
Concept: Movement expression and creativity.
Biologic efficiency: Coordination.
Movement skill: Locomotion and nonlocomotion.

Children pretend their heads are hammers and hammer a nail into the wall. They continue exploring percussive movement by using other body parts as a hammer.

Children select other ideas for exploring percussive movement, such as knocking on a door, stamping a peg into the ground, jumping on something to break it, or popping a balloon.

Children work together to show sudden, sharp movement. For example, two children may act out a fist fight by facing each other, one advancing with percussive steps and striking at the other as the second child retreats with percussive steps, dodging with sharp, thrusting movements of the body.

MOVEMENT QUALITIES

Behavioral goal: To explore movement qualities, using ideas.
Concept: Movement expression and creativity.
Biologic efficiency: Coordination; flexibility.
Movement skill: Locomotion and nonlocomotion.

Children use ideas to stimulate movement that illustrates different qualities. For example:

(1) Using the trunk as the pendulum of a clock, swing rhythmically from side to side. The clock begins to run down until the pendulum is moving in slow motion. Suddenly, the spring snaps and parts of the clock shoot off explosively. The spring vibrates by itself.

(2) An old freight train is chugging along, vibrating as it goes over the bumpy track. The signal begins to swing, the train slows down for the crossing, and the whistle in the signal tower pops up and down vigorously.

(3) A horse trots in short, quick, percussive movements, swinging its head from side to side impatiently. It slows down, gets to its knees, lies on its side, and rolls from side to side.

(4) A sailboat sails smoothly on the ocean, the waves swinging it rhythmically from side to side. It crosses the wake of another boat, bumping sharply up and down. A sudden breeze whips the sail about and the boat shudders and vibrates until it rights itself, then sails smoothly away.

(5) The wheel of the sewing machine swings round and round, the needle bobs up and down in short percussive jabs on the cloth, which moves slowly through the machine.

Exploring Time and Space[5]

Experimentation with movement through the exploration of time and space factors may include several elements: speed, distance and direction, level, range, and shape.

Speed, the swiftness or rate of motion through space, may be thought of as a time-space element, moving on a continuum from fast to slow. Distances may be described as far or near, and directions as up, down, forward, backward, or sideward. Levels may be described as high or low, and range as large or small. Shape of the movement in space is effected by combinations of the other four elements.

An additional factor related to spatial elements is that of focus, the point to which attention is directed by the movement. The focus may remain constant, or it may change with each movement.

LARGE AND SMALL

Behavioral goal: To experiment with range of movement.
Concept: Movement expression and creativity.

[5] Modified from Latchaw and Pyatt, op. cit.

Biologic efficiency: Flexibility; coordination.
Movement skill: Locomotion and nonlocomotion.

   Children crouch on the floor, curling into as small a space as possible.
Then they begin moving forward, expanding with each step.   When they are
as large as possible, and fill as much space as possible, they suddenly become
very small again.
   Children experiment with different ways of using very little and very much
space, in stationary positions, and traveling in different directions.

RANGE OF MOTION

Behavioral goal: To experiment with range of motion.
Concept: Movement and creativity.
Biologic efficiency: Flexibility; coordination.
Movement skill: Locomotion and nonlocomotion.

   Teacher and children list some familiar movements, such as batting a ball,
riding a surfboard, eating a banana, dribbling a ball, combing one's hair,
and so on.   Each child selects one movement and performs it.   Then he performs his movements in as small a space as possible, using very tiny actions,
and then in as large a space as possible, using very large actions.
   Children explore range further by using movement patterns such as walk,
hop, and jump, increasing and decreasing the range of movement as they
perform the patterns.   For example, a child may jump forward, his body
curled as much as possible.   Then he may gradually increase the range of
movement by jumping higher and farther, arms and body very wide, and
using as much space as possible.
   Children may form groups and select an activity or activities to perform.

They may work out movements that show a change of range from small to medium to large; or they may reverse the procedure, starting large and moving to small.   Children may start with the normal position, then change the range to very small, then to very large.

Children may select movements they wish to repeat together or individually.   They may choose accompaniment, using words or sounds, music, or percussion.   They may vary the movements by using different speeds as they change the range of movement.   They may move in many different directions as they perform large and small movements.

SPACE PEOPLE

Behavioral goal: To experiment with speed of motion.
Concept: Movement expression and creativity.
Biologic efficiency: Flexibility; coordination.
Movement skill: Locomotion and nonlocomotion.

Children pretend that they are on a planet in space where their bodies are much heavier than on earth.   They lift an arm as though it weighed a great deal, walk as though their bodies were twice as heavy as they are.

Children select a familiar game such as tag, softball, or dodge-ball and play the game on the strange planet, using slow motion because of their increased weight.   The teacher may use a gong to help children maintain sustained movement.   Each movement should continue for as long as the child can hear the sound of the gong.

SLOW MOTION

Behavioral goal: To experiment with slow motion.
Concept: Movement expression and creativity.
Biologic efficiency: Coordination; flexibility.
Movement skill: Locomotion and nonlocomotion.

Children pretend that they are moving in a jar of molasses or heavy syrup. They try to swim through the syrup, walk through it, sit down and stand up, throw a ball, push a table.

Children select a story, poem, or any idea, and act it out in slow motion, like actors in a movie being projected at slow speed. Then they pretend that the movie is projected at fast speed, and repeat their movements rapidly.

FAST AND SLOW

Behavioral goals: To experiment with contrasting speeds.

Concept: Movement expression and creativity.
Biologic efficiency: Coordination; flexibility; agility.
Movement skill: Locomotion and nonlocomotion.

Children select something that can change speed—an automobile, a train, a boat, an animal, a person, the wind.   Each child chooses one thing and moves as it does, following the beat of the teacher's drum.   Teacher gradually accelerates drumbeat, then decelerates until it is very slow.

Children walk in a circle to the drumbeat, moving into a run as the beat picks up speed, and slowing to a walk as the beat slows down.

Children sit on the floor and move as slowly as they possibly can, as rapidly as they possibly can, as "medium" as they possibly can.

Children divide into groups, and each group chooses something that moves at different rates of speed.   They work out movements to show what their object is, how it moves at different speeds, and how it relates to other objects.   For example, if a group selects the wind, one child may be the wind and others in group may be things the wind moves, such as signboards (swinging), windmills (turning), weather-vanes (turning), a line of clothes (blowing), trees (swaying), leaves (tossing about), or people leaning into or away from the wind.   The wind may be a gentle wind, a strong wind, a tornado or hurricane.

MY NAME IS ――――

Behavioral goal: To form letters in space.
Concept: Movement expression and creativity.
Biologic efficiency: Coordination; flexibility.
Movement skill: Locomotion and nonlocomotion.

Each child writes his own name on an imaginary chalkboard with an imaginary piece of chalk. Then he writes his name with the chalk attached to his elbow, then to his head, knee, foot.

Child writes his name on the floor by walking it as a floor pattern. He writes it as if he felt sad, happy, angry, tired. Other children try to guess the feeling he is showing as he writes his name.

SPACE SHAPES

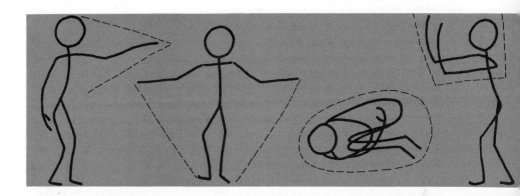

Behavioral goal: To experiment with different ways of making shapes in space.

Concept: Movement expression; creativity.

Biologic efficiency: Coordination; flexibility.

Movement skill: Locomotion and nonlocomotion.

Children explore different body shapes:

(1) Make the body into a point, first using the whole body, then individual body parts;

(2) Make the body into a ball, using the whole body, then individual parts;

(3) Make the body into a brick wall, using the whole body, then individual parts;

(4) Make the body into a plane, a flat surface, using the whole body, then individual parts.

Children explore different air shapes that can be made by movement:

(1) Make a curved shape in the air, using the whole body, then individual parts;
(2) Make a straight line in the air;
(3) Make a squared shape in the air;
(4) Make a round shape in the air;
(5) Make a triangular shape in the air;
(6) Make a twisted shape in the air;
(7) Make a spiral in the air;
(8) Make other shapes by combining curves, squares, spirals, lines, and so on.

Children draw pictures of objects in space, using the whole body as the pencil, then using individual body parts. Children experiment with space pictures, starting the picture with one part of the body as the pencil, and completing it with other parts of the body.

Children make shapes in space, varying range and speed:

(1) Make shapes using very small, then very large movements;
(2) Make shapes in space, using very quick movements, then very slow movements.

Children make shapes in space, varying movement patterns of running, throwing, jumping, kicking, and so on.

IN THE JELLY GLASS

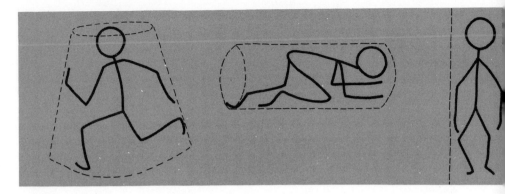

Behavioral goal: To experiment with different shapes in space.
Concept: Movement expression and creativity.
Biologic efficiency: flexibility; coordination.
Movement skill: Locomotion and nonlocomotion.

Children imagine that they are sleeping on the bottom of a jelly glass. The glass is just large enough for them to touch its sides in every direction by stretching as hard as possible.

Children awaken and decide to explore the sides of the jelly glass for cracks. Lying on the bottom they explore all sides carefully by stretching as far as possible. Then very slowly, moving up from the bottom, they explore all sides carefully by stretching as far as possible. After their exploration, they break out of the jelly glass by kicking the sides and breaking the glass.

They experiment with different shapes in space:

(1) Exploring the sides of a box;
(2) Exploring a very low tunnel by creeping, crawling, or moving through on the stomach;
(3) Exploring the sides of a high, narrow tunnel which they can get through only by standing and moving sideways, making themselves as thin as possible.

LINE DRAWINGS

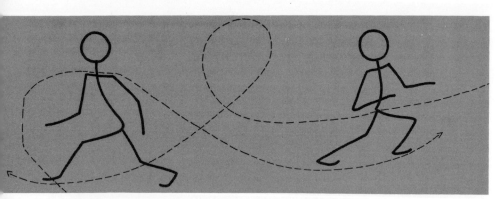

Behavioral goal: To experiment with various shapes of floor patterns.
Concept: Movement expression and creativity.
Biologic efficiency: Coordination.
Movement skill: Locomotion and nonlocomotion.

Each child draws a simple, unbroken line on a piece of paper. Then he walks in a floor pattern corresponding to his line.

Two children work together, drawing two lines that overlap or cross each other. Each child moves in a floor pattern corresponding to one of the lines.

Three children work together, each with his own line crossing or paralleling the others, and all moving on their individual floor patterns.

EXPLORING DIRECTIONS

Behavioral goal: To experiment with moving in different directions.
Concept: Movement expression and creativity.

Biologic efficiency: Coordination.
Movement skill: Locomotion and nonlocomotion.

Children move in many different directions—forward, backward, side-ward, diagonal, around.

Children explore directions, using combinations of locomotions, such as: walk forward three steps, backward two steps, hop sideward, ending with a jump-turn. They repeat the pattern several times, fast and then slow, with small and large movements.

Children plan a sequence of movement patterns, with different parts of the body leading on each directional change. For example, they may walk forward leading with the nose, then sideward, leading with the elbow, then backward, leading with the hip, and so on.

Children form groups, select an idea, and work out a movement sequence, using different directions.

UP AND DOWN AND IN-BETWEEN

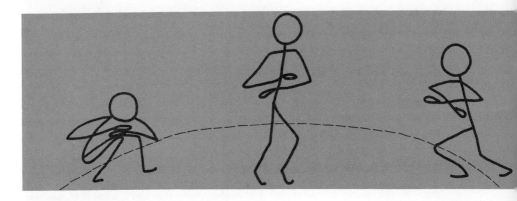

Behavioral goal: To explore levels in space.
Concept: Movement expression and creativity.
Biologic efficiency: Coordination; flexibility.
Movement skill: Locomotion and nonlocomotion.

Children explore up and down and in-between. For example, "down" may be lying on the floor and "up" may be standing, with "in-between" either sitting or kneeling. Then using a body part, such as the arm, they show up and down and in-between.

Children explore high and low and middle, using locomotion, by, for example, walking in a circle with body as low as possible, as high as possible, and at levels between the two extremes.

Children select a game using levels, and act it out in movement.   For example, they may choose softball where the batter reaches for a high or low ball, the baseman fields a grounder, the catcher reaches for a high wild pitch, and so on.

WHAT AM I WATCHING

Behavioral goal: To explore ways of moving while focusing on an object.
Concept: Movement expression and creativity.
Biologic efficiency: Coordination; flexibility.
Movement skill: Locomotion.

Children form groups of three or four.   One child in each group is IT.   IT closes his eyes and turns himself around.   When he stops turning, he opens his eyes and focuses on some object.   Then he moves about, twisting and turning in many directions, but watching his object all the time.   Other children in the group try to guess his object, and the child who first guesses correctly is the new IT.

Each group of children then chooses an object upon which to focus.   They watch the object continuously while trying many movements—away from the object, toward the object, around the object; standing on tiptoe, moving with knees bent, and so on.   After exploring many ways to move while focusing on an object, the group may combine a series of movements into a dance, and perform in unison.   For example, they may skip toward the object, slide around it, crawl away from it, jump in place, and finally walk away from the object, looking at it over their shoulders.   Each group may plan accompaniment for their dance.   Groups may show their dances to the class, permitting the class to try to guess the object.

Summary

The behavioral goal for each activity described in this chapter is experimentation with many different ways of moving.   The purpose is to provide opportunities for the experimental and creative development of each child.   The teacher should use the "guidelines and criteria for a creative environment" described in Chapter 5, "Movement Expression," to provide an atmosphere for nurturing creative movement expression in the child.

The concepts developed in this chapter are those of movement expression and creative experimentalism, and the interrelation between sensation and movement.   These concepts are described in Chapter 5, "Movement Expression," and Chapter 6, "Sensation and Movement."

These activities contribute to the development of certain aspects of biologic efficiency and movement skill, although these learnings are necessarily incidental to the experimental objective, and should not be emphasized to the detriment of the creative learnings.   Succeeding chapters in this book provide activities whose primary goals are the development of biologic efficiency and movement skills.

14 RUNNING ACTIVITIES

Running activities contribute to the development and maintenance of organic endurance. The degree to which they contribute to endurance depends upon how the activities are performed. If the purpose is to develop endurance, the activities should include running for increasingly longer periods of time, or at faster speeds. If an entire class is to benefit from the running, activities in which all children run for the maximum time should be selected. In some games, only two children run at a time, and this continues until one of the children is tagged. During this performance, other class members stand in some formation, waiting for their turns to run. It is apparent that the development of endurance is not the primary goal when such games are used.

It is advisable to alternate group running with individual running games, with emphasis on group running when the development of endurance is desired. This allows for increased increments by using the physical education period for running longer distances or at faster speeds.

Tagging activities emphasize the skills of starting and stopping, dodging, changing direction, running with the body at varying levels, and maintaining and regaining stability while in the process of moving rapidly. For example, the individual being chased must be able to swerve, start rapidly, stop and change direction, stretch away from the chaser, bend and duck under the hand of the chaser, and so on. The chaser must be able to anticipate the action of the one he is trying to tag, to move with him, block his movement, and successfully overtake and tag him.

Activities for Kindergarten

Many four and five years olds may find tagging games difficult in both organization and skills involved. Movement exploration without high organization is more to their liking, particularly if there is adequate space for running, jumping, and moving with the whole body. When children progress in their skill competencies and in their abilities to understand game boundaries, rules, and formations, they are ready to perform successfully in tag games.

Some simply organized activities that provide opportunities for kindergarten children to develop some of these skills and understandings are suggested in this section.

WILD HORSE RACE

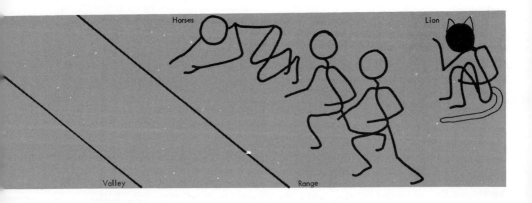

Behavioral goal: To run fast and stop without losing balance.
Concept: Gravity and movement; stability.
Biologic efficiency: Coordination; endurance.
Movement skill: Running.

Children are wild horses, grazing on the range. A mountain lion frightens them, and they race to the valley where they are safe.

To develop endurance, game may be repeated several times and running distances may be increased.

SPACE SHIP

Behavioral goal: To start fast and run rapidly in a circle.
Concept: Newton's laws of motion.
Biologic efficiency: Coordination; endurance.
Movement skill: Running.

Children are space ships. On the countdown, "Five, four, three, two, ONE!" the rocket blasts the space ships off the ground, they quickly pick up speed and go into orbit. After one orbit, they return to earth and "splash-down."

Game may be repeated any number of times, with space ships flying any number of orbits.

WHISTLE STOP

Behavioral goal: To run and stop on a signal.
Concept: Newton's laws of motion; gravity and movement.

Biologic efficiency: Endurance.
Movement skill: Running, stopping.

Children are scattered around field, within predetermined boundaries. On signal, "Run!" children run until the whistle blows, then stop immediately. They start again on the signal, "Run!" Children must be able to run and stop on appropriate signals, staying within the boundaries, and avoiding other runners.

Variations:

(1) When the whistle blows, stop; then obey the command, such as:
    (a) Run in a circle;
    (b) Run to a boundary;
    (c) Run sideward;
    (d) Run backward;
    (e) Run toward the fence (tree, school);
    (f) Run away from the fence (tree, teacher);

(2) When whistle blows, stop and clap hands;

(3) When whistle blows, stop and do a trick;

(4) When whistle blows, stop and wave at teacher;

(5) When whistle blows, stop and walk toward school;

(6) Other.

TIGERS RUN

Behavioral goal: To run fast on signal from one goal to another, increasing the distance from day to day.

Concept: Increasing endurance.

Biologic efficiency: Endurance.
Movement skill: Running.

Two goals are designated, 20 to 30 feet apart. Children stand back of one goal. Teacher says, "Tigers run once!" Children run to opposite goal. Teacher says, "Tigers run two times," and children run back to original goal. Teacher continues to call, "Tigers run three times," and so on until children tire.

A record may be kept of the number of "tiger runs," and each succeeding day children try for an increasing number of runs. As they improve in endurance, the distance between the goals may be extended.

OLYMPIC RUNNERS

Behavioral goal: To run for endurance.
Concept: Increasing and maintaining endurance.
Biologic efficiency: Endurance.
Movement skill: Running.

Mark off a large oval area, the "track." Children run around the track as many times as they can without stopping. When they are tired, they stop and tell the teacher whether they ran all the way around, half around, twice around, and so on.

Each succeeding day, the children try to run farther than before.

BEANBAG TAG

Behavioral goal: To overtake and tag another, and to avoid being tagged by others.
Concept: Laws of motion; gravity and movement.
Biologic efficiency: Coordination; endurance.
Movement skill: Running; dodging.

One child is IT and carries a beanbag as other children chase him. If someone tags IT, the tagger takes the beanbag and becomes IT, and all other children chase him.

If IT chooses to do so, he may toss the beanbag away. The child who catches or picks up the beanbag is IT and is chased by the others.

RED LION

Behavioral goal: To tag successfully and avoid being tagged.

Concept: Laws of motion; gravity and movement.
Biologic efficiency: Coordination; endurance.
Movement skill: Running; dodging.

One child is the red lion. The red lion is in his den, inside a circle, behind a tree, under a bush, and so on. Children gather round the den and chant, "Red lion, red lion, come out of your den."

When he chooses to do so, the lion charges out of his den and tries to catch a player. When he tags someone, they both go back to the den. The tagged player also becomes a lion and helps tag others. Game continues until all are tagged. Last player caught is new lion.

FROG IN THE SEA

Behavioral goal: To move quickly to tag others and avoid being tagged.
Concept: Laws of motion; gravity and movement.
Biologic efficiency: Coordination; endurance.
Movement skill: Running, dodging.

One child is the frog and sits in center of the circle. Players dare the frog by running in close to him and saying, "Froggie in the sea, can't catch me!"

If a player is tagged by the frog, he also becomes a frog and sits in the circle beside the first frog. Frogs must tag from the sitting position.

Game continues until four players are tagged. Then first frog chooses new frog from players who were not tagged.

Behavioral goal: To tag another and avoid being tagged.
Concept: Laws of motion; gravity and movement.
Biologic efficiency: Coordination; endurance.
Movement skill: Running in a circle.

Children stand in a circle. One child is IT and walks around the outside of the circle touching each person lightly and saying, "Gray owl," as he touches them. When he touches someone and says, "White owl," that person chases IT around the circle. If chaser can tag IT before IT reaches the vacant place in the circle, the tagger becomes IT. If tagger does not catch him, IT walks around the circle again.

If first IT is not tagged after two tries, he chooses a new IT from the children in the circle.

Activities for Grades 1, 2

The running-tagging activities suggested here can be performed successfully by most six and seven year olds. As with the activities suggested for kindergarten, the games are simple both in organization and skills involved.

JET RACES

Behavioral goal: To run fast and stop without losing balance; to start quickly on signal.
Concept: Gravity and movement.
Biologic efficiency: Coordination; endurance.
Movement skill: Running.

Children are jet pilots and stand with both feet back of starting line. On signal, "Take-off!" jets zoom to finish line. First jet to cross line is the winner, and gives the signal for the next race.

HUNTSMAN

Behavioral goal: To run fast on a signal.
Concept: Newton's laws of motion.

Biologic efficiency: Coordination; endurance.
Movement skill: Running.

One child is huntsman, and says to the other children, "Come with me to hunt bears." Other players fall into line behind him and follow in his footsteps as he leads them away from the goal line. When huntsman says, "Bang!" other players run to goal while huntsman tries to tag as many as possible. As each child is tagged, huntsman calls out child's name. Huntsman chooses new huntsman from players who reached base safely.

FLYING IN SPACE

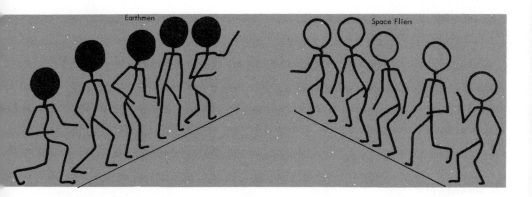

Behavioral goal: To overtake and tag others, and avoid being tagged.
Concept: Newton's laws of motion.
Biologic efficiency: Coordination; endurance.
Movement skill: Running.

Players are divided into two groups, the Earthmen and space fliers. Earthmen stand on one goal line and space fliers on the other. Space fliers choose the name of an object in space such as rocket, space ship, moon, earth, stars, meteors, astronaut, and so on; then they walk to a line three feet from the Earthmen. Space fliers say, "Earthmen, who are we?" Earthmen guess until they guess the correct object, then they chase the space fliers back to their goal.

Any fliers caught by the Earthmen become Earthmen and return to the goal with them. Space fliers who were not caught choose a new space object, and game continues until all are caught.

Game is repeated, with original Earthmen becoming space fliers, and vice versa.

DOGCATCHER

Behavioral goal: To overtake and tag others, and avoid being tagged.
Concept: Newton's laws of motion; gravity and movement.
Biologic efficiency: Coordination; endurance.
Movement skill: Running, dodging.

Children stand behind one goal line. Child who is dogcatcher stands in area between goals. Each child chooses the name of a dog. Dogcatcher calls, for example, "Poodles run!" Children who are poodles run to opposite goal. Any poodle caught by dogcatcher is put in the dog pound.

After dogcatcher has called several different names, he calls, "Dogs run!" and all remaining children run to opposite goal. New dogcatcher is chosen from among children who reached the goal safely, and game is repeated.

POM-POM-PULLAWAY

Behavioral goal: To overcome and tag another, and to avoid being tagged.

Concept: Newton's laws of motion.
Biologic efficiency: Coordination; endurance.
Movement skill: Running; dodging.

One child is IT, and stands in the area between two goals. All other children are behind one goal line. IT calls, "Pom-pom-pullaway! Come away or I'll pull you away!" and all players must run to opposite goal. Any children who are caught help IT catch others, when he calls again. IT is only player who can call.

When all children are caught, last one to be caught is new IT. If it is difficult to judge which child is last to be caught, IT may choose a new IT.

STONE

Behavioral goal: To move quickly from sitting to standing to running, and overtake and tag others; to avoid being tagged.
Concept: Newton's laws of motion; gravity and movement.
Biologic efficiency: Coordination; agility.
Movement skill: Running; changing body position quickly.

One child is "stone" and sits in center of a circle. Other players skip around stone. When stone jumps up, players run to either goal and stone chases them. Any player tagged by stone before reaching a goal becomes a stone too, and sits in circle with first stone. The other players continue to skip around the stones. No stone may move until the first stone moves.

Game continues until all children are caught.

HOW MANY ORBITS?

Behavioral goal: To run as many orbits as possible, without stopping.
Concept: Increasing endurance.
Biologic efficiency: Endurance.
Movement skill: Running.

Children are space ships trying for an endurance record in circling the earth. Each ship carries several tags with the name of the pilot (child who is the runner) on each tag. Each time the ship completes an orbit, it drops a tag in a box at the starting point. (Or the teacher may check off the child's name on a chart as he runs past.)

A record is kept from day to day, so that each child can see his increase in endurance as he becomes able to run greater distances. Comparisons are made with the child's own record, not against other runners.

Activities for Grades 3, 4

Most eight and nine year olds enjoy the activities suggested in this section. Activities range in order from simple to more difficult. It may be helpful to review some of the games for earlier grades, or to ask the children to suggest some familiar games that they enjoy before presenting new activities.

FLYING DUTCHMEN

Behavioral goal: To run swiftly with a partner.
Concept: Newton's laws of motion.
Biologic efficiency: Coordination; endurance.
Movement skill: Running with a partner.

Children stand in a circle, hands joined. Two children with hands joined are IT and walk around outside the circle. The child nearest the circle tags the joined hands of two circle players. IT couple runs around the circle in the same direction they were walking; tagged couple, hands joined, runs around the circle in opposite direction from IT couple.

Couple first reaching vacant place in circle is IT for next game.

MAN FROM MARS

Behavioral goal: To tag others and avoid being tagged.

Concept: Newton's laws of motion.
Biologic efficiency: Coordination; endurance.
Movement skill: Running; dodging.

Child who is man from Mars stands in center of playing area. Players stand on a boundary line and call, "Man from Mars, may we chase you to the stars?" Man from Mars responds, "Yes, if you're wearing blue" (or black, or red, or have red shoes, or any other colored object he chooses to name). All children with stated color or object chase man from Mars around play area, staying within predetermined boundaries. Child who tags him is the new man from Mars and game starts again.

BEAR IN THE PIT

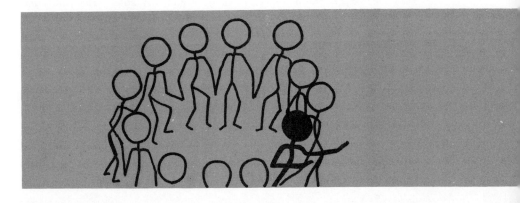

Behavioral goal: To break out of the circle and avoid being tagged; to overtake and tag a runner. ·
Concept: Newton's laws of motion.
Biologic efficiency: Agility; endurance.
Movement skill: Running.

One child is the bear and is inside the circle, or pit. He tries to break out by crawling under, stepping over, or breaking through arms and hands of circle players. When bear breaks out, other players chase him around the play area. Child who catches him is new bear.

HILL DILL, COME OVER THE HILL

Behavioral goal: To tag and avoid being tagged.
Concept: Newton's laws of motion.
Biologic efficiency: Coordination; endurance.
Movement skill: Running

Half the players stand behind each goal line. IT calls, "Hill Dill, come over the hill," and players run to opposite goals. Any players tagged by IT join him in the center of the play area and help him tag others. IT is only chaser who can give the call. New IT is last player tagged.

HEN AND CHICKENS

Behavioral goal: To move in unison with others while avoiding being tagged; to move quickly to tag another.
Concept: Newton's laws of motion.

150

Biologic efficiency: Coordination; endurance.
Movement skill: Dodging; changing direction and level quickly.

One child is the hen.   Other children—chickens—line up in single file behind the hen, each with his hands on the shoulders of the one in front. Child who is fox tries to tag the last chicken in line.   Hen tries to protect her chicken from being tagged by spreading her arms and dodging in front of the fox, with the line of chickens still in formation.

When the fox tags the last chicken in the line, the tagged chicken becomes fox and fox becomes hen.

RENDEZ-VOUS IN SPACE

Behavioral goal: To run swiftly and avoid a chaser while meeting a partner; to overtake and tag an opponent.
Concept: Newton's laws of motion.
Biologic efficiency: Coordination; agility.
Movement skill: Running; dodging.

Children who are space ships line up in pairs, facing child who is enemy interceptor standing with his back toward the others, eyes straight ahead. When interceptor calls, ''Rendez-vous!'' the pair at the end of the line run to the front and try to join hands before the interceptor tags either one.

If one space ship is tagged, the chaser takes the other partner and they take their places at the head of the line; child tagged is the new enemy interceptor.   If the chaser is unsuccessful, he continues to be IT and space ships who successfully completed the rendez-vous go to head of line.

SAVE THE SHEEP

Behavioral goal: To use guarding tactics effectively by moving quickly to intercept opponents.

Concept: Newton's laws of motion.

Biologic efficiency: Coordination; agility; endurance.

Movement skill: Running; dodging.

Two children are wolves, one child is sheep dog, one child is sheepherder. All other children are sheep. Sheep are grazing in the valley until the sheepherder calls out, "Wolves!" Sheep try to get to sheep fold without being caught by wolves. Sheepherder and sheep dog try to protect sheep from wolves by placing themselves between sheep and wolves. Wolves try to dodge around them and tag as many sheep as possible.

Wolves, sheepherder, and sheep dog may not touch, push, or rough each other. New wolves, sheepherder, and sheep dog are chosen from among sheep who were not caught.

RUNNING IN PLACE

Behavioral goal: To lift knees high and run in place for increasing periods of time.

Concept: Attaining and maintaining endurance.
Biologic efficiency: Endurance.
Movement skill: Running in place.

On signal, "Run!" children run in place, continuing as long as possible. Teacher uses watch to time running, calling off every 15 seconds. When child stops, his score to the last 15-second interval is called.

Running should be done with knees lifted as high as possible, touching the hands, which are held level with the elbows. Individual scores should be recorded, so that each child can attempt to better his own record.

SMUGGLER'S GOLD

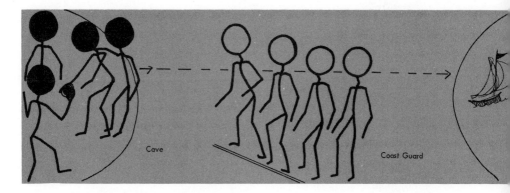

Behavioral goal: To run swiftly, overtake, and tag another; to avoid being tagged.
Concept: Newton's laws of motion.
Biologic efficiency: Coordination; endurance.
Movement skill: Running; dodging.

Half the group are smugglers, half are Coast Guard. Boundaries (locations of cave and ship) are set up and agreed upon by both sides.

Smugglers stand close together in cave and pass gold (marble or coin) to one of their players, keeping Coast Guard from knowing who has the gold. Then smuggler captain shouts, "Run!" The smugglers scatter around the play area, and Coast Guard begins searching for the smuggler with the gold. The gold may not be transferred to another player after smugglers leave cave.

If a smuggler is tagged, he is told, "Hand over the gold." If he has it, he must show it, and the Coast Guard wins the game. If the smuggler with the gold gets safely to the ship, the smugglers win the game.

Game is repeated with roles reversed.

KICK THE CAN

Prison

Behavioral goal: To have the endurance to chase and tag many runners; to have the endurance to avoid being tagged.

Concept: Endurance.

Biologic efficiency: Endurance; coordination; agility.

Movement Skill: Running; dodging.

A can is placed in center of play area with a "prison" near by. IT covers his eyes and counts to ten by ones, as all other players scatter around the play area, staying within the defined boundaries. Upon the count of ten, IT may chase and try to tag any number of players. Those so tagged must go to prison, where they must remain until completion of the game.

There are no safe areas for the runners. If one runner, however, can get close enough to kick the can, all other players are safe and the game is finished. IT's score is the number of players in prison upon the completion of the game.

IT chooses a new IT and the games continue until each player has had a turn to be IT. Player with highest score is the winner of the group.

Activities for Grades 5, 6

Ten, eleven, and twelve year olds enjoy games with more complex organization, using many types of skills. They are more interested in adult sports, particularly team activities. The games suggested here are challenging to these children. They also provide many opportunities for the children to improve their skills.

MONSTER'S CHOICE

Behavioral goal: To tag and avoid being tagged.
Concept: Newton's laws of motion.
Biologic efficiency: Coordination; endurance.
Movement skill: Dodging.

Children are in groups of four, with one child designated as the monster. Other three children in group join hands, with monster outside the circle. Monster chooses one child in the circle as the one he wishes to tag.

Teacher calls, "Monster's choice!" and all monsters try to tag their designated choices, while each circle moves to prevent the monster from tagging the designated child. Monsters may go around one side or the other, but may not go through or over in tagging.

If the designated child is tagged, he becomes the new monster in his group for the next game. If he is not tagged by the time the teacher calls, "Stop!" the old monster continues when the new game starts.

BEATER GOES ROUND

Behavioral goal: To run rapidly and avoid being beaten; to overtake and beat another.

155

Concept: Newton's laws of motion.
Biologic efficiency: Coordination; agility.
Movement skill: Running.

Children stand in a circle, facing the center, hands behind backs. IT runs around outside the circle, carrying a towel with one end knotted, which he drops into the hands of a child. The person receiving the towel turns at once toward one of his neighbors and chases him around the circle, beating him with the towel as often as he can. If the neighbor can outrun the chaser he may avoid being beaten.

When the runner returns to his place, IT takes the beater's place in the circle, and the beater becomes IT, dropping the towel into the hands of another person. The game continues until all have been beaters.

BRONCO TAG

Behavioral goal: To dodge in unison with two others; to move quickly to tag another.
Concept: Newton's laws of motion.
Biologic efficiency: Coordination; agility; endurance.
Movement skill: Dodging; running.

Children scatter around play area in groups of three, the players in each group in single file, with hands around the waist of the one in front. The third child in line is the bronco's tail, the first is the head, and the second the body.

Two children are the runner and the chaser. To save himself from being tagged, the runner must catch hold of a bronco's tail. If he succeeds, the head of the bronco becomes the new runner. The bronco tries to keep his tail out of reach of the runner by dodging around.

If the chaser tags the runner before he can catch the bronco's tail, the runner becomes the chaser.

WALK-RUN FOR DISTANCE

Behavioral goal: To improve endurance by moving as far and as long as possible.

Concept: Attaining and maintaining endurance.

Biologic efficiency: Endurance.

Movement skill: Walking; running.

A circular course is marked out around the play area and is divided into fourths for scoring purposes. Children start at starting line and walk ten steps, then run ten steps, continuing to walk-run for as many laps as possible. Child's score is the number of quarter-laps he completes without stopping.

Each child may have a partner who scores for him, and he in turn scores for his partner. Thus, half the class may run at one time.

Individual rather than group scores should be emphasized, with each child trying to improve from day to day.

SNATCH

Behavioral goal: To use strategy in out-maneuvering another player, and score a point for one's own team.

157

Concept: Newton's laws of motion; gravitation and movement.
Biologic efficiency: Coordination; agility.
Movement skill: Running; dodging.

Players are divided into two equal teams with players on each team numbered consecutively. Each team stands on its own goal line. A beanbag or Indian club is placed halfway between the goal lines.

The teacher calls a number. Children from each team having that number run to the beanbag and try to carry it safely across their own goal lines without being tagged by the opposing runner. If a runner carries the beanbag safely to his goal, he scores one point for his team. If he is tagged before crossing the goal, the tagger scores a point for his team.

If either player merely touches the beanbag, or picks it up and drops it, the opposing player can score by tagging him before he reaches the goal. If both players hesitate for a time in picking up the beanbag, other players may count aloud in unison to ten, upon which both players retire to their own goal lines and no score is recorded for either side.

JUMP THE SHOT

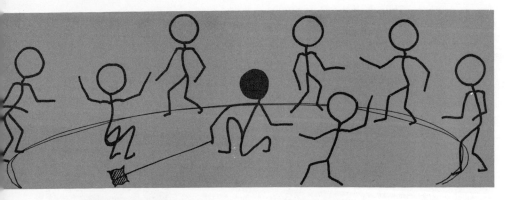

Behavioral goal: To jump quickly to clear the rope.
Concept: Skills of locomotion.
Biologic efficiency: Endurance; coordination; agility.
Movement skill: Jumping.

Children are divided into even teams, each team forming a circle and facing center. Each team sends one player to another team to swing the "shot." The shot is a soft tennis shoe or beanbag tied to the end of a 12 to 15-foot rope.

On signal, "Go!" the player kneels in the center of the circle and starts swinging the shot around the circle. As it nears a circle player, he must jump into the air to clear it. Any player tagged by the shot must drop out of the game. Team that can keep players in the circle longest is the winner.

The shot must be swung so that it never is more than 5 to 6 inches off the floor. Children should practice swinging the shot before playing the game.

CAPTURE THE FLAG

Behavioral goal: To capture the opponents' flag and protect one's own flag from the enemy.

Concept: Skills of locomotion.

Biologic efficiency: Coordination; endurance.

Movement skill: Running; dodging.

Players are divided into two equal teams. Each team has its own court with its own flag on the back line of its court. Each team also has a prison marked off in the back part of its court.

Each team tries to capture the opponents' flag, and prevent the capture of its own flag. If a player manages to get the opponents' flag and carry it safely into his own court without being tagged, his team wins the game.

If a player is tagged while in enemy territory, he must go into the enemy prison. A teammate may rescue a prisoner by going into the prison, taking his hand, and running home with him. If rescuer and prisoner are tagged while in enemy territory, both become prisoners. Only one prisoner may be rescued at a time, and the rescuer may not take the flag while he is rescuing a prisoner.

BUNNY TAILS

Prison   Neutral Ground   Prison

Behavioal goal: To overtake an opponent and steal his tail, while protect-
ing one's own tail from thievery.
Concept: Skills of locomotion.
Biologic efficiency: Coordination; endurance.
Movement skill: Running; dodging.

Children are divided into two or more equal teams. Each team has a
goal (safety area) and a prison for captives, with neutral ground between the
goals. Each player has a bunny tail (piece of colored cloth) tucked into the
belt at the back. Members of each team use tails of the same color for
identification. Tails may not be *tied* to the belt.

Players go into neutral ground to steal tails from other teams. When a
tail is taken from a player, he becomes a prisoner of the person who
snatched it and must go to that team's prison.

Team that captures all the opponents, or team that has the most prisoners
at the end of a given playing time, is the winner.

Summary

The behavioral goals for the activities described in this chapter deal
generally with overtaking and capturing or tagging an opponent, and in
avoiding being tagged or captured. In some instances this is done by
cooperating with other team members and by using strategy to outwit and
overcome opponents.

The concepts covered in this chapter are those of moving one's own body
through space, using the laws of motion and of gravitation, and the laws of
attaining and maintaining endurance. These concepts are described in
Chapters 3, "Mechanics of Movement," and 8, "Endurance."

These games contribute in some degree to those aspects of biologic efficiency related to endurance, coordination, and agility, described in Chapters 3 and 8. The movement skills used in these activities are the skills of locomotion, dodging, starting, and stopping. Analysis of these skills is presented in Chapter 4, "Movement Analysis of Selected Skills"; and a description of human locomotion is presented in Chapter 2, "Human Movement." Instruction in performance of these skills is important if children are to attain the greatest benefits from the activities.

15   RELAYS AND RACES

Relays and races involve moving quickly from one place to another, either individually or as a team member. The child may race against time, his score being the number of seconds it takes him to move a given distance; or he may race against another child or children to determine who is the winner.

Relays and races may contribute to the development of endurance if the child moves rapidly enough over a long enough period of time to place stress upon his cardiovascular system, that is, to become "out of breath." The kind of endurance needed to run a short relay race is different from the endurance needed for running a long race. Both types of endurance are dependent upon the ability of the lungs, heart, and circulatory system to transport oxygen and carbon dioxide to and from the muscles.

Any type of locomotor movement lends itself to relays and races. Frequently used at parties and other recreational events, these activities are fun for adults and children alike. Relays and races use many movement skills. In addition to the specific mode of locomotion, such as walking, running, or hopping, these activities emphasize starting quickly, stopping, and often changing direction (as in the shuttle races).

Activities for Kindergarten

Four and five year old children are strongly individualistic, and team activities of any nature are difficult for them to understand. Consequently, races rather than relays are more suitable for children of this age.

Races should be simple, of short duration, and with a minimum of organization. Locomotor patterns used in the races should be those that the children can manage with ease. The children are usually excited by the competition, and the racing atmosphere is not conducive to learning new and difficult locomotor skills.

Three types of races for the kindergarten child are suggested here. Teacher and children may substitute seasonal or holiday characters, storybook characters, familiar locomotor skills, and the like, in any of the racing events described.

TYPE ONE RACE: WALK-RUN RACE

Behavioral goal: To walk quickly and run fast in racing others a given distance.

Concept: Skills of locomotion.

Biologic efficiency: Coordination and endurance.

Movement skill: Walking; running.

In this race, children use locomotor skills to move from one line to another. All children line up side by side on the starting line. On signal, "Go!" they walk rapidly to the opposite line, then turn and run back to the starting line. Winner is the first child to return to the starting line who has performed the locomotor patterns correctly.

This may be simplified by having the children run from the starting line and finish on the opposite line, rather than returning.

Suggested Variations:

(1) Crawl-run race, crawling on hands and knees to opposite line and running back;

(2) Skip-run race;

(3) Hop-run race;

(4) Backward-forward race, walking backward to the opposite line and walking forward on the return trip;

(5) Bunny-hop race, hopping or jumping to the opposite line, with winner being the first bunny to reach the line;

(6) Bear-walking to the opposite line;

(7) Elephant-walking to the opposite line and running back;

(8) Wild horse galloping race;

(9) Jumping jack race;

(10) Birds race, flying to opposite line and back;

(11) Witches race, riding a broomstick across the line;

(12) Caterpillar race, inching along like a caterpillar;

(13) Other storybook characters.

TYPE TWO RACE: BRING HOME THE BEANBAG

Behavioral goal: To retrieve an object and carry it back across the starting line, moving as fast as possible.

Concept: Newton's laws of motion.

Biologic efficiency: Endurance.

Movement skill: Running; changing direction rapidly.

This type of race involves retrieving an object and carrying it back across the starting line. Runners line up side by side on the starting line. A bean-bag is placed opposite each runner on a line 20 to 30 feet from the starting line.

On signal, "Go!" runners run to their beanbags, each runner picks up his beanbag and carries it back across the starting line.   First runner to cross the line *with beanbag in his possession* is the winner.

Variations:

(1) Bring home the valentine;
(2) Bring home the toy;
(3) Bring home an Easter egg;
(4) Bring home a Christmas tree;
(5) Bring home the Jack-o-lantern;
(6) Bring home the turkey;
(7) Other holiday or storybook characters.

TYPE THREE RACE: CHALLENGE RACE

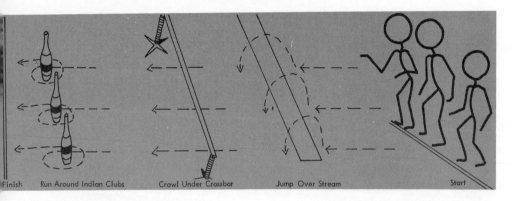

Finish   Run Around Indian Clubs   Crawl Under Crossbar   Jump Over Stream   Start

Behavioral goal: To perform the various challenges as quickly as possible.
Concept: Human locomotion; Newton's laws of motion.
Biologic efficiency: Endurance.
Movement skill: Locomotion.

This type of race provides various challenges or obstacles to be overcome. Children line up at starting line.   On signal, "Go!" they try to reach the finish line as fast as possible, overcoming each obstacle in the pathway to the finish line.   The obstacles are a stream to be jumped or leaped over, a bar to be crawled under, and an Indian club to be circled.

First child to reach the finish line after performing the challenges correctly is the winner.

Variations:

(1) Over and through a row of barrels or boxes;

(2) Climb over or crawl through or around favorite pieces of playground apparatus;

(3) Walk a balance beam or chalk line;

(4) Perform stunts at various stations, such as a sit-up at one place, a push-up at another, a forward roll at another, and so on.

Activities for Grades 1, 2

The same types of races suggested for kindergarten are also interesting and challenging for the six and seven year old child. The team organization required for relay races demands cooperative endeavor which is usually undeveloped in many children of these age groups. Some of these children may enjoy racing as a team member if they can compete with an individual member from another team, contributing toward a team score when they win. An example of this type of team race is the first game suggested in this section, "Tag the Line Race." Another type of team race is that in which all team members run at the same time, keeping in some predetermined order, or ending in the starting order.

It is suggested that the teacher of this age group continue with variations of the three types of races suggested for the kindergarten age group, following these races with the team-type races.

TAG THE LINE RACE

Behavioral goal: To race an opponent, contributing a score as a team member.

Concept: Skills of locomotion.
Biologic efficiency: Endurance; coordination.
Movement skill: Running.

Players are divided into teams of 6 to 8 members.   Each team lines up on starting line, standing in file formation, one behind the other.

On signal, "Go!" first player in each team runs to opposite line, touches it with his foot and runs back across the starting line.   First player back is the winner of the race and scores a point for his team.   On signal "Go!" second players on each team run, and the winner is determined.   This continues until all have run.

Team with most points wins.

THREAD THE NEEDLE

Behavioral goal: To run fast, staying in formation with other team members.
Concept: Skills of locomotion; Newton's laws of motion.
Biologic efficiency: Coordination; endurance.
Movement skill: Running.

Children line up in groups of 5 to 6.   Members of each group line up in file formation on starting line, with hands on shoulders of teammate in front. This line of players is the "thread."

An Indian club is on the ground about 40 feet in front of each team, with a second Indian club placed 2 feet beyond the first.   (See illustration 99.) The space between the two clubs is the eye of the needle.   On signal, "Go!" children drop hands and, staying in their positions in line, run between the Indian clubs, through the eye of the needle, and back to their starting positions, ending with hands on shoulders of player in front.

Team who is first back into original starting position is the winner, if the team members have stayed in line while running. If a team member knocks over an Indian club, it must be replaced immediately, before team can continue threading the needle.

Variations:

(1) Train race, with trains making a straight run from one station to another, or making a circular or figure eight run;

(2) Santa's reindeer pulling Santa Claus in his sleigh, with eight children as reindeer and one child at end of line as Santa Claus;

(3) Centipede race, with each child being a leg of the centipede.

ESCAPE FROM THE ZOO RACE

Behavioral goal: To race home from the zoo as fast as possible.

Concept: Newton's laws of motion.

Biologic efficiency: Coordination; endurance.

Movement skill: Running.

Children are divided into three or four groups. Each group takes the name of a zoo animal, and all stand within the boundaries of a designated area. On the signal "Go!" they break out of their cages and run to their homes in the forest. All animals of the winning group reach home before all animals of the other groups.

Variations:

(1) Toy race, with children taking names of toys;

(2) Bird race, with birds represented;

(3) Halloween race, with Halloween characters represented.

Activities for Grades 3, 4

Most eight and nine year olds find relays and races appealing. The team aspect of the relay is interesting to the children because of the developing gang spirit of these age groups, and because the organization of the relay is usually simple for them to perform successfully.

RUN THE BASES

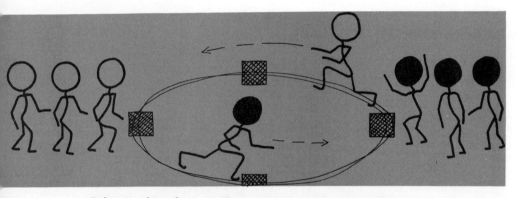

Behavioral goal: To run fast and defeat the other teams.
Concept: Newton's laws of motion; skills of locomotion.
Biologic efficiency: Coordination; endurance.
Movement skill: Running.

Children divide into two teams. One team lines up in single file in back of first base, and the other team in back of third base (see illustration). On signal "Go!" the first player of each team circles the bases, tagging each base with his foot as he passes it. When he returns to his team he touches the next player in line who circles the bases. First team to get all players back into original positions wins.

JUNGLE RELAY

Behavioral goal: To run with the body in an unusual position.

Concept: Newton's laws of motion; gravity and movement.

Biologic efficiency: Agility; endurance.

Movement skill: Running, with center of gravity in different positions.

Children divide into even teams of 4 to 6 players per team. Teams line up on starting line in file formation. Each team member imitates a predetermined (real or imaginary) animal as he races to the opposite line and returns, touching off the next runner in his team.

For example, the first runner in each team may be a lion running on all fours; second runners may be monsters with stiff legs and arms, and center of gravity to the side; third runners may be kangaroos, jumping with feet together; fourth runners may be space birds, hopping and cackling, and so on.

On signal "Go!" first runners go to opposite line and return, touching next runner in line. Team which finishes first wins.

RESCUE RELAY

Behavioral goal: To run fast with a partner.

Concept: Newton's laws of motion.
Biologic efficiency: Coordination; endurance.
Movement skill: Running.

Players divide into even teams. Each team has a leader who stands on "leader's line" facing other teammates, who are lined up in file formation on "player's line." (See illustration.)

On signal, "Go!" leader runs to first player on his team, takes his hand and runs with him back to leader's line. Leader remains on this line, and rescued player runs back to team and brings next player to leader's line with him. This continues until all are rescued.

First team to get all players behind leader's line wins.

SHUTTLE RELAY

Behavioral goal: To run fast and help team win.
Concept: Newton's laws of motion; skills of locomotion.
Biologic efficiency: Coordination; endurance.
Movement skill: Running.

Children divide into even teams, 6 to 10 per team. Half of each team faces other half, as in illustration 104.

On signal, "Go!" first player on starting line runs and touches off first player on opposite line and goes to end of line. Player touched off runs to starting line and touches off next player in that line. This continues until both halves are back in original positions.

First team to get all players back to original positions wins.

FIGURE EIGHT RELAY

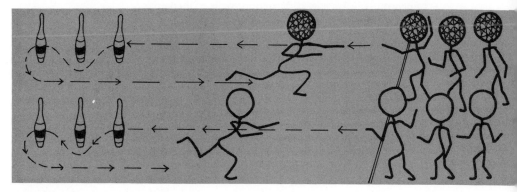

Behavioral goal: To run fast and help team be a winner.
Concept: Newton's laws of motion; skills of locomotion.
Biologic efficiency: Coordination; endurance.
Movement skill: Running.

Children divide into even teams, 6 to 10 per team. Each team stands in file formation behind starting line. Three Indian clubs or beanbags are placed in line with each team, 30 feet from starting line, and 5 feet apart.

On signal, "Go!" first player in each team runs to his team's clubs and, going to the right of the first club, weaves through them in a figure eight. Then he weaves back and touches off next runner.

First team to return to original line-up wins.

CHALLENGE COURSE RACE

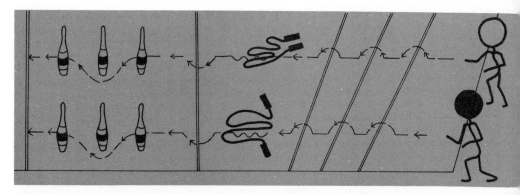

Behavioral goal: To perform the various challenges in appropriate sequence, and as quickly as possible.

Concept: Newton's laws of motion; skills of locomotion.
Biologic efficiency: Coordination; endurance.
Movement skill: Locomotion.

Children line up at starting line. On signal, "Go!" they try to reach the finish line as fast as possible, overcoming each obstacle in the path on the way to the finish line.

The obstacles are three hurdles to be leaped over, a rope to be jumped three times, a bar to be crawled under, three Indian clubs to weave through; children must hop to the finish line.

Other challenge courses may be set up, using different obstacles. See Type Three Race described for kindergarten (above).

Activities for Grades 5, 6

Ten, eleven, and twelve year olds are interested in the team competition inherent in the relay races. The locomotor skills needed to compete in these events are challenging to these children, and the desire to excel in motor activities is a motivating factor, encouraging good performance in these areas.

AROUND THE WORLD

Behavioral goal: To start quickly and run rapidly.

Concept: Newton's laws of motion; skills of locomotion.
Biologic efficiency: Agility; coordination; endurance.
Movement skill: Running.

Children divide into even teams, with each team standing in a circle facing the center. Each team member is given a number in consecutive order, beginning with number 1. Teacher calls a number and players with this number run around outside their circles and back to place. Player who arrives first is winner and scores a point for his team. Winning team is the first to score 11 points, or the team with most points when all have run.

JUMP ONE-TWO-THREE RELAY

Behavioral goal: To run, jump a rope rapidly, and return quickly.
Concept: Newton's laws of motion; skills of locomotion.
Biologic efficiency: Agility; endurance.
Movement skill: Jumping.

Children divide into even teams and line up single file on starting line. Three jump ropes are placed in front of each team, the first rope 30 feet from the starting line, the second rope 10 feet from the first, and the third rope 10 feet from the second.

On signal, "Go!" the first player on each team runs to first rope, picks it up and jumps over it once, replaces it and runs to second rope, jumps it twice, then to third rope and jumps it three times. Player replaces each rope after using it, returns to team and touches next player in line, who continues the jumping. Team finshing first wins.

Variation: An obstacle or challenge course similar to those described for earlier grades may be used.

POTATO RACE

Behavioral goal: To maintain equilibrium while picking up objects and changing direction quickly; to run fast.

Concept: Gravity and movement; Newton's laws of motion.

Biologic efficiency: Agility; endurance.

Movement skill: Running.

Children divide into even teams and line up single file behind starting line. A box, base, or circle drawn on the ground may be used as container for the potatoes (beanbags). From starting line to first potato is 24 feet; second potato is placed 32 feet away, and in line with first potato. (See illustration.)

On signal, "Go!" first player on each team retrieves either potato and places it in box on starting line. Then he gets other potato, touches box on starting line with it, and returns it to its original place. He returns to box on starting line, gets potato from it and returns it to its original position. Then returning to starting line he touches off next runner who continues the process. Potatoes may be taken and replaced by each runner in turn, in any order the runner chooses.

Team finishing first wins.

JUMP THE STICK RELAY

Behavioral goal: To perform skillfully in helping one's team win.
Concept: Skills of locomotion.
Biologic efficiency: Agility; endurance.
Movement skill: Jumping; running.

Children divide into even teams with team members in file formation. Teams should stand about 10 feet apart. First player in each team holds a stick or wand. On signal, "Go!" first player hands other end of wand to second player in line, and holding it between them they run the length of their line, dragging the stick under the feet of their teammates. Players in line jump over stick as it reaches their feet.

When players with stick reach end of line first player lets go of stick and stays at end of line. Second player runs back to head of line with stick and hands other end to third player. These two run down line as first two did. This continues until player number 1 is back in his original position at head of line. Team to finish first wins.

Summary

The behavioral goals for the activities described in this chapter are those of starting quickly and moving rapidly in the performance of certain locomotor tasks. Some of the activities are individual in that one person races another; some are in the nature of team activities, where an individual cooperates with team members to win the race or relay.

The concepts covered are those of the skills of locomotion, found in Chapter 2, "Human Movement," and Chapter 4, "Movement Analysis of Selected Skills," and the laws of motion and gravitation found in Chapter 3, "Mechanics of Movement."

These activities contribute in varying degrees to development of coordination, agility, and endurance. The movement skills used in these activities were the skills of locomotion, chiefly that of running.

16 STUNTS AND TESTS

This chapter constitutes a potpourri of activities variously designated as stunts, tumbling, tests, self-testing activities, combative activities, exercises, and the like. The purpose of these activities is to test performance of basic movements of the body involving equilibrium or balance, use of levers, range of motion in joints, and such various physiologic factors as strength, endurance, flexibility, coordination, and agility. Some of the skills included in human locomotion and overcoming inertia of other objects are used in the performance of these activities.

Some of these activities may be performed by one individual working alone, others require a partner; still others are designed for a group of individuals working cooperatively. Some of the activities need no equipment and may be performed in the classroom or on the play field. Others require specific types of equipment, and a special type of surface for landing, taking off, rebounding balls, etc.

Many of the activities in Chapter 13, "Movement Exploration," are useful in preparing children for stunts of a more complex nature. The individual races suggested in Chapter 15, "Relays and Races," are tests in themselves if they are performed against time.

Activities for Kindergarten

The stunts and tests suggested for kindergarten involve the use of the body in different positions, with and without the use of apparatus. Many of

the problems suggested in Chapter 13, "Movement Exploration," present interesting movement possibilities to the four and five year old; these may be
added to the specific activities suggested here for kindergarten children.

TIGHTROPE WALKER

Behavioral goal: To balance on a beam in stationary and moving positions.
Concept: Gravity and movement.
Biologic efficiency: Coordination; balance.
Movement skill: Walking.

Children walk forward on a balance beam or a line drawn on the floor,
in the following ways:

(1) Heel-toe walk, placing the heel of one foot at the toe of the other,
    moving forward;
(2) Giant steps, taking long steps forward;
(3) Baby steps, taking short steps forward;
(4) Balance on two feet for a count of 5;
(5) Balance on one foot for a count of 5.

The balance beam may be approximately 8 to 10 inches from the floor,
a safety factor if the child should lose balance.   A 2 inch × 6 inch board may
be used, stabilized on each end, and approximately 10 to 12 feet long.
(See illustration 112.)

Before walking on the beam, children may first try walking on a line on
the floor.   Arms may be extended to the sides to help in balancing the body.

Children may invent other stunts to do on the beam, using different locomotor patterns, changing direction and level.

LOG ROLLING

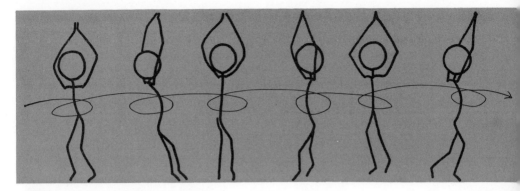

Behavioral goal: To roll several times, keeping body straight.
Concept: Newton's laws of motion.
Biologic efficiency: Coordination.
Movement skill: Rolling.

Each child lies on a mat, or on the grass, arms stretched overhead. He rolls, turning his shoulders and hips in the direction he wishes to go.

He will roll straight if he turns the shoulders and hips simultaneously. As he continues to roll, momentum will help him move. After rolling several times in one direction, he rolls back to his original position.

SQUASH

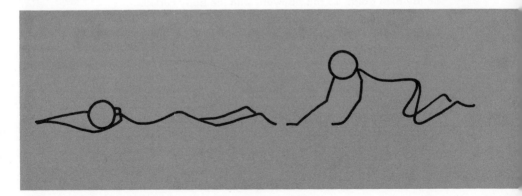

Behavioral goal: To fall flat from a kneeling position.

Concept: Overcoming inertia of one's own body; relaxation.
Biologic efficiency: Coordination; relaxation.
Movement skill: Falling; landing.

Children kneel on mats on hands and knees. On signal "Squash," they fall forward by extending arms forward and legs backward at the same time.

Child should keep his head up to avoid hitting his face or chin. If he relaxes and "gives" with the fall, he will not receive as great a shock when his body hits the mat.

EASTER EGG ROLL

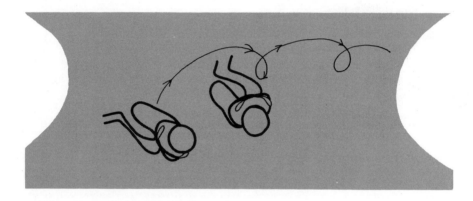

Behavioral goal: To roll sideward with the body curled.
Concept: Newton's laws of motion.
Biologic efficiency: Coordination.
Movement skill: Rolling.

Child kneels on mat, arms folded and elbows resting on mat. He pushes with arms and knees, rolls to his side, then to his back, to his other side, and to knees (original position).

By keeping his body curled, he will lose equilibrium and roll faster, with momentum assisting him in continuing the roll. By pushing hard with his arms and legs, he can overcome body inertia and start his motion.

WRING THE DISHRAG

Behavioral goal: To turn under arms with a partner.
Concept: Levers of the body.
Biologic efficiency: Coordination; flexibility.
Movement skill: Turning.

Partners join hands, facing each other. Raising one pair of joined arms they turn under the raised arms, in a back-to-back position. Then, raising other pair of joined arms, they turn under to face partner in original position.

OVER THE HEAD

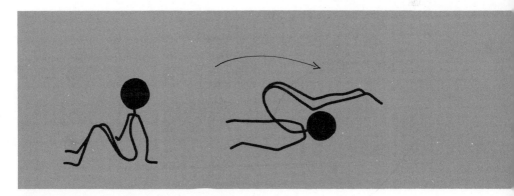

Behavioral goal: To roll backward, touching feet to floor over head.
Concept: Newton's laws of motion; levers of the body; flexibility.
Biologic efficiency: Flexibility.
Movement skill: Rolling.

Child sits on mat, knees bent, arms at sides. He pushes with his feet, rolling backward and swinging his legs over his head to touch the floor behind his head with his toes.

Variation: Start from a lying position, knees bent, and feet on the floor.

OVER THE FENCE

Behavioral goal: To swing legs in air while supporting weight on hands.
Concept: Gravity and movement; Newton's laws of motion.
Biologic efficiency: Arm strength; balance; coordination.
Movement skill: Swinging.

Child stands on one side of a line drawn on the floor, with his side toward the line, or "fence." He bends down and puts his nearest hand over the fence, turns his body and puts the other hand over the fence. Keeping his hands on the floor, he swings his legs over the fence, finishing in the standing position.

DUCK WALK

Behavioral goal: To walk in a squat position.
Concept: Mechanics of movement; flexibility.
Biologic efficiency: Balance; flexibility.
Movement skill: Walking.

Child squats with knees apart, hands placed under armpits for wings. He flaps wings, swings legs forward and outward like a duck, keeping body close to floor.

SEAL WALK

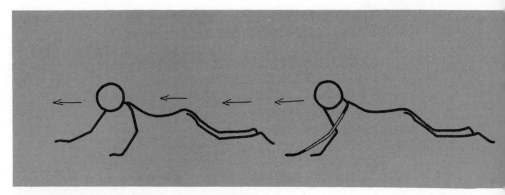

Behavioral goal: To pull body forward with hands.
Concept: Attaining strength; endurance.
Biologic efficiency: Arm strength; endurance.
Movement skill: Walking on hands.

Child positions himself on the floor, weight on hands and toes, back straight. He walks forward with his hands, dragging his legs and toes. His back should be straight, his head up. Hips may swing as he moves.

Child walks as many steps as possible, trying to walk farther each day.

FROG HOP

Behavioral goal: To hop forward in squat position; using hands and feet alternately.

Concept: Flexibility.

Biologic efficiency: Flexibility; coordination.

Movement skill: "Hopping"; jumping.

Child squats, placing hands on floor between knees. He moves forward by putting hands ahead of feet, then bringing feet up to the hands. After hopping forward several times, he hops backward.

Keep "hops" short by putting hands a short distance ahead of feet, swinging feet easily up to hands.

ELEPHANT WALK

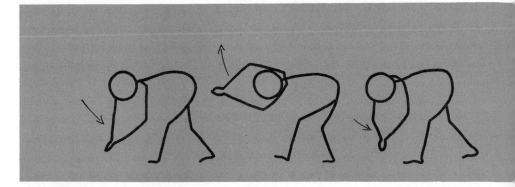

Behavioral goal: To walk with arms swinging rhythmically, touching floor with hands.

Concept: Flexibility; range of motion.

Biologic efficiency: Flexibility.

Movement skill: Walking.

Children stand with bodies bent forward, hands clasped, arms hanging like an elephant's trunk. On each step, the arms swing from side to side, hands touching the floor.

Variations:

(1) Walk with knees bent, back rounded, hands touching floor on each swing.

(2) Walk with knees straight, back straight, arms swinging on each step.

MEASURING WORM

Behavioral goal: To walk, alternating hands and feet.

Concept: Flexibility; range of motion.
Biologic efficiency: Flexibility.
Movement skill: Walking on all fours.

Child gets on all fours, putting weight on hands and feet. He walks forward on his hands, keeping his feet stationary until his body is in a straight line. Then, flexing his hips, he walks his feet up to his hands. This continues, alternating hands and feet for as long as possible.

Keep knees and elbows straight throughout entire walk.

Activities for Grades 1, 2

Six and seven year olds are capable of twisting their bodies into many different positions because of wide range of movement in the joints. Their shorter legs place the center of gravity near the base of support, which gives them good stability in balancing activities. Wild and White, pioneers in the field of elementary physical education suggest that the head stand is more easily taught at the first grade level than at any later time.[1]

This is the golden age of childhood for exploring and experimenting, experiencing many different body positions and movement skills.

WALKING THE PLANK

Behavioral goal: To balance on a beam in various positions.

[1] Monica R. Wild and Doris E. White, *Physical Education for Elementary Schools*, rev. ed. (Cedar Falls, Iowa: Iowa State Teachers College, 1950).

Concept: Gravity and movement.
Biologic efficiency: Balance; agility.
Movement skill: Walking.

Walk on a balance beam, a line drawn on the floor, or a plank placed on the floor in the following ways:

(1) Walk forward on heels, backward on tiptoes;
(2) Crawl forward, then backward on all fours;
(3) Walk to center of plank, balance on one foot for count of 3, then walk backward to place;
(4) Walk to center of plank, kneel on one knee for count of 5, then walk backward to place;
(5) Walk to center of plank, squat for count of 5, walk backward to place;
(6) Run on the plank;
(7) Make up new stunts on the plank.

A plank 2 inches square and 10 feet long may be used; taping it to the floor will make it more stable.

FORWARD ROLL

Behavioral goal: To roll forward with body curled.
Concept: Newton's laws of motion.
Biologic efficiency: Coordination; flexibility.
Movement skill: Rolling.

Child squats facing mat, feet apart and toes touching mat. He places hands on mat just ahead of toes. He bends his head forward, looking between his legs. Keeping his body curled, he pushes with hands and feet and rolls forward, transferring weight from feet to shoulders. He crosses his feet in midair and rolls to a sitting position on the mat.

Variations:

(1) Roll to a sitting position with feet together;

(2) Roll to a standing position, giving a push on the mat with the hands as weight rolls over feet.

BACKWARD ROLL

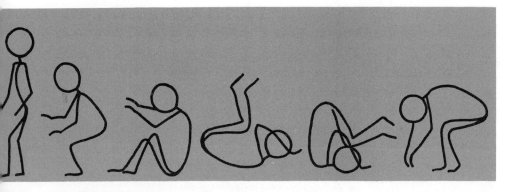

Behavioral goal: To roll backward with body curled.

Concept: Newton's laws of motion.

Biologic efficiency: Coordination; flexibility.

Movement skill: Rolling.

Child sits at edge of mat, knees bent, feet on the floor. He places his hands at his shoulders, palms up, thumbs toward neck. He pushes with his feet, tucks his head and rocks backward, bringing knees close to chest. As his hips rock over his shoulders, he pushes against the mat with his hands, drops his toes on the mat in back of his head, taking his weight on them, and finishing in squat position.

Variation: Keep body curled during the roll as described above, then catch the weight on the toes and slide the feet back so that the body is extended, finishing in an extended position, face down.

HUMAN BALL

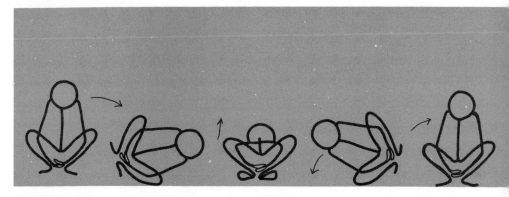

Behavioral goal: To roll sideward in a curled position.
Concept: Newton's laws of motion.
Biologic efficiency: Flexibility; coordination.
Movement skill: Rolling.

Child sits on floor, knees bent, arms through legs and around outside of legs with hands clasped in front of ankles. Start momentum by swaying from side to side, then roll on side of thigh and shoulder, continuing momentum by rolling to back, to opposite side, and back to original position. A circle is made in two complete rolls.

Be sure to roll to the side first. If the body rolls first to the back, the momentum to continue sideways will be lost and it will be difficult to complete the roll.

SHOULDER STAND

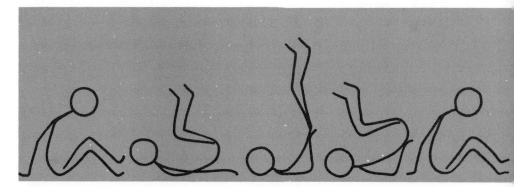

Behavioral goal: To balance on shoulder and arms with legs extended vertically.

Concept: Gravity and movement.
Biologic efficiency: Balance.
Movement skill: Balancing.

Child lies on his back on the mat. He lifts his hips above his shoulders, bracing his hands against his body to help support the hips. When he is in balance, he slowly extends his legs until they are straight above his head, his weight resting on his shoulders, neck, and elbows. Then he tucks his knees to his chest, rounds his back, and rolls back to the mat to his original position.

DOUBLE SHOULDER STAND

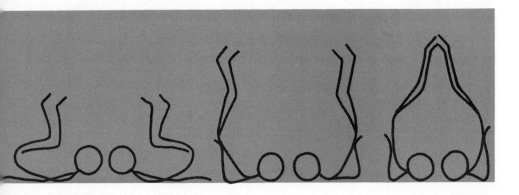

Behavioral goal: To raise the body to a shoulder stand with a partner.
Concept: Gravity and movement.
Biologic efficiency: Balance.
Movement skill: Balancing.

Partners lie on mat, heads toward each other and about two feet apart. On signal, raise body to shoulder stand position, feet extended to meet partner's feet to form an arch. Brace feet against partner's feet, legs straight, toes pointed. Tuck and return to original position.

TIP-UP

Behavioral goal: To balance body on hands.
Concept: Gravity and movement.
Biologic efficiency: Balance; arm strength.
Movement skill: Balancing.

Child squats, knees apart, hands between knees and placed on floor, just beneath shoulders. He braces his elbows against his knees, leans forward, and slowly centers his weight over his hands, feet off the mat. He balances in this position.

HEADSTAND

Behavioral goal: To balance body with weight on head and hands.
Concept: Gravity and movement.

193

Biologic efficiency: Balance.
Movement skill: Balancing.

Child takes tip-up position just described. He then places his head on the mat, about 10 to 12 inches in advance of his hands; this is called a "tripod" position. The head and hands form a triangle base with the weight of the body over the center of the triangle. Child then slowly raises his legs until they are straight and above his head, arching his back evenly to keep his center of gravity over the base of support.

To come down, child bends legs and drops them to the floor; or, he may tuck his head, curl, and do a forward roll.

CARTWHEEL

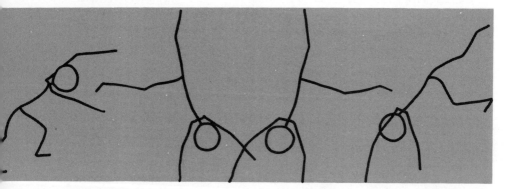

Behavioral goal: To extend legs and swing them sideward in a circle while supporting weight on hands.
Concept: Gravity and movement; Newton's laws of motion.
Biologic efficiency: Arm strength; balance; coordination.
Movement skill: Swinging.

Child first reviews "Over the Fence," described on page 184. Then he stands with his side to the mat, bends down, and puts nearest hand on mat, pushing from mat with opposite leg and extending it upward. Then he pushes from mat with other leg, rocks weight to other hand, which is now placed on mat. Legs continue to swing over his head as he pushes from mat with hand and comes to a standing position.

This is sometimes easier to perform if momentum is gained by starting from a short run.

PYRAMID

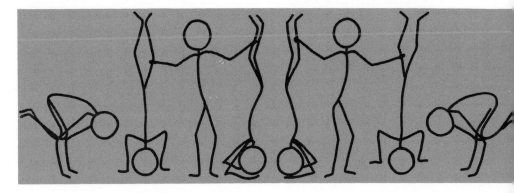

Behavioral goal: To cooperate with others in performing a group balancing stunt.

Concept: Gravity and movement.

Biologic efficiency: Balance.

Movement skill: Balancing.

Children design a pyramid, using balancing stunts they have mastered. For example, two children may perform a double shoulder stand in the center of the pyramid, a child may stand on his head on either side, with a child standing between to assist in balancing; and a child may do a tip-up at either end of the pyramid.

Children plan and execute other pyramids.

KANGAROO HOP

Behavioral goal: To jump forward in squat position.

Concept: Skills of locomotion.
Biologic efficiency: Leg strength; agility.
Movement skill: Jumping.

Child squats, arms folded across his chest.   From this position, keeping the knees bent, he jumps forward several times.

CRAB WALK

Behavioral goal: To walk on hands and feet in supine position.
Concept: Newton's laws of motion.
Biologic efficiency: Coordination.
Movement skill: Walking.

Child sits down, knees bent, and places hands flat on floor in back of him.   Then, raising his weight, he walks forward on hands and feet, body facing upward.

Move right foot and hand together, then left foot and hand together.

LAME DOG WALK

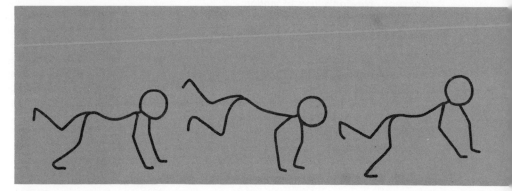

Behavioral goal: To walk on both hands and one foot.
Concept: Newton's laws of motion.
Biologic efficiency: Coordination.
Movement skill: Walking.

Child gets down on all fours.   He lifts one leg off the floor and extends it backward.   He pushes with the foot on the floor and moves both hands forward, then supports his weight on both hands and brings the foot forward.

Move in short hops both forward and backward.   Repeat, using opposite leg for support.

WHEELBARROW

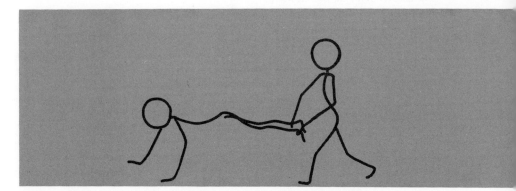

Behavioral goal: To walk on hands with a partner supporting the feet.

Concept: Newton's laws of motion.
Biologic efficiency: Arm strength.
Movement skill: Walking.

Child gets down on all fours. Partner grasps his ankles and raises his feet and legs off floor. Children move forward, first child walking on his hands and partner supporting his legs.

Keep body straight from head to feet. Move forward several steps, then backward to original position.

HALF-TOP

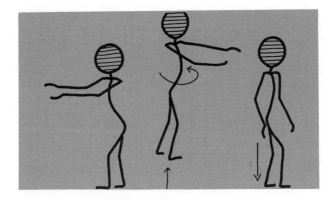

Behavioral goal: To execute a half-turn in the air.
Concept: Skills of locomotion.
Biologic efficiency: Coordination.
Movement skill: Jumping.

Child stands on a line on the floor, feet apart comfortably. He jumps into the air, taking off from both feet, turns in the air and lands on the line facing the opposite direction from the starting position.

Swing arms and body in direction of the turn; land with feet apart to maintain balance, and knees bent to decrease shock of landing.

O'LEARY

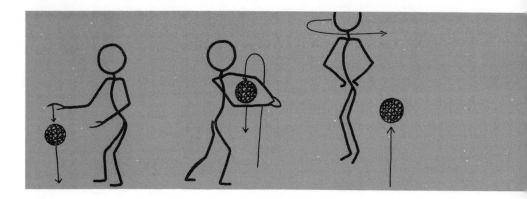

Behavioral goal: To bounce a ball rhythmically to a chant.
Concept: Skills of overcoming inertia of external objects.
Biologic efficiency: Coordination.
Movement skill: Bouncing a ball.

Each child has an 8- or 10-inch rubber playground ball. He bounces it with one or two hands, chanting the rhyme and bouncing rhythmically:

> One and two and three O'Leary
> Four and five and six O'Leary
> Seven and eight and nine O'Leary
> Ten O'Leary Postman.

On the word "postman," he gives one hard bounce and catches the ball. Variations:

(1) Throw one leg over the ball on O'Leary;
(2) Turn around on O'Leary;
(3) Make circle with arms and let ball bounce through on O'Leary;
(4) Change to opposite hand on O'Leary;
(5) Improvise other variations.

CHINESE GET-UP

Behavioral goal: To cooperate with a partner in moving up and down.
Concept: Gravity and movement; Newton's laws of motion.
Biologic efficiency: Coordination.
Movement skill: Sit and stand.

Two children stand back-to-back with elbows locked. Bracing against each other's back, they bend knees, walk two or three small steps away from each other, sinking slowly to the floor. Keeping arms locked and knees bent, they bring the feet close to the body. Then, bracing feet against the floor and pushing against the partner's back, they extend legs and rise to the original position. Repeat several times.

ROCKING HORSE

Behavioral goal: To cooperate with a partner in rocking forward and backward.

Concept: Newton's laws of motion.
Biologic efficiency: Coordination.
Movement skill: Rocking.

Two children sit on the floor facing each other. First child bends knees and slides feet under second child; second child also slides feet under first child, keeping legs outside partner's legs. They bend knees, sit as close as possible, grasping each other's shoulders.

First child rocks back, pulling second child forward off floor, feet in contact with partner's body; then second child rocks back, lifting first child off floor. Continue rocking back and forth; momentum will make rocking easy if motion is continued.

Variation: Progress across the floor by extending legs each time before they reach the floor.

TURK STAND

Behavioral goal: To stand and sit with arms and legs crossed.
Concept: Newton's laws of motion; gravity and movement.
Biologic efficiency: Leg strength; balance.
Movement skill: Stand and sit.

Child stands with arms and legs crossed. He sits down and rises to standing at once.

On first time, keep hands at sides to avoid injury by sitting too fast. When sitting, carry weight on outer side of feet. Get center of gravity over feet by leaning forward when rising.

HAND REST

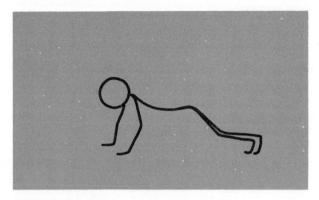

Behavioral goal: To support weight on hands and toes.
Concept: Attainment of strength, endurance.
Biologic efficiency: Arm strength and endurance.
Movement skill: Supporting body weight.

Child gets down on floor, supporting weight on hands and toes. Then he walks his feet backward until there is a straight line from head to toes.

Body should not sag at waist, and hips should not be elevated. Maintain position for a count of 5; then hold for increasingly longer periods on successive days.

SIT-UP

Behavioral goal: To sit up from a back-lying position with knees bent.
Concept: Attainment of strength, endurance.

Biologic efficiency: Abdominal strength; endurance.
Movement skill: Sitting up and lying down.

Child lies on back, knees bent, and feet flat on the floor. He places his hands on his shoulders, elbows pointing upward. A partner holds his feet to the floor. Child curls forward, raising head and shoulders, and sits up touching elbows to top of knees; then returns to lying position. This constitutes one sit-up. He continues doing sit-ups for as long as possible, trying to increase the number on succeeding days.

When able to do 20 or more consecutive sit-ups without difficulty, clasp the hands behind the head with elbows held back, to increase the resistance.

PUSH-UP

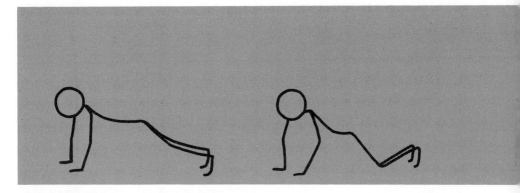

Behavioral goal: To lift and lower the body weight.
Concept: Attainment of strength, endurance.
Biologic efficiency: Arm and shoulder strength; endurance.
Movement skill: Push-up.

Child lies face down on the floor with hands, palms down, placed on the floor under his shoulders. Body is held in a straight line from toes to shoulders as force is exerted against the hands until the arms are extended. Then, while the elbows slowly bend, the body is lowered until the chin touches the floor. This constitutes one push-up.

Child continues doing push-ups for as long as possible, trying to extend the number on succeeding days.

If child has difficulty raising body, he may bend his knees, keeping the body in a straight line from knees to shoulders, as he straightens his arms and pushes up from the floor. Girls usually use the knees as the point of contact with the floor; boys are frequently able to push up from the toes.

FLYING RINGS

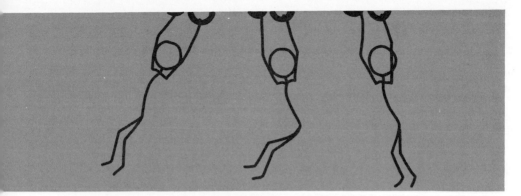

Behavioral goal: To swing on the rings while hanging from the hands, then drop off safely.

Concept: Newton's laws of motion; human locomotion.

Biologic efficiency: Arm and shoulder strength.

Movement skill: Swinging on rings.

Child grasps the rings with each hand, and starts momentum by running a few steps, or with a push from a helper. He pumps with the body by arching and extending the legs. He continues swinging, pulling slightly on the rings at the height of the forward swing to aid momentum.

When ready to drop off, he keeps his body extended and at the height of the backswing he pulls on the rings, releases grip and drops off to a stand, giving with the knees and ankles to minimize the jar of landing.

It is important to have adult supervision while the child is learning this skill, since he may need help in starting the momentum and in dropping from the rings. A trapeze may be used in place of the rings.

SPINNING ON THE BAR

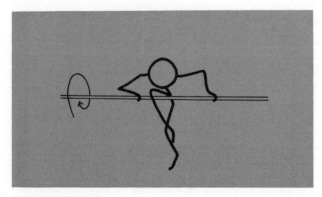

Behavioral goal: To spin on the low bar.

Concept: Newton's laws of motion.
Biologic efficiency: Coordination.
Movement skill: Spinning on the bar.

Child mounts low bar, hooking one knee over it and leaving other leg straight, palms of hands facing body. He thrusts straightened leg backward and head and trunk forward simultaneously, causing body to spin entirely around bar and back to original position.

Be sure to use a spotter while child is learning this stunt; his hands may slip, or he may need help in stopping.

TREADMILL

Behavioral goal: To run in place from a hand rest position.
Concept: Attainment of endurance.
Biologic efficiency: Endurance.
Movement skill: Running.

Child takes hand rest position, supporting weight on hands and toes, legs extended in back. Keeping the hands stationary, he runs in place by alternately bending one leg while extending the other. Repeat until mildly fatigued, trying to lengthen the period from day to day.

BLOW UP THE BALLOON

Behavioral goal: To stretch the lower back.
Concept: Attainment of flexibility.
Biologic efficiency: Flexibility of lower back, hip joints.
Movement skill: Stretching.

Child stands with feet comfortably apart, then squats, placing hands on floor in front of feet. Then, keeping hands flat on floor, he tries to straighten his legs as much as possible, pushing his hips upward and contracting his abdominal muscles.

HAND TUG-OF-WAR

Behavioral goal: To try to pull an opponent over a line.
Concept: Gravity and movement; Newton's laws of motion.
Biologic efficiency: Strength.
Movement skill: Pulling

Two children stand facing each other from opposite sides of a line drawn on the floor. They grasp right hands and on signal, "Go!" try to pull the opponent over the line. Child who wins two "falls" out of three is the victor of the match.

TICK-TOCK

Behavioral goal: To jump over a rope that is swinging back and forth.
Concept: Skills of locomotion.
Biologic efficiency: Coordination; endurance.
Movement skill: Jumping.

A 20-foot rope is swung slowly back and forth like a pendulum. The rope is gradually raised higher and higher as the jumper jumps to the following chant:

Tick-tock, tick-tock, what's the time
By the clock?
It's one, two, three . . . . ,

and so on to twelve o'clock, or until the child misses.

When jumper jumps to twelve o'clock, he runs out and becomes a turner. If he misses on a number before twelve, he is out and becomes a turner.

JUMPING A SHORT ROPE

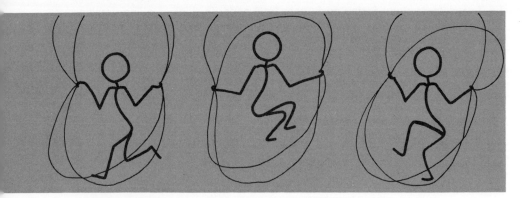

Behavioral goal: To jump a short rope, using various movements.
Concept: Newton's laws of motion; skills of locomotion.
Biologic efficiency: Coordination; endurance.
Movement skill: Jumping; hopping; leaping.

Each child has a rope twice long enough to reach from his hips to the ground. He turns the rope for himself as he performs various stunts:

 (1) Rocking, by leaping forward over the rope, then shifting weight to back foot;
 (2) Jumping in place, taking off from and landing on both feet together as the rope swings under the feet;
 (3) Hopping on one foot, swinging the rope under the foot;
 (4) Jumping forward, running while jumping;
 (5) Swinging the rope backward and jumping it.

FRONT DOOR, BACK DOOR

Behavioral goal: To run into a turning rope, jump several times, and run out.

Concept: Newton's laws of motion.
Biologic efficiency: Coordination; endurance.
Movement skill: Jumping.

Two children turn a 15 to 20-foot rope for other children to run into and jump. When the rope swings toward the jumper from above, it is called "front door" and when it swings toward him from below it is called "back door." Jumper runs into the front door immediately after the rope touches the ground, and into the back door immediately after it passes his body.

Perform the following stunts:

(1) Run in the front door, jump one, run on through and out the other side;
(2) Run in the front door and jump to the jingle, then run out the other side:

Teddy Bear, Teddy Bear
Turn around (turn while jumping).
Teddy Bear, Teddy Bear
Touch the ground (squat and touch ground once).
Teddy Bear, Teddy Bear
Show your shoe (raise leg and show shoe).
Teddy Bear, Teddy Bear
Run on through (run out other side).

(3) Run in back door, jump once, run through;
(4) Run in back door and jump to jingle, then run through:

I asked my mother for fifty cents
To watch the monkey jump the fence,
He jumped so far he reached the stars
And then came back as the man from Mars.

Activities for Grades 3, 4

Many of the activities suggested for younger children may also challenge eight and nine year olds. It is impracticable to state an absolute degree of difficulty of any stunt, since much depends upon the body structure, development, attitude, and previous experiences of the individual attempting the stunt. Some children may find it difficult, if not impossible to perform a given stunt because of physiologic, anatomic, or psychologic barriers, described in Chapter 12, "Movement and the Biologic Condition."

Designation of grade levels is to help the teacher make a selection for a given group. It must be remembered, however, that any of the activities may be suitable for any particular grade level, and may even be challenging to adults.

THE BALANCE BEAM

Behavioral goal: To balance on a beam while performing stunts.
Concept: Gravity and movement.
Biologic efficiency: Balance; agility; coordination.
Movement skill: Balancing.

Children perform the following stunts on the beam:

(1) Walk forward several steps ending in stride position, pivot without lifting feet from beam, and return;
(2) Jump on the beam;
(3) Hop on one foot;
(4) Stand on one leg, swinging other leg forward and backward;
(5) Sit, facing length of beam;
(6) Sit, knees bent, then knees straight;
(7) Swan dive, standing on one leg and bending trunk forward with other leg straight in air in back of body;
(8) Duck walk, squatting and taking three or four steps;
(9) Gallop several steps;
(10) Measuring worm: with weight on all fours, first walk forward with the hands while keeping feet stationary, then walk feet up to meet hands.

If a beam is not available, use a line on the floor, or a plank fastened to the floor. Balance beam should be no more than 8 to 10 inches from the floor; mats should be on either side for safety.

HEEL CLICK

Behavioral goal: To jump or leap into the air, clicking heels together before landing.

Concept: Skills of locomotion, mechanics of movement.

Biologic efficiency: Balance; coordination.

Movement skill: Jumping; leaping.

Child jumps from both feet, clicks heels together once before landing. Variations:

(1) Jump and click heels twice before landing; arm swing upward helps to achieve height;

(2) Cross one foot in front of other; spring upward from forward foot, lifting other foot sideward, clicking heels before landing on take-off foot;

(3) Extend one foot forward, jumping from other foot and clicking heels, landing on take-off foot;

(4) Extend one foot to the rear, leap from other foot and click heels in this position, landing on take-off foot.

ONE-LEGGED SQUAT

Behavioral goal: To squat and return to standing, sustaining the weight on one leg.

Concept: Gravity and movement; Newton's laws of motion.

Biologic efficiency: Leg strength; balance; flexibility.

Movement skill: Squatting.

Child stands on mat, arms extended at sides for balance. He lifts one leg in front of him with knee straight and, bending knee of supporting leg, squats low, then returns at once to standing position.

KNEE DIP

Behavioral goal: To lower and raise body with weight supported on one leg.

Concept: Gravity and movement.

Biologic efficiency: Leg strength; balance; agility.
Movement skill: Squatting.

Child lifts one leg behind back, grasping ankle with opposite hand, and touching knee to mat by bending supporting leg. He returns to standing position immediately.

THROUGH THE STICK

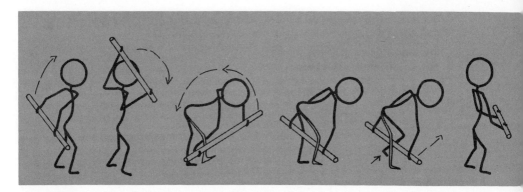

Behavioral goal: To maneuver the body into positions necessary to perform the stunt.
Concept: Flexibility; basic movements of the body.
Biologic efficiency: Flexibility.
Movement skill: Bending; stretching; twisting.

Child holds stick behind back, hands wide apart, palms forward. Hands continuing to grasp the stick, he brings stick over his head in front of body. He lowers stick toward right foot, swings right foot around right arm and steps over stick, so that right leg is between the two hands. Then, raising left hand, he passes stick over his head and behind his back, sliding stick over the right knee and back. Then he stands, stepping back over the stick with the left foot, finishing with stick in front of body. At no time does he release the stick.

TRUNK TWIST

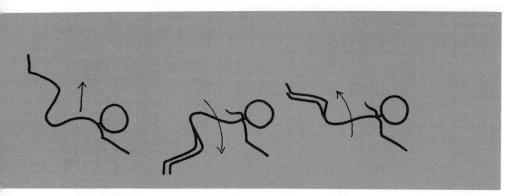

Behavioral goal: To lie flat on the back and twist trunk from side to side.
Concept: Strength.
Biologic efficiency: Strength of abdomen, trunk.
Movement skill: Twisting.

Child lies on floor on his back, arms outstretched at sides, palms down. He raises his knees to his chest, then lowers his hips alternately from side to side, touching the floor each time.

When this can be executed easily 10 to 12 times in succession, add more resistance by directing child to perform with legs straight.

HIP WALK

Behavioral goal: To move across floor walking on hips.

Concept: Skills of locomotion; human locomotion.
Biologic efficiency: Coordination.
Movement skill: Walking on hips.

Child sits on floor, back straight, legs extended in front, arms folded over chest. He walks forward on his hips, moving first one side then the other.

KNEE WALK

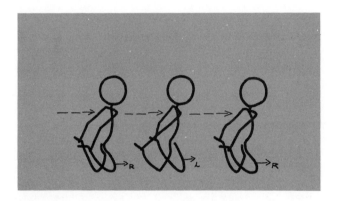

Behavioral goal: To move forward by walking on knees.
Concept: Human movement.
Biologic efficiency: Balance; coordination.
Movement skill: Walking on knees.

Child kneels on mat on both knees, holding ankles or toes with hands. He walks forward to edge of mat on knees.

Balance is more easily maintained if one moves quickly.

CHINNING

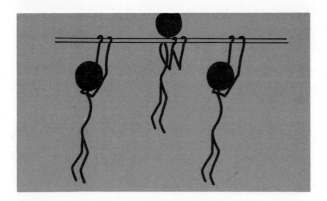

Behavioral goal: To lift the body weight with hands and arms, with or without support.

Concept: Strength.

Biologic efficiency: Arm and shoulder girdle strength.

Movement skill: Chinning.

Child jumps and grasps a bar placed slightly higher than a standing reach. The bar may be gripped with a front or reverse grip of the hands. The individual then pulls himself toward his hands in an attempt to place his chin over the bar. The body is lowered back to the hanging position. The child repeats the pulling up and lowering down movements until he can do no more.

Chinning with support: Chins may be difficult for some children, and modified chins with the feet on the ground can be used until they develop the necessary strength for regular chinning. In the modified chin, the child grasps a low bar, palms toward him. He extends his legs in front with knees bent at right angles, weight supported by feet and arms. He bends his elbows until chin is level with bar, then extends arms to original position. He continues for as long as possible.

CORKSCREW

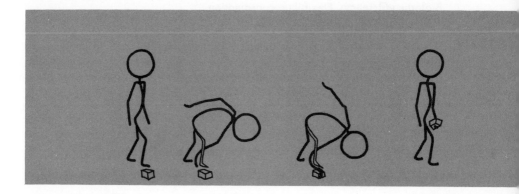

Behavioral goal: To twist body into position to pick up object.
Concept: Flexibility.
Biologic efficiency: Flexibility.
Movement skill: Twisting.

Child stands with feet apart, an object placed near toe of right foot. He brings left arm across body, around outside of right leg, then reaches through legs and retrieves object. He may move in any way he wishes, as long as feet remain flat on floor.

SKIN THE SNAKE

Behavioral goal: To cooperate with others in performing the stunt.
Concept: Flexibility.

Biologic efficiency: Flexibility; coordination.
Movement skill: Lying down; standing up.

Five children line up, one behind the other, legs in wide stride position. All reach right hand between legs and left hands forward, grasping hands of children in front and back. The last one in line lies down on his back, still holding the hand of the child in front of him. Walking backward in wide stride position, children keep hands linked and, as each person reaches the end of the line, he lies down. The last child in line to lie down gets up at once and walks forward, straddling the bodies of the others. Retaining their hand grasps, children rise in turn until all are standing again.

FULL TOP

Behavioral goal: To do a complete turn in the air.
Concept: Skills of locomotion; Newton's laws of motion.
Biologic efficiency: Coordination.
Movement skill: Jumping; twisting.

Child stands on a line on the floor, feet comfortably apart. He jumps into the air, taking off from both feet simultaneously, spins completely around, and lands on line facing same direction as in starting position.

Swing arms and body in direction of the turn; land with feet apart to maintain balance, and with knees bent to decrease shock of landing.

JUMP IN PLACE

Behavioral goal: To jump repeatedly, landing lightly.
Concept: Attainment of endurance.
Biologic efficiency: Endurance.
Movement skill: Jumping.

Child jumps in place, taking off from both feet simultaneously and "giving" as he lands. He should bounce lightly, with a minimum of noise on the landing.

Continue until mildly fatigued. Repeat on continuing days, trying to increase the length of time.

JUMP AND REACH

Behavioral goal: To jump vertically in the air and reach as high as possible.
Concept: Skills of locomotion.

Biologic Efficiency: Coordination; agility.
Movement skill: Jumping.

Child stands facing the wall, feet flat on the floor and both hands raised upward, placing a chalk mark at the height of the reach.   Child then turns sideward to the wall and jumps as high as he can, placing a chalk mark at the height of the jump, as far up the wall as possible.   The measure of the distance between the two marks is his score.

SHUTTLE RUN

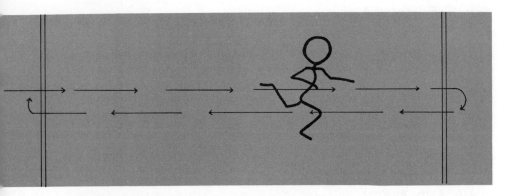

Behavioral goal: To run fast, stopping and changing direction quickly.
Concept: Skills of locomotion; Newton's laws of motion.
Biologic efficiency: Speed; endurance.
Movement skill: Running; changing direction.

Child stands with both feet behind the starting line.   On signal, "Go!" he runs to opposite line, returns to starting line, and continues running back and forth a given number of times.   His time is taken with a stop watch, calibrated in tenths of seconds, with the score recorded to the nearest tenth.

Lines should be 20 to 30 feet apart; each child runs back and forth two or three times without stopping.

Variation: Score may be number of trips completed in a given number of seconds.

SOFTBALL DISTANCE THROW

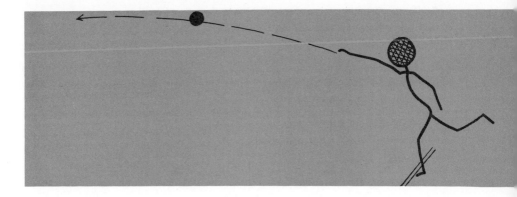

Behavioral goal: To throw a softball as far as possible.
Concept: Skills of overcoming inertia of other objects.
Biologic efficiency: Arm strength; coordination.
Movement skill: Throwing.

Child stands behind a throwing line and throws a softball as far as possible, using an overhand throw. Throw is measured in feet, from throwing line to place where ball first touches ground. Child is given three trials, and his score is the best of the three.

Variation: Underhand or side-arm throws may be used. Objects other than balls, such as beanbags or rings, may be thrown for distance.

FORWARD ROLLS FROM A RUN

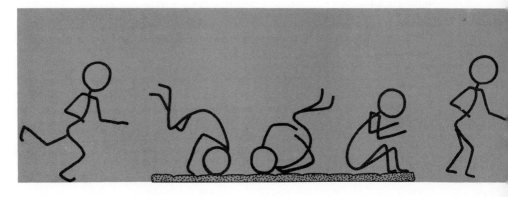

Behavioral goal: To execute continuous forward rolls, starting from a short run.

Concept: Gravity and movement; Newton's laws of motion.
Biologic efficiency: Flexibility; coordination.
Movement skill: Forward roll.

Child takes short run forward toward mat, springs from both feet, landing on hands on mat. Then, elbows bend, head tucks under, and he rolls over. At finish of roll, keeping body curled, he rocks weight over feet and immediately rolls forward again. He continues rolls for length of mat, leaping to his feet after last roll.

CONTINUOUS CARTWHEELS

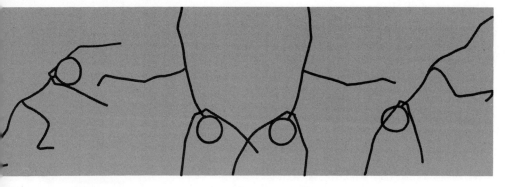

Behavioral goal: To perform several cartwheels in a straight line.
Concept: Gravity and movement; Newton's laws of motion.
Biologic efficiency: Arm strength; balance; coordination.
Movement skill: Turning a cartwheel.

Child first reviews turning a cartwheel, described for Grades 1, 2, p. 194. When he can execute this successfully, he performs one cartwheel, following it immediately with another. By rapidly whipping arms down and legs up, he gains momentum for each succeeding cartwheel.

MULE KICK

Behavioral goal: To support weight on hands and kick both feet into the air.
Concept: Gravity and movement.
Biologic efficiency: Arm strength; balance; coordination.
Movement skill: Balancing.

Child bends forward, placing both hands on floor, arms straight. He kicks both feet into the air, holding weight on hands, hips vertically above the head before the legs are extended upward. When handstand position is reached, he bends the hips, pushes from the floor with hands, and springs back to the feet.

PUSH OUT OF THE CRATER

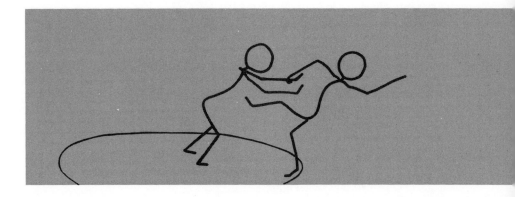

Behavioral goal: To push another out of the circle.

223

Concept: Gravity and movement; Newton's laws of motion.
Biologic efficiency: Strength; coordination.
Movement skill: Pulling; pushing.

A circle, 8 to 10 feet in diameter, is drawn on the floor. Paired contestants stand facing each other in center of circle. On the signal, "Go!" each child tries to push or pull the other out of the circle, while keeping both his own feet inside the circle.

CROSSED ROPES

Behavioral goal: To run into two ropes turning simultaneously and run out; to jump short rope inside long ropes.
Concept: Newton's laws of motion.
Biologic efficiency: Coordination; endurance.
Movement skill: Jumping.

Children review jumping front door and back door using a single rope, described for Grades 1, 2, p. 208. Two ropes are crossed at right angles to each other. Swingers synchronize ropes so that both are turning toward jumper from above (front door), and are touching the ground simultaneously. Child runs into front door to center where ropes cross, jumps several times, and runs through.

Variations:

(1) Run in the front doors, jump to the jingle, then run through:
   One, two, buckle my shoe
   Three, four, shut the door
   Five, six, pick up sticks

Seven, eight, lay them straight
Nine, ten, run out again;
(2) Run in back doors (ropes both swinging toward jumper from below) and jump to the jingle, then run out;
(3) Run in back doors carrying short rope, and jump short rope in center of crossed ropes;
(4) One child jumps short rope in center of crossed ropes, and a partner runs in and jumps with him.

FRONT CROSS–BACK CROSS

Behavioral goal: To jump a short rope, executing "front cross" and "back cross."

Concept: Newton's laws of motion.

Biologic efficiency: Coordination; endurance.

Movement skill: Jumping.

Child reviews jumping short rope, described for Grades 1, 2, p. 208. For front crosses, he swings the rope forward over his head, crossing his arms at elbows in front of his body on alternate jumps.

For back crosses, he swings the rope backward over his head, crossing his arms in front of his body on alternate jumps.

JUMPING FROM AN OBJECT

Behavioral goal: To jump from an object, landing in various ways.
Concept: Skills of locomotion.
Biologic efficiency: Coordination; flexibility.
Movement skill: Jumping.

Child sits or stands on a box, balance beam, horse, low ramp, low bar, or other object. He gets off in the following ways:

(1) Jump off, landing softly;
(2) Jump off, "walking" in air;
(3) Jump off, bringing knees to chest, then straightening legs before landing;
(4) Jump off, making a turn in the air;
(5) Jump off, turning a forward roll after landing;
(6) Jump off with a partner.

WALKING ASTRONAUT

Behavioral goal: To "walk" while in suspension.

Concept: Human movement; strength; postures.
Biologic efficiency: Arm strength; coordination.
Movement skill: Walking while hanging.

Child grasps bar with hands and hangs with arms and legs fully extended, feet completely off ground. From this position, child raises first one knee, then the other, continuing to walk without stopping. He receives one score for each step. Knee should be raised until thigh is parallel with floor.

The hanging position may help the child to attain a kinesthetic feeling for good body alignment from head to toes, if the presence of the "feeling" is brought to his attention.

STRADDLE SPIN

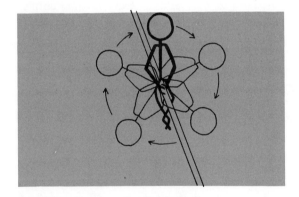

Behavioral goal: To spin on the bar in straddle position.
Concept: Newton's laws of motion.
Biologic efficiency: Arm strength; coordination.
Movement skill: Spinning on the bar.

Child straddles the bar, body erect, feet several inches from the ground. He takes his weight on his hands, which are close to the body, and crosses legs, hooking one toe behind the other heel. Keeping body and legs straight, he swings trunk to one side of bar, and swings legs to opposite side, turning completely around bar and back to original position.

Continue turning several times in succession. It is important to keep body in a straight line, legs and trunk extended, to facilitate spinning on bar.

HORIZONTAL LADDER

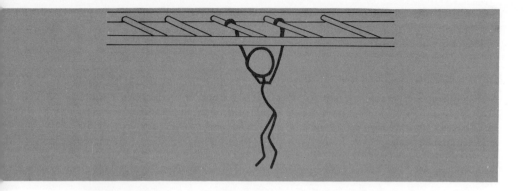

Behavioral goal: To move across horizontal ladder with hands.
Concept: Newton's laws of motion.
Biologic efficiency: Arm strength; coordination.
Movement skill: Walking with hands across ladder.

Child climbs steps and grasps first rung of ladder. From hanging position he reaches with one hand for next rung and continues "walking" across ladder, alternating hands from rung to rung.

Other stunts to be performed on the ladder:

(1) Walk across ladder with hands, skipping every other rung;
(2) Travel sideways, grasping one side of ladder with both hands;
(3) Travel forward, grasping both sides of ladder;
(4) Make a half turn with the body while swinging from rung to rung.

Activities for Grades 5, 6

Ten, eleven, and twelve year olds are eager to test their strength, speed, endurance, and flexibility, and are interested in improving their performance in activity areas. Their growing bodies are causing changes in the center of gravity, which affects their performance in activities requiring balance and stability. Compensating for this is the accompanying maturation and growth of motor areas, which gives them good muscular development and control in movement activities. Adapting to a changing body becomes one of the goals for this age group, and stunts and tests provide useful opportunities for helping them to achieve this goal.

THE BALANCE BEAM

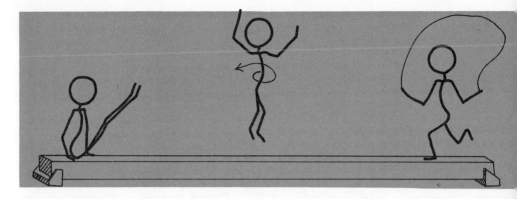

Behavioral goal: To balance on the beam while performing stunts.
Concept: Gravity and movement.
Biologic efficiency: Balance; agility; coordination.
Movement skill: Balancing on the beam.

Children review activities on the beam learned in previous grades. Children perform the following stunts:

(1) Hop on one foot forward and backward;
(2) Turn on beam in squat position by crouching with one foot ahead of other; then make a half pivot turn without rising;
(3) V-sit on the beam by sitting, then lifting both legs until body and legs form position of V;
(4) Perform half-top on beam, jumping into air and turning half way around;
(5) Jump rope on the beam;
(6) Improvise stunts.

BUILDING PYRAMIDS

Behavioral goal: To work with a group in designing pyramids.
Concept: Gravity and movement.
Biologic efficiency: Balance; strength.
Movement skill: Activities involving balance, strength.

Children design their own pyramids, using balance stunts and following these pointers:

(1) Stronger, larger children are the supports or "bases";
(2) Light children are on top;
(3) When standing or kneeling on a child who is the base, avoid placing weight on joints such as spine or neck—kneel or stand on padded body parts, such as buttocks;
(4) Use mats to avoid injury;
(5) Pyramids may be designed with the height in the center, at either end, or both;
(6) Add interest by performing moving stunts such as forward rolls and cartwheels under and through the pyramid.

WALKING CHAIR

Behavioral goal: To walk in crouched position, moving with others.
Concept: Levers of the body; gravity and movement.
Biologic efficiency: Balance; coordination.
Movement skill: Walking.

Five or six children line up, one behind the other, hands at waist of person in front. Last child bends knees as if sitting in a chair. Child in front of him backs up to him and takes same position, back of his legs against first child, each child supporting his own weight. Other children take similar position. On signal, "Walk!" all children move forward with right foot and continue to walk, keeping in step with each other.

DORSAL ARCH

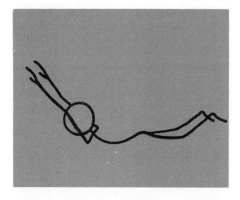

Behavioral goal: To perform the stunt correctly.
Concept: Attaining flexibility, strength.

Biologic efficiency: Strength of back extensors.
Movement skill: Arching back.

Child lies face down, hands over head. He raises his head and toes from the floor, attempting to clear his chest and thighs from the floor. He holds the position for a count of 3, then returns to original position.

Repeat several times.

WOODCHOPPER

Behavioral goal: To perform the exercise correctly.
Concept: Attainment of strength.
Biologic efficiency: Strength of knee, hip, and trunk extensors.
Movement skill: Swinging forcefully.

Child stands with feet apart and directly under shoulders, arms overhead, and hands clasped. He swings the arms forcefully downward toward feet, as though chopping wood, allowing hands to swing between legs. Then he returns to extended position.

Repeat several times, adding further repetitions on consecutive days.

FORWARD ROLL OVER A MAT

Behavioral goal: To perform a forward roll over a mat.
Concept: Newton's laws of motion.
Biologic efficiency: Flexibility; coordination.
Movement skill: Rolling.

A rolled-up mat is placed at the edge of another mat. Child takes several running steps toward mat; when about a foot from it, he jumps forward and upward, and lands with hands on other side of obstacle. He bends elbows, tucks head, and rolls over the obstacle, returning to feet.

Variations: When child can perform the above easily, he may try such other dives as:

(1) Dive over one person lying flat on edge of mat;
(2) Dive over one person crouched on hands and knees;
(3) Dive over one person raised on hands and knees;
(4) Dive over two people, and so on.

HANDSTAND

Behavioral goal: To support weight in inverted position on hands.

Concept: Gravity and movement.
Biologic efficiency: Arm strength; balance.
Movement skill: Balancing.

Review "Mule Kick," described for Grades 3, 4, p. 223.   Place hands on floor or mat, shoulder distance apart, fingers pointing forward, and spread to enlarge the base of support.   Move legs close to body with hips vertically above head, as in mule kick.   Kick one leg over head, followed immediately by other leg.   To help catch balance, keep head up with back slightly arched. Balance in this position for a few seconds, then bend hips and drop legs to floor one at a time.

TIGER STAND

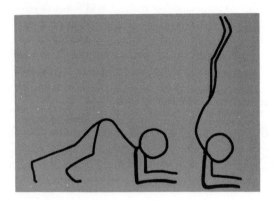

Behavioral goal: To support weight on forearms.
Concept: Gravity and movement.
Biologic efficiency: Balance.
Movement skill: Balancing.

Child places forearms on mat, shoulder width apart, palms down.   He walks up to arms with feet, until hips are nearly vertical, then kicks legs up over head.   He maintains balance by keeping head up, and arching back slightly.   He descends by dropping one leg to the mat, then the other.

JUMP AND SLAP

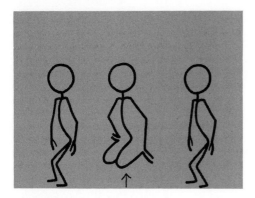

Behavioral goal: To jump into air and slap heels before landing.
Concept: Skills of locomotion.
Biologic efficiency: Balance; coordination.
Movement skill: Jumping.

Child stands with hands at sides, then jumps into air bringing heels up to sides, and slaps heels with hands before landing.

JUMP TO HEELS

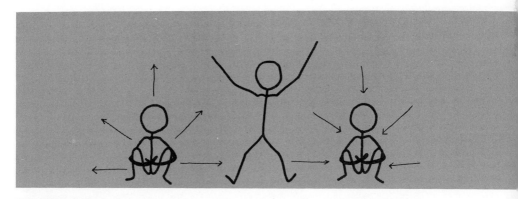

Behavioral goal: To spring into air from squat position, landing on heels.
Concept: Skills of locomotion.
Biologic efficiency: Flexibility; coordination; balance.
Movement skill: Jumping.

Child squats, then jumps into air, landing with feet in stride position with weight supported on heels. Then he rocks weight to ball of foot and returns to squat position.

BEAR DANCE

Behavioral goal: To shift weight from foot to foot in squat position.
Concept: Newton's laws of motion.
Biologic efficiency: Strength; coordination; balance.
Movement skill: Leaping in squat position.

Child squats, hands on hips, one foot extended in front of him. He pushes against the floor, raising his weight and extending the opposite foot. He continues "dancing," by changing from foot to foot in the squat position.

JUMP THE STICK

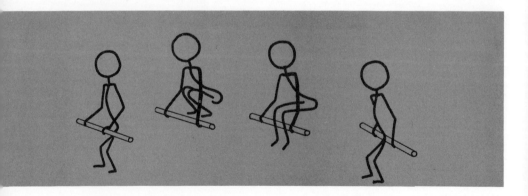

Behavioral goal: To jump over a stick held in the hands.
Concept: Skills of locomotion.
Biologic Efficiency: Flexibility; coordination.
Movement skill: Jumping.

Child holds stick in front of his body, palms down.   He jumps into air, bringing knees close to chest, simultaneously swinging stick under his feet.   He finishes with stick behind him.   Stick must be held with both hands during entire stunt.

KNEE SPRING

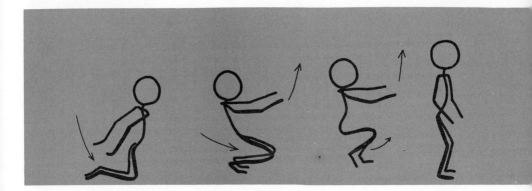

Behavioral goal: To spring to standing position from knees.
Concept: Skills of locomotion.
Biologic efficiency: Coordination.
Movement skill: Jumping from knees.

Child kneels on mat, ankles and toes extended, back straight.   He swings his arms backward, then forcefully forward and upward, pushing from mat with feet.   He springs upward, pulls feet under body and lands in standing position.

JUMP THE FOOT

Behavioral goal: To spring over foot supported by wall.
Concept: Skills of locomotion.
Biologic efficiency: Coordination.
Movement skill: Jumping.

Child stands with one side to the wall, with outside foot flat against wall and in front of inside leg. He springs from inside foot and jumps over outside leg.

ANKLE THROW

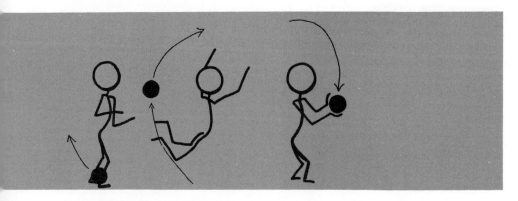

Behavioral goal: To toss an object over the head, throwing it from the level of the ankles.
Concept: Skills of locomotion.
Biologic efficiency: Coordination.
Movement skill: Jumping.

Child holds beanbag or ball between his feet. He jumps into the air, kicking his feet backward and propelling the object over his head. He catches the object as it comes down in front of him.

EGGBEATER

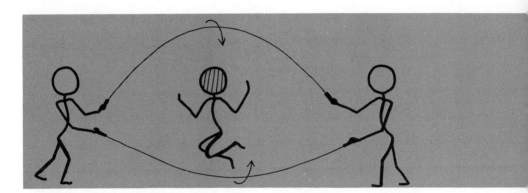

Behavioral goal: To jump two ropes turning toward each other.
Concept: Newton's laws of motion; skills of locomotion.
Biologic efficiency: Coordination; endurance.
Movement skill: Jumping.

Two children, holding the end of a rope in each hand, turn two long ropes alternately toward each other. A child runs into the center and jumps the ropes. He must jump rapidly in order to jump over both ropes as they come under his feet in sequence.

When child is adept at this, he may run into eggbeater carrying a short rope, simultaneously jumping his short rope and the long ropes.

SKIN THE CAT

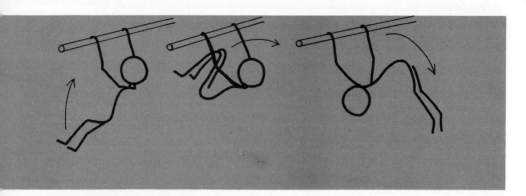

Behavioral goal: To turn over on the low bar.
Concept: Newton's laws of motion.
Biologic efficiency: Arm strength.
Movement skill: Turning on the bar.

Child grasps bar, palms of hands toward him. He lifts knees up between arms and, bringing them to his chest, lowers his head and simultaneously swings legs through arms, turning over the touching the ground with his toes. Then he releases bar and stands.

Variation: After turning over, retain grasp on bar, touch toes to ground, and immediately turn body back to original position, bringing legs back through arms and ending in standing position facing bar.

HAND WRESTLE

Behavioral goal: To cause the opponent to lose balance.

Concept: Gravity and movement; Newton's laws of motion.
Biologic efficiency: Strength; balance; coordination.
Movement skill: Pushing; pulling.

Two children stand facing each other in forward stride position, right feet placed side by side, and right hands grasped. On signal, "Go!" each tries to push or pull the other to make him move his feet or lose balance. Winner is one who wins two falls out of three.

TRAVELING RINGS

Behavioral goal: To move by swinging from one ring to the next.
Concept: Moving in suspension.
Biologic efficiency: Arm and shoulder strength; coordination.
Movement skill: Traveling on rings.

Child grasps two rings, body extended and hanging. He pulls on first ring, starting swing, then releases first ring, grasping second ring with both hands; he releases other hand and grasps third ring, and so on, until he has traveled to end of rings. He may either drop off, or he may travel back to the starting point.

Variation: Pull on first ring, release, and turn body to face opposite direction; grasp next ring, and continue to end, turning forward and backward.

STICK WRESTLE

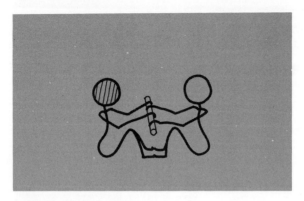

Behavioral goal: To overcome an opponent by pulling him from the floor.
Concept: Newton's laws of motion.
Biologic efficiency: Strength; coordination.
Movement skill: Pulling.

Two children sit facing each other on the mat, toes braced against opponent's toes. A stick is placed between them and each takes a firm grasp on it. On signal, "Go!" they both pull on stick, each trying to pull the other to a standing position. Winner is one who wins two bouts out of three.

HAND SLAP

Behavioral goal: To cause opponent to lose balance.
Concept: Newton's laws of motion; gravity and movement.
Biologic efficiency: Balance; coordination.

Movement skill: Balancing.

Two children face each other, arms' distance apart, right arms extended forward with palm facing opponent's palm. Children touch right palms, left hands behind backs, and one foot raised backward. On signal, "Go!" they try to slap opponent's hand, causing him to lose balance and touch raised foot to floor. Winner is one who wins two bouts out of three.

ELBOW DIP

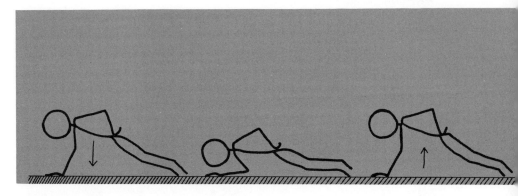

Behavioral goal: To raise and lower body weight.
Concept: Newton's laws of motion; attainment of strength; endurance.
Biologic efficiency: Arm strength; endurance.
Movement skill: Raising and lowering body.

Child lies on side, body in a straight line. He pushes up from mat with both hands, then places left hand on hip and supports weight with right hand and feet, keeping body in a straight line. Then he bends his elbow to lower his body to the mat and pushes up again immediately. He repeats for as long as possible, extending the number from day to day.

SQUAT-THRUST

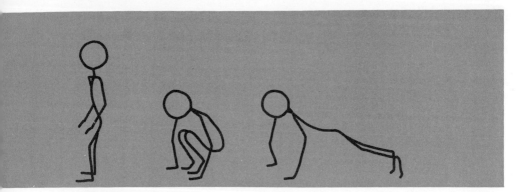

Behavioral goal: To improve endurance.
Concept: Attainment of endurance.
Biologic efficiency: Endurance.
Movement skill: Bending; stretching.

Child stands with arms at sides. He performs the squat-thrust as follows:

Count 1—Squat, placing hands on floor;
Count 2—Extend both legs to rear simultaneously, body straight;
Count 3—Return to squat position;
Count 4—Return to standing position.

He repeats the squat-thrusts rapidly for as long as possible, trying to extend the number of repetitions on successive days.

WAISTLINER

Behavioral goal: To rotate the upper body, keeping feet stationary.

Concept: Attainment of flexibility.
Biologic efficiency: Flexibility.
Movement skill: Twisting.

Child stands in easy stride position, toes parallel to each other. He raises arms to shoulder height, then bends elbows, bringing hands in front of chest. Keeping feet stationary, he rotates body from side to side, twisting as far as possible.

LEG LIFT

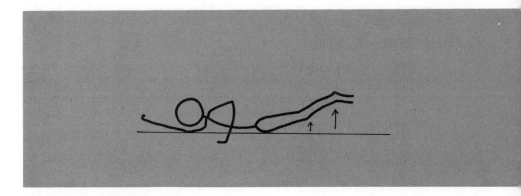

Behavioral goal: To raise legs from floor.
Concept: Attainment of strength.
Biologic efficiency: Leg and hip strength.
Movement skill: Raising and lowering legs.

Child lies on side on floor, head resting on arm extended under him, top hand on floor at chest. Keeping body in a straight line, he lifts both legs from floor as high as possible, holding for a count of four. Repeat as often as possible. Then repeat, lying on opposite side.

STANDING BROAD JUMP

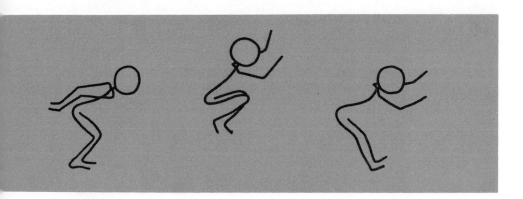

Behavioral goal: To jump forward as far as possible.
Concept: Newton's laws of motion; skills of locomotion.
Biologic efficiency: Coordination.
Movement skill: Jumping.

Child stands at edge of mat or jumping pit, feet in back of take-off line. He swings his arms, bends his knees, and jumps forward as far as possible. His score is the number of inches measured from the take-off line to the heel, or nearest point touched by his body in landing. Child is allowed three trials, and the best score of the three is recorded.

CHINESE JUMP ROPE

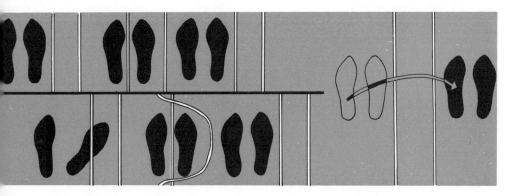

Behavioral goal: To jump the three "floors" successfully.
Concept: Newton's laws of motion; skills of locomotion.

Biologic efficiency: Coordination.
Movement skill: Jumping.

The equipment used for this game is an elastic jump rope about two yards long, tied at the ends to make a circle. Two chairs or two people are used to hold the rope. The rope is kept taut off the ground, held by two front chair legs or by two people's legs (people standing in stride position facing each other).

The game is played on three "floors," ankle height, knee height, and thigh height. If the rope is stepped upon while jumping, or if the jumper fails a step, he loses his turn and next time around starts off on whichever floor he was at the time he missed.

First Floor. The rope is held taut about 4 to 6 inches from the ground.

Step I. Assume starting position with right ankle against left side of rope.
Jump and land with right foot inside rope.
Jump back to starting position.
Catch left rope over right instep, jump and land with right rope between feet. Left rope has been carried over by right foot.
Jump back to starting position.
Repeat *rapidly* a total of three times. Then hop completely over rope so that left ankle is against right rope.
Repeat above directions three times starting with left foot, performing Step I in reverse.

Step II. Place both feet under right side of rope.
Jump across left side of rope, carrying right rope over left.
Turn to your right.

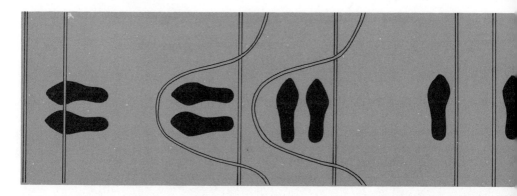

Jump so that rope springs back to position, and land with one foot on each side of rope.

Step III. Place one foot on each side of rope.

Slide feet close together.

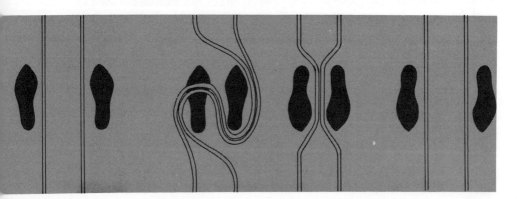

Turn around to your right until facing the opposite direction with rope wrapped around ankles. It will be in front of the left ankle and behind the right ankle.

Jump so that rope springs back to position and feet land on either side of rope, as in starting position.

Second Floor The rope is slid higher, so that it is just below the knees of the jumper. Repeat all the steps of the first floor.

Third Floor The rope is slid higher, so that it is at the thighs of the jumper.

Step I. Start on left side of rope.

Jump to land with right foot between ropes.

Jump to land with left foot between ropes and right foot outside right rope.

Jump to land with right foot between ropes and left foot outside left rope.

Jump back to starting position on left side of rope.
Step II. Both feet on left side of rope.
    Jump so that left rope is carried over right rope and right foot is
    between them.
    Jump back to starting position on left side of rope.

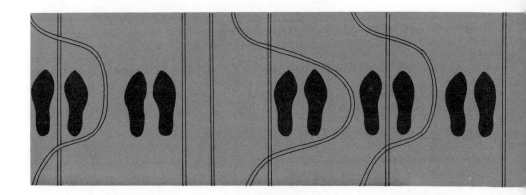

Jump both feet over right rope, carrying left rope over right rope.
Step left foot back over right rope.
Jump to return to starting position.

As children become adept at this game they will invent many variations.

Summary

The activities in this chapter contribute primarily to such aspects of biologic efficiency as strength, endurance, flexibility, balance, agility, and coordination. These factors are frequently considered to be measures of "physical fitness" or "physical performance."

Concepts relating to these activities are those of development of strength, endurance, and flexibility, found in Chapters 7, 8, and 9, and the principles of moving one's own body described in Chapters 2 and 3. Emphasis is on equilibrium, momentum, and application of force.

Movement skills include the basic movements of bending, stretching, and twisting, and the movement patterns needed to give impetus to self that were described in Chapters 2 and 4.

17 THROWING ACTIVITIES

The materials in this chapter are focused on the achievement of the specific movement skills of throwing and catching various types of objects. These activities use underhand throws, overhand throws, the bounce pass, push passes and shots, and catching objects of many different sizes and shapes, such as beanbags, balls, rings, and the like.

Activities are presented ranging from simple to more complex, and are grouped by grade levels. The teacher is encouraged to ignore grade boundaries, however, and select activities to meet the particular needs and goals of the group on the bases of abilities and previous experience of the children.

Activities for Kindergarten

Kindergarten children enjoy manipulating objects to find out how they "feel" and what they can do. Balls of different sizes and weights, beanbags, and rings should be available for them to handle, bounce, toss, roll, or use in any other ways they devise. Four and five year olds may prefer to select and manipulate an object individually rather than joining into group activities using objects.

The simplest group activities for children of this age are those of handling the equipment, rolling or pushing balls, and bouncing balls. The activities included in this section provide opportunities for group participation in the use of these skills.

PETER RABBIT AND FARMER BROWN

Behavioral goal: To pass different sized objects around a circle without dropping them.

Concept: Skills of overcoming inertia of other objects.

Biologic efficiency: Coordination.

Movement skill: Passing and receiving objects.

Children and teacher sit in a circle on the floor. Teacher tells story as she passes objects around the circle. Objects should be handed from child to child and returned to the teacher after they have been passed around the circle.

"Mother Rabbit started to look for Peter who had been gone from home for some time." (Teacher begins passing a large ball slowly around circle while she talks.)

"She couldn't find him, so she decided to wait for him at home." (Teacher places ball back in box when it returns to her.)

"Meanwhile, Peter was taking a walk in Farmer Brown's lettuce garden." (Pass small ball around circle slowly.)

"Farmer Brown saw him, and took after him to chase him away." (Pass large ball after small ball, moving both balls as rapidly as possible around the circle.)

If Farmer Brown overtakes Peter before he gets home, Peter is caught. He may escape and get home, Mother Robbit may find him, or the story may end in any way the teacher and children decide.

Other characters may be added to the story, such as "Flopsy" (a bean-bag), the fox (a block), and so on.

HOT BALL

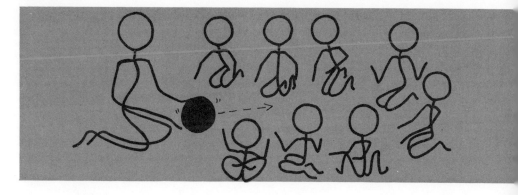

Behavioral goal: To push or roll ball away from self quickly.
Concept: Skills of overcoming inertia of other objects.
Biologic efficiency: Coordination.
Movement skill: Pushing or rolling a ball.

Teacher and children sit in circle. Teacher places both hands on rubber playground ball, resting in front of her. She says, "I am warming the ball." Then she suddenly says, "The ball is hot!" and quickly pushes it away from her, using both hands. As it rolls across the circle to a child, the child pushes it away with both hands. This continues until the ball rolls away or teacher starts a new game.

Teacher may ask a child to warm the ball and start the game. Game may be varied by pushing with only one hand.

I'LL ROLL THE BALL TO ———

Behavioral goal: To roll the ball to another person; to stop the ball with
two hands, one hand.

Concept: Overcoming inertia of external objects.
Biologic efficiency: Coordination.
Movement skill: Rolling; catching.

Teacher and children sit on floor in circle.   Teacher has a rubber playground ball.   She says, "I'll roll the ball to Mary," and rolls the ball to the designated child.   Child stops ball with both hands, then rolls with both hands to another child, saying first, "I'll roll the ball to ————."

Game continues until all have received the ball several times.   Then teacher takes a different size ball and starts a new game, using only one hand to roll the ball.   Children stop the ball with one hand, using same hand to roll it to someone else.

BOUNCE AND CATCH

Behavioral goal: To bounce and catch a rubber playground ball.
Concept: Overcoming inertia of external objects.
Biologic efficiency: Coordination.
Movement skill: Bouncing; catching.

Each child has a rubber ball.   He bounces it and catches it, using both hands.   He repeats it several times.   Then children try to bounce ball to a partner and catch the partner's return bounce.

Children bounce a ball against a wall and catch it as it bounces back.   Teacher places several children in a line and bounces to each in turn.   Children experiment with other ways of bouncing and catching.

Activities for Grades 1, 2

Six and seven year olds are capable of tossing, bouncing, and catching balls and other objects. These activities may be performed in relation to: self, a wall, a receptacle, a target, and another person. Each game that follows involves one or more of these aspects of throwing and catching.

HIT THE BUCKET

Behavioral goal: To toss a ball into a basket from a given distance.
Concept: Overcoming inertia of external objects.
Biologic efficiency: Coordination.
Movement skill: Tossing a ball.

Each child, in turn, tries to toss a ball into a basket from a position out-side of circle. He may use one or two hands. When he is successful, he scores 1 point.

Child in center of circle is retriever; he gets ball and passes to next player. Child who is scorekeeper keeps each player's score. After all players have had an equal number of turns, child with highest score is winner.

If teams are playing against each other, the team with most points at end of a given time period is winner.

BEANBAG THROW FOR DISTANCE

Behavioral goal: To throw a beanbag as far as possible.
Concept: Skills of overcoming inertia of external objects.
Biologic efficiency: Coordination; arm strength.
Movement skill: Throwing.

Six or eight children line up on throwing line. On signal, "Throw!" each throws his beanbag as far as he can into the field, then runs and stands beside his own beanbag.

Then another group line up and throw, and this continues until all have thrown. If a beanbag hits a player in the field, it stays where it drops. Winner is player who threw farthest.

HIT THE MOON

Behavioral goal: To throw a beanbag into a circle and hit a target.
Concept: Skills of throwing.

Biologic efficiency: Coordination.
Movement skill: Throwing.

Each child stands on inner circle and, in turn, tries to hit the "moon" with the beanbag. If he is successful, he moves to the outer circle, throwing from there when his turn comes again.

When a child makes a successful throw, he moves to or remains on the outer circle. When he is unsuccessful he remains on or returns to the inner circle. Each successful throw from the inner circle counts 1 point, and from the outer circle, 2 points.

Center player is retriever, and throws beanbag to each player in turn. After beanbag has gone around circle once, retriever chooses player from outer circle to be new retriever and exchanges places with him.

LION AND MOUSE

Behavioral goal: To pass and receive different sized balls, moving them as rapidly as possible.
Concept: Skills of overcoming inertia of external objects.
Biologic efficiency: Coordination.
Movement skill: Throwing; catching.

Children stand several feet apart in a circle formation. The "mouse," a small ball, is started first and is passed from child to child around the circle. When the mouse is halfway around the circle, the "lion," a large ball, is started. Balls may be tossed or bounced to the next player.

If the lion catches the mouse, the lion wins. If the mouse overtakes the lion, the mouse wins. If one ball is dropped and the other ball passes it before it is back in action, the ball that passed scores a win.

Variation: Use three different sized balls, a mouse, a cat, and a lion.

TEACHER'S CHOICE

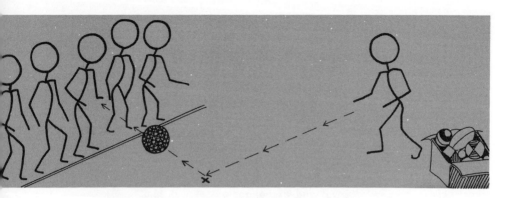

Behavioral goal: To throw and catch different sized balls.
Concept: Skills of overcoming inertia of external objects.
Biologic efficiency: Coordination.
Movement skill: Throwing; catching.

Children stand in line, facing child who is "teacher." Teacher chooses any ball he wishes to use and throws or bounces it to each child in turn. When each child has received the ball, teacher goes to end of line, and child who is at head of line becomes new teacher, choosing ball to be used. Game continues until each child has been teacher.

CALL BALL

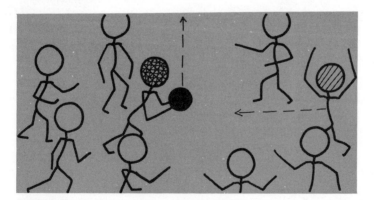

Behavioral goal: To toss a ball straight up, and to catch a ball on the bounce or on the fly.
Concept: Skills of overcoming inertia of external objects.

Biologic efficiency: Coordination.
Movement skill: Throwing; catching.

Children stand around outside a circle with one child in center, holding 8-inch rubber playground ball. Child in center calls name of a circle player, simultaneously tossing the ball straight into the air.

Player whose name is called must catch ball on the fly before it touches the ground. If he is successful, he becomes IT and goes to center to call a name. If player who is called misses the ball, he remains where he is and original IT may toss again.

A legal toss is one that goes at least 6 feet over the head of the tosser and would land inside the circle. If the toss is not legal, child whose name was called is IT whether or not he catches the ball.

If children are not skillful enough to catch the ball on the fly, one bounce may be permitted.

FOX AND SQUIRREL

Behavioral goal: To toss objects rapidly around the circle.
Concept: Skills of overcoming inertia of external objects.
Biologic efficiency: Coordination.
Movement skill: Throwing; catching.

Children stand in a circle. A ball, the "fox," is held by a child in the circle opposite a child who is holding the "squirrel," a beanbag. On signal "Go!" both objects are started around the circle in the same direction, the fox trying to overtake the squirrel. The fox may change direction around the circle at any time. The squirrel must then change direction to avoid being caught.

Activities for Grades 3, 4

Eight and nine year olds are interested in refining the tossing, bouncing, and catching skills. They are also capable of using underhand and overhand throws in simple team activities. Children of this age group should learn how to perform throwing and catching skills correctly, establishing good habit patterns in the use of these skills.

SPUD

Behavioral goal: To hit a stationary target with a ball.
Concept: Newton's laws of motion; skills of throwing.
Biologic efficiency: Coordination.
Movement skill: Throwing.

Children stand inside a circle; in center, one child holds an 8-inch rubber ball. Child with ball tosses it high into the air, calling another child's name. The child called runs to catch the ball while other children scatter into the playing field.

When child catches the ball he calls, "Stop!" All other children must stop and freeze in their positions. Child with ball takes aim and tries to hit one of the others with the ball. If he hits a player fairly, below the waist, he takes ball back to center of circle; other children then return to circle, and he calls a name and tosses the ball. If he misses the player at whom he aimed, that person may toss the ball from center and call a name.

If a player is hit fairly, he has a "spud" on him. After a player gets three spuds, he must pay a predetermined forfeit. The forfeit may be to

sing a song, run around the field, do a dance, stay out of the game until someone else gets three spuds, and so on.

Variation: If needed, a rule may be added permitting thrower one or
two giant steps toward the target before throwing.

INS AND OUTS

Behavioral goal: To hit a moving target with a ball, using overhand or
underhand throw with one or two hands.

Concept: Newton's laws of motion; skill of throwing.

Biologic efficiency: Coordination; agility.

Movement skill: Throwing; dodging.

A circle is drawn on the floor.   Half the children—the "outs"—stand
outside the circle, and half—the "ins"—stand inside the circle.   Outs, standing with both feet outside circle, try to hit Ins with an 8-inch rubber ball.
Ball must strike below waist of person who is hit.

When an In is hit, he joins the Outs and tries to hit other Ins.   Winner
is the In who can stay in circle longest.   Game is repeated with players who
were Ins becoming Outs and Outs becoming Ins.   Game may end in a play-
off between the two winners if desired.

CIRCLE DODGE BALL

Behavioral goal: To hit a moving target with a ball.
Concept: Newton's laws of motion; skill of throwing.
Biologic efficiency: Coordination; agility.
Movement skill: Throwing; dodging.

Children stand outside a circle with one child on the inside. Outside players try to hit child in the center of the circle, using an 8-inch rubber ball. A fair hit is one that strikes below the waist and is thrown by a player with both feet outside the circle.

When the center player is hit fairly, he exchanges places with the thrower who hit him and the game continues.

BOMBARDMENT

Behavioral goal: To hit a stationary target with a ball; to guard a target from being hit.
Concept: Newton's laws of motion; skill of throwing.

Biologic efficiency: Coordination; agility.
Movement skill: Throwing; catching; dodging.

Group is divided into two teams, one team in each court. Players may move freely on own court. One player holds rubber ball. On signal "Go!" he tries to hit and knock down opponents' Indian clubs with the ball, at the same time protecting own clubs. Players continue throwing at opponents' clubs until one team knocks down all clubs of other team. If the game is played for time, team wins who knocks down most clubs within time limit.

TAIL OF THE WOLF

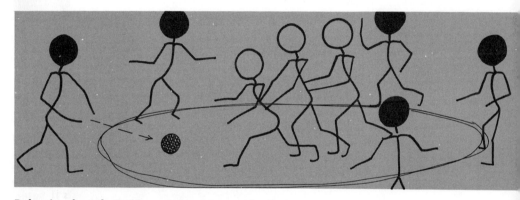

Behavioral goal: To hit a moving target with a ball.
Concept: Newton's laws of motion; skill of throwing.
Biologic efficiency: Coordination; agility.
Movement skill: Throwing; dodging.

Three children stand in the center of the circle, each holding the waist of the one in front. The lead child is the head of the wolf, the middle child is the body, and the last child is the tail. Other children stand outside the circle.

Players on outside try to hit the tail of the wolf, using an 8-inch rubber ball. A fair hit is one that strikes below the waist. The thrower must have both feet outside the circle. The wolf may dodge and swing around to protect his tail from being hit. If the tail is hit fairly, the child who is the tail joins the throwers, the thrower who hit him becomes the wolf's head, the head becomes the body, and the body becomes the new tail.

If a child lets go of the waist of the player in front of him, he must join the throwers, and a new player is chosen to take his place.

Variation: The circle may be enlarged to make room for several wolves in the center; two or three balls may be used by the throwers.

OVER THE LINE

Behavioral goal: To throw a beanbag as far as possible.
Concept: Levers of the body; gravity and movement.
Biologic efficiency: Coordination; arm strength.
Movement skill: Throwing.

A throwing box is drawn on the field. A line is drawn 20 to 30 feet from the box. One child is IT and stands in the field back of the line. Other children, each holding a beanbag, wait by the throwing box.

Each child, in turn, steps into the throwing box and, using an overhand throw, throws his beanbag across the line as far as he can. Any beanbags that do not go over the line are "dead." IT tries to catch all beanbags that go over the line before they hit the ground. Those he catches are also "dead." If IT can catch all the beanbags thrown over the line, he is IT again. Otherwise, the player who throws an uncaught beanbag farthest over the line is the new IT.

OVERTAKE

Behavioral goal: To pass and receive a ball rapidly.

Concept: Overcoming inertia of external objects.
Biologic efficiency: Coordination.
Movement skill: Throwing; catching.

A double circle is drawn on the floor.   Half the children stand on outer circle and half on inner circle, both circles facing each other.   Each circle counts off by twos.   All number 1 players in both circles are one team, and number 2 players are the other team.

On signal, "Go!" player from one team who is standing on outer circle and a player from other team who is standing on the inner circle start the balls in motion.   Each starter passes to his teammate on the opposite circle. Both balls are passed in same direction, around the circle from player to player.   Balls must make two complete trips around the circle.   The team finishing first (with the ball back in hands of starter) scores 1 point.   If either team overtakes the other, an additional point is given.   First team scoring 5 points is winner.

PRISONER'S BALL

Behavioral goal: To throw a ball, placing it out of reach of opponents; to catch a thrown ball.
Concept: Levers of the body; Newton's laws of motion.
Biologic efficiency: Coordination; agility.
Movement skill: Throwing; catching.

Divide into two teams, each team stationed in one court.   Between courts is "neutral ground."   Each team has a prison on the side of its court.   Ball is started by a player on one team who calls the name of an opponent and throws ball across neutral ground into opponents' court.   Ball must be caught before it touches the ground, or the player whose name was called must go to prison.   Any player on the team may catch the ball.   If it is caught, the catcher calls an opponent's name and throws the ball into opponents' court.

A team may free a prisoner by calling a prisoner's name as the ball is thrown into opponents' court.   If ball is not caught, the prisoner may return to his own team.

If ball lands in neutral ground, it is dead.   Team opposite the thrower recovers the ball.   Game continues for 10 minutes.   At end of time period, team with most prisoners in its prison is the winner.

HEAD MAN

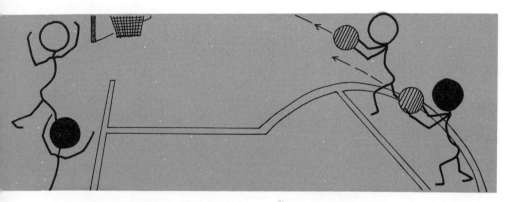

Behavioral goal: To shoot a basket before opponent scores.
Concept: Levers of the body; Newton's laws of motion.
Biologic efficiency: Coordination.
Movement skill: Throwing.

Players divide into two teams, 4 to 6 players per team.   Number 1 player for each team is called "head man," and takes position in back of free throw line.   Last man on each team stands under basket, retrieves ball for his head man, and passes back to him.

On signal, "Go!" both head men begin to shoot, and continue shooting until one of them makes a goal, or until each one has shot three times. Player who first makes goal scores a point for his team.   If neither player scores after three tries, number 2 players become new head men and number 1 players become retrievers.   Game continues until all have been head man. Team with most points wins.

NEWCOMB

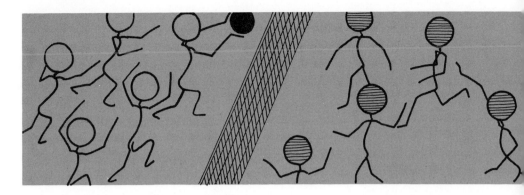

Behavioral goal: To throw a ball over the net, placing it out of reach of opponents; to catch a ball.

Concept: Overcoming inertia of external objects.

Biologic efficiency: Coordination; agility.

Movement skill: Throwing; catching.

Players divide into two teams. Each team as its own court, about 25 × 25 feet; top of net is about 5 feet from ground. Players arrange themselves to cover area on own court.

An 8-inch rubber playground ball is given to a player on one team and on signal, "Go!" player throws ball over net into opponents' court. Opponents try to catch ball before it strikes the ground and throw it back over the net. If the ball hits the ground in either court at any time, it is one point for the other team. Ball is started again on the side where it hit the ground.

Out-of-bounds ball is brought in on side where it went out, and is put into play again. Players may not walk with the ball. They may pass to other teammates if they wish; but if ball hits ground on their court, it scores a point for the opponents.

Penalty for walking with the ball is that the ball is awarded to the other team.

Team with most points after a 10-minute playing period is the winner.

Activities for Grades 5, 6

Ten, eleven, and twelve year old children are capable of performing many different types of overhand and underhand throws using various sizes and types of balls. They are interested in improving their throwing-catching skills to facilitate successful performance in many of the culturally acceptable sports such as football, basketball, and softball. These status activities are particularly important to boys of this age group, and their need to excel in one or more of these sports is a motivating factor toward improving skills and working on new skills.

BOMBER

Behavioral goal: To hit a moving target.
Concept: Skill of throwing.
Biologic efficiency: Coordination.
Movement skill: Throwing.

Two children are the bombers and stand opposite each other outside the circle. Other players are inside the circle. Bombers try to hit other players with the ball. A fair hit must strike below the waist, and the ball must have been thrown from outside the circle.

When a player is hit fairly, he joins the bombers outside the circle and helps hit the remaining players.

The two players who remain longest in the circle become bombers for the next game.

FIVE PASSES

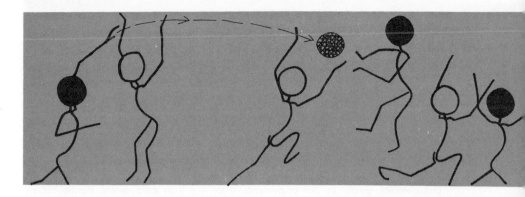

Behavioral goal: To accurately pass and catch a basketball while being guarded by opponents.

Concept: Overcoming inertia of external objects; Newton's laws of motion; levers of the body.

Biologic efficiency: Coordination; agility.

Movement skill: Throwing; catching; dodging.

Children divide into two equal teams of 6 to 8 members. Referee tosses basketball to captain of one team who passes to a team member. Ball is passed from player to player, while opposing team tries to intercept passes and obtain ball.

If five successive passes are completed by one team without interception by the opponents, the team completing the passes scores a point. Referee then tosses ball to opposing team captain and game continues.

Fouls are tripping, pushing, kicking, holding, or roughness of any form. Penalty for such fouls is ball awarded to opposing team.

Team with highest score at end of playing period wins.

END DODGE BALL

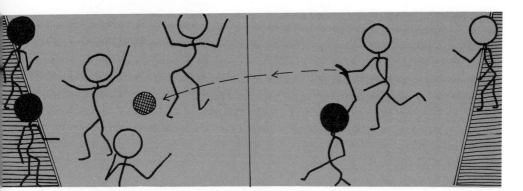

Behavioral goal: To hit opponents with the ball and avoid being hit by opponents.

Concept: Skills of locomotion; overcoming inertia of other objects.

Biologic efficiency: Coordination; agility; endurance.

Movement skill: Throwing; catching; dodging.

Players divide into two teams, each team on its own court. Ball is put into play by one team. Any player hit fairly by the ball must go to end zone behind opponents' court. He may continue to play from the end zone. A fair hit must strike below the waist and must be direct; a rebounding ball is dead and does not count. A player may save himself by catching the ball on the fly, in which case the thrower must go to the opponents' end zone. If the thrower is already in the end zone, the catcher may send any free opponent to the end zone.

First team to send all opponents to end zone wins.

PASSING SMORGASBORD

Behavioral goal: To pass and catch a basketball quickly and accurately, using various types of passes.

Concept: Skills of overcoming inertia of external objects.
Biologic efficiency: Coordination.
Movement skill: Passing; catching.

Children divide into equal teams, 6 to 8 per team. First player in each team stands inside a circle; the members of his team are lined up facing him. Each team member is assigned a specific type of pass before the game starts, for example:

Number 1 member—chest pass
Number 2 member—shoulder pass
Number 3 member—bounce pass
Number 4 member—overhead pass
Number 5 member—underhand pass, using two hands
Number 6 member—underhand pass, using one hand

On signal, "Go!" first player passes to each team member in turn, using his assigned type of pass. When ball reaches last player on team, that player runs with ball to circle and first player runs to head of line. Game continues until each player has had the circle position, and has passed to each team member in turn, using his designated pass.

First team to get all players back to original positions wins.

TWENTY-ONE

Behavioral goal: To shoot a basket successfully.
Concept: Overcoming inertia of external objects; levers of the body.
Biologic efficiency: Coordination.
Movement skill: Throwing.

Children are divided into groups, 4 to 6 per group. Each player has a number and takes his turn in order. Each turn consists of three successive throws at the basket.   The first throw is made from the free throw line, and scores 5 points if successful.   The next two throws are made from wherever the ball is recovered from the rebound.   Second throw, if successful, scores 3 points; third throw, 1 point.

Game continues until one player reaches the exact score of 21.   If player shoots more than 21 points, his score reverts to zero.

FREEZE OUT

Behavioral goal: To shoot a basket successfully.
Concept: Levers of the body; Newton's laws of motion.
Biologic efficiency: Coordination.
Movement skill: Throwing.

Children divide into groups, 4 to 6 per group.   Each player has a number and takes his turn in order.   Each turn consists of taking one shot at the basket from any position on the court.   When a player makes a basket, however, the player following him must also make a basket from the same spot, or he is "frozen out," and has to drop out of the game.   Winner is last player left in game.

Players who are out help to retrieve balls and pass to shooters.   This game is more interesting if players of like abilities are grouped together.

END BASKETBALL

Behavioral goal: To make long, accurate passes; to catch passes successfully.
Concept: Levers of the body; Newton's laws of motion.
Biologic efficiency: Coordination; arm strength.
Movement skill: Throwing.

Children divide into two teams, half of each team on its own court and other half in end zone behind opponents' court. Ball is put into play by one team, which tries to complete a successful pass to a player in the end zone. Each completed pass from a court player to one of his end zone players counts 1 point.

After each point is scored, the end zone player must pass the ball to the opponents, who put it into play. Fouls are: (1) taking more than one step when the ball is in possession, and (2) holding the ball more than 3 seconds. Penalty for fouls is ball awarded to opponents.

After 5 minutes of play, players rotate, with court players going to end zone and end zone players going to court. Game continues for another 5 minutes. Team with most points at end of 10 minutes of play wins.

KING OF THE COURT

Behavioral goal: To use passing, shooting, and guarding skills in a game situation.

Concept: Basketball rules and skills.

Biologic efficiency: Coordination; agility; endurance.

Movement skill: Throwing; catching; dodging; running.

Children divide into two teams, 8 players per team, with 3 forwards, 3 guards, 1 king of the court who does all the shooting for basket, and 1 goal defender. Game is played on basketball court, each team playing on half a court. The forwards play on their own half court, guards play on opponents' court and guard opponents' forwards. King of the court plays on his own half court in the free throw circle only, and goal defender guards the opponents' king, playing also in the free throw circle only of the opponents' court.

King is the only player who can shoot for basket, and defender is only player who can guard him and attempt to regain ball for his own team. King and goal defender are only players who can be in the free throw circle, and they are not permitted to move out of the circle at any time.

In general, the rules of basketball govern fouls, penalties, and playing situations. The limited dribble may be used if desired, but this is primarily a passing game.

Ball is thrown by referee alternately to forward of each team. Forward receives throw while standing in center circle, and is unguarded while receiving throw. The throw-in is used to start the game, and after each score is made. After each score, positions are rotated for team making score, with goal defender becoming king, number 1 forward becoming goal defender, and king rotating to number 3 guard position, the last position in the rotation.

Violations include: (1) taking more than one step with the ball in hands; (2) pushing, tripping, or roughing opponent; (3) playing in wrong playing area. Penalty for first and third violations is ball awarded to opposing team. Penalty for second violation is free throw awarded to player who was fouled against.

Each successful basket made from the field counts 2 points; each free throw going into the basket counts 1 point. Team with most points at end of playing time wins. Playing time may be two five-minute halves, or it may be until everyone has rotated to king position once.

FOOTBALL GOAL PASS

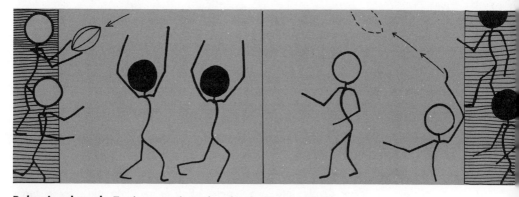

Behavioral goal: To throw and catch a football successfully.
Concept: Levers of the body; skills of throwing.
Biologic efficiency: Coordination; arm strength.
Movement skill: Throwing; catching.

Children divide into two teams. Three players from each team are goal players and are in goal area back of opponents' field. Remaining players are in own field. Ball is given to goal player on one team, who starts game on signal, "Go!" by passing to his own field players. One score is made when a field player completes a pass to his goal player, providing passer is in his own field and receiver on his own goal.

Opponents try to intercept and pass to their own goal players. Players may not step into opponents' area to intercept ball. Field players may pass to own field players, but all passes must be made from spot where ball was caught.

Out-of-bounds ball is brought in at place where it went out and is played from there. Penalty for violating any rules is ball given to opposing goal player, who then puts it into play.

Team with most scores at end of playing period wins.

TEAM FORWARD PASS

Behavioral goal: To pass and catch a football; to intercept passes.
Concept: Newton's laws of motion; levers of the body.
Biologic efficiency: Coordination; agility.
Movement skill: Throwing; catching.

Playing field is around 150 feet long, with two end lines and a center circle. Children divide into two teams. Ball is put into play by a team member standing in center circle and passing to a teammate, while opponents try to intercept the pass. Every completed pass gives the receiver the right to take three steps toward opponents' goal line before passing the ball. Every pass intercepted, touched, knocked down, or caught causes the ball to be returned to the center circle, and the team intercepting the pass puts the ball into play.

A goal is made when the ball is passed over the opponents' end line and is not caught by opponents after it passes the end line. If ball is caught behind goal line, it is thrown back into field and is in play again.

BATTER'S CHOICE

Behavioral goal: To make a long throw into the field and run the bases successfully.

Concept: Levers of the body; skill of throwing.

Biologic efficiency: Coordination; arm strength.

Movement skill: Throwing; running.

Children divide into two teams, one at bat and the other in the field. Fielders play regular softball positions. A box of different types of balls—football, softball, basketball, rubber playground balls of different sizes, and so on—is placed back of home plate. The "batter" chooses any ball he wishes and throws it into the field, then runs to first base, second, third, and home without stopping on any base. If he gets home without being put out, he scores a point for his team.

Batters are out if:

(1) Fielder catches a fly ball;
(2) Fielder throws the ball to a baseman before the runner reaches the base (the ball must be thrown in order from first base to second, to third, to home, and each baseman must have one foot touching his base as he throws to the next base);
(3) Batter throws foul ball outside the playing area;
(4) Base runner neglects to touch a base.

Three outs retire the batting team, and fielding team comes to bat. Team with most points after an equal number of innings have been played wins.

NO-BAT SOFTBALL

Behavioral goal: To use throwing, catching, and running skills in a softball game situation.

Concept: Skill of throwing; softball rules and strategy.

Biologic efficiency: Coordination; arm strength; endurance.

Movement skills: Throwing; catching; running.

Children divide into two teams, one at bat and the other in the field. The rules of softball govern fouls, penalties, and playing situations, with the following exceptions:

(1) The batter stands with one foot on home plate and throws the softball into the field rather than batting a pitched ball;

(2) The pitcher does not pitch, he serves only as a fielder, covering the pitching position.

TOUCH FOOTBALL

Behavioral goal: To use passing, kicking, and running skills in a football game situation.

Concept: Skills of overcoming inertia of external objects; rules and strategy of football.

Biologic efficiency: Coordination; agility; endurance.

Movement skill: Passing; catching; kicking; running; dodging.

Children divide into two teams, 7 players per team. One team, players' backs toward their own goal, starts the play by kicking or passing from their own half of the field. The ball may be advanced by a running play, a forward pass, or by kicking. To start each play, the center must pass the ball backward to a teammate before any player may advance beyond the line of scrimmage, which is an imaginary line crossing the field from the spot where the center passes the ball.

In general, the rules of football govern fouls, penalties, and playing situations.

Tackling is not permitted and "touching" is substituted for it. This occurs when the ball carrier is touched or tagged on some part of his body below the neck by an opponent. *Both hands must touch simultaneously.*

The size of the field, number of players, type of football, and modification of rules should be governed by the ability and experience of the players. For elementary-age children, a junior football or soccer ball may be used, and the field length should be roughly 60 yards. The game may be played in 5 to 8-minute quarters, with rest periods between quarters. Players should wear rubber-soled tennis shoes and jerseys or pinnies to identify the teams easily. *No spiked shoes, shoulder pads, or helmets should be worn.*

For official football rules, write to the National Federation of State High School Athletic Associations, 7 South Dearborn St., Chicago, Illinois.

Summary

The materials in this chapter are focused on the achievement of specific movement skills of throwing and catching objects. Chapters 2, "Human Movement," 3, "Mechanics of Movement," and 4, "Movement Analysis of Selected Skills" provide information to help the teacher understand the concepts of giving and receiving impetus of external objects, the mechanics of movement, and the specific analysis of throwing and catching objects.

The activities in this chapter contribute primarily to the aspects of biologic efficiency evinced in coordination, agility, strength, and endurance.

18   STRIKING ACTIVITIES

Kicking-striking skills are in themselves more complex than the running or throwing skills, and some children may find difficulty in mastering the coordinations needed to contact a moving target, such as a pitched ball, with a bat or even with the hand.   Kicking or striking a stationary target is less demanding than contacting a moving target, and games may be simplified by substituting a stationary ball for a pitched ball when children are unable to contact the moving ball successfully.

Activities are presented ranging from simple to more complex, and are grouped by grade levels, although grade boundaries may be crossed at any time in selecting activities for a particular group of children.

Activities for Kindergarten

Kicking-striking activities for the kindergarten child are exploratory in nature.   Balls of various types should be made available, and the child should be encouraged to use them in ways that he chooses.   For example, a child may decide to play "football."   He may kick the ball, then chase it, and fall on top of it; or he may kick it to another child, who may pick it up and run for a goal.

Rubber balls may be bounced on the ground or into the air.   Balloons may challenge the child, as he tries to keep them in the air by striking them with his hands.

Organized activities using the kicking-striking skills are generally un-successful with this age group because they demand both organizational and movement skills that the typical four or five year old neither possesses nor has interest in.

Activities for Grades 1, 2

Six and seven year olds are capable of participating in simple kicking games using stationary objects, and in games such as O'Leary, p. 285, which involve bouncing a ball. Some children in this age group are interested in trying to strike a ball with a bat or paddle. The coordination needed for success in batting, however, is much better developed in the more mature child, and games using this skill are usually not included in activities for the younger age group.

KICKAWAY

Behavioral goal: To kick a ball across the circle without lofting it.
Concept: Overcoming inertia of external objects.
Biologic efficiency: Coordination.
Movement skill: Kicking

Children stand around a circle. One player has ball on ground in front of him with his foot resting on it. Suddenly he says, "Kick-away!" and kicks it across the circle.   The child receiving the ball kicks it quickly away from him to another child; children continue to kick ball until it goes outside the circle, or is lost in some way.   Player who retrieves the ball brings it back to the circle and starts it again.

A large rubber ball should be used, and children should be helped to kick in back of the ball rather than under it, to avoid lofting the ball.

FREE BALL

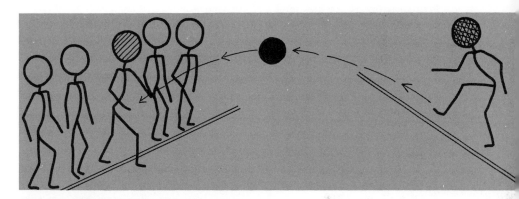

Behavioral goal: To loft a ball, kicking at a target.
Concept: Newton's laws of motion.
Biologic efficiency: Coordination.
Movement skill: Kicking.

Two parallel lines are marked 30 to 40 feet apart.   Child who is IT stands back of one line, facing other players who stand back of opposite line.

IT calls a player's name and lofts a large rubber ball toward the opposite line, using a punt or kicking the ball from the ground.   Player whose name is called tries to catch ball and kick it back to IT.   This continues until IT has kicked once to each player.   Then IT calls, "Free Ball!" and kicks toward the opposite line.   Player who catches or stops the ball is the new IT.

This game is most successful if played with only 4 to 6 players per group.

OVER THE WALL

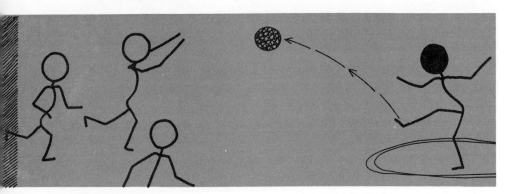

Behavioral goal: To kick the ball "over the wall."
Concept: Skills of kicking.
Biologic efficiency: Coordination.
Movement skill: Kicking.

The "wall" is a 25-foot line drawn a distance of 30 to 50 feet from the kicking circle. One player is kicker and stands in the kicking circle. Other players scatter in playing field in front of wall.

Kicker places ball on ground inside kicking circle, calls, "Over the wall!" and kicks toward the wall. Any fielder who can catch or stop the ball before it goes over the wall is the new kicker. If the ball crosses the line, or wall, the original kicker kicks again. If no one stops the ball after he has kicked three times, he chooses a new kicker.

If ball goes out of bounds (over an imaginary line from the circle to each end of the wall), fielders call, "Chase it yourself!" and run to kicking circle. First fielder to reach circle is new kicker. Original kicker must chase his own out-of-bounds kick and return ball to new kicker.

This game should be played with 5 to 8 players per group; this makes it possible for all to have a turn at kicking.

KICK AND RUN

Behavioral goal: To kick a ball so far that player can run around all four bases before ball is retrieved.

Concept: Newton's laws of motion; skills of kicking.

Biologic efficiency: Coordination; strength; endurance.

Movement skill: Kicking; running.

Children divide into two teams, one in field and one at bat. First player on fielding team goes into field and first player of batting team places ball in kicking circle. When fielder is ready, kicker kicks ball into field and runs around bases and home. Fielder fields ball and runs directly to home base. When he reaches it he calls, "Home!"

Kicker scores 1 point for each base he touches before fielder calls, "Home!" For example, if kicker touches first base only, he scores 1 point; if he runs past second base, he scores 2 points, and so on.

After each player on the kicking team has had one turn at bat, the kickers become fielders and fielders become batters. Each player on fielding team has also had one turn in the field.

If individual scores are kept, winner is player with highest score; if a team score is kept, team with higher score wins.

O'LEARY

Behavioral goal: To bounce a ball rhythmically to a chant.

Concept: Skills of overcoming inertia of external objects.

Biologic efficiency: Coordination.

Movement skill: Bouncing a ball.

For description of game see p. 199.

Kicking and striking activities are challenging to eight and nine year olds. Children of this age group are capable of mastering soccer skills, such as dribble, punt, drive, and trap. Boys are particularly eager to excel in the kicking skills, which receive high cultural approval for males in the United States, particularly in football.

Many eight and nine year olds are successful in bouncing or batting a ball with the hand or with a paddle. Although boys are impatient for baseball experiences because of cultural expectations, many of this age group may have difficulty in batting a softball or in volleying a volleyball.

It is important to provide opportunities for children to try their hands at many activities; and it is equally important to avoid forcing children beyond their abilities to perform successfully.

HIT THE CIRCLE

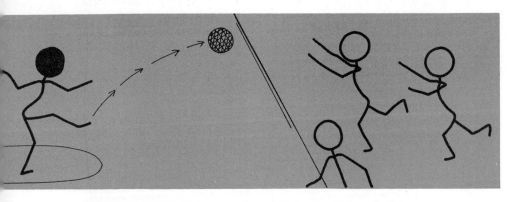

Behavioral goal: To punt or place kick for as far as possible.
Concept: Skills of overcoming inertia of external objects.
Biologic efficiency: Coordination; strength.
Movement skill: Kicking.

One player is the kicker and stands in the kicking circle with a soccer ball. Other players scatter in the field. A 5-foot "roll-in" line is marked 20 to 30 feet from the kicking circle. The kicker punts or place kicks the soccer ball into the field. The fielder who stops the ball tries to roll it across the kicking circle, using his hands. He may carry the ball to the roll-in line, or he may roll it from the place where he stopped it, whichever is most advantageous. If he succeeds, he becomes the kicker. If he misses, the original kicker continues; if the latter is not put out after three turns, he chooses another kicker and goes into the field.

If a fielder catches a fly ball, he becomes kicker immediately, without the roll-in.

FOUR SQUARES

Behavioral goal: To bounce a ball successfully in a game situation.
Concept: Newton's laws of motion.
Biologic efficiency: Coordination.
Movement skill: Striking.

A court consisting of four squares is marked on a surface that will rebound a rubber ball. Each square is approximately 5×5 feet.

One child stands in each square. The game starts when player D bounces the ball to any other player. The ball must land in the opponent's square; and it must be played after the first bounce, with the receiving player bouncing to any other player. The ball must bounce once in a square before it may be returned. The ball may not be held or caught.

Play continues until a player fouls by:

(1) Bouncing the ball on a line or out of the court;
(2) Hitting the ball with the fist;
(3) Holding the ball;
(4) Failing to return the ball that lands in one's square;
(5) Being hit by the ball—the player who is hit is down, not the server.

Penalty for any foul: The player who fouls goes to square D, and other players move in regular rotation from D to C to B to A. If the player in D fouls, he is out and goes to end of waiting line. Player at head of waiting line goes into D. Player in square D always starts the ball when play is resumed.

SOCCER KEEPAWAY

Behavioral goal: To cooperate with team members in keeping the soccer ball from the opposing team members.

Concept: Skills of overcoming inertia of external objects.

Biologic efficiency: Coordination; endurance.

Movement skill: Kicking.

Divide players into two teams. Team with ball tries to kick it in such a way that they pass it among themselves and keep it away from opposing team.

Players may not touch ball with hands, but must block it with body. They may dribble, advancing the ball with short kicks, and trap or stop the ball with the feet. Kicks should be with the inside of the foot rather than with the toe. Players may not kick, push, or rough each other.

SOCK-BALL

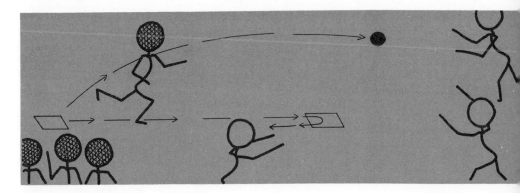

Behavioral goal: To strike a ball in such a way that a home run can be made.
Concept: Newton's laws of motion; levers of the body.
Biologic efficiency: Coordination; strength; speed.
Movement skill: Striking; running.

Players divide into two teams, one team in the field and one at bat. First player of team at bat strikes the ball into the field with his hand and runs to base and home in one complete trip. He may not stop on the base but must continue to home. If he makes the trip without being put out, he scores a run for his team.

Runner is out if:

(1) Fielder catches a fly ball;
(2) Fielders hit the runner below the waist with the ball before he reaches home, but fielders are not allowed to run with the ball.

When the team at bat makes three outs, it goes into the field and team in field comes to bat. Team with most scores at end of playing period (after an equal number of innings) wins.

Variation: A football may be punted into the field by the team at bat, with the runner being out if a fly ball is cought or if a fielder holding the ball touches home plate before the runner.

KEEP IT UP

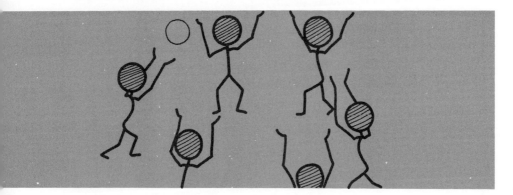

Behavioral goal: To cooperate with others in keeping a volleyball in the air as long as possible.

Concept: Overcoming inertia of external objects.

Biologic efficiency: Coordination.

Movement skill: Striking.

Divide children into teams, 5 or 6 per team. Each team has a volleyball. On signal, "Go!" a team member tosses the ball into the air. Players keep striking it up into the air, using both hands. Team which keeps the ball up the longest wins 1 point. Team which makes most points at end of playing period is the winner.

Variation: If this is difficult for the children, simplify game by permitting one bounce between each hit.

KICK TAG

Behavioral goal: To kick a soccer ball at a moving target.

Concept: Overcoming inertia of external objects; kicking; blocking.
Biologic efficiency: Coordination.
Movement skill: Kicking; blocking.

Boundaries of the playing area are determined and marked off.   Players scatter within playing area.   Three or four players are IT, and they kick the soccer ball at the other players, trying to tag them below the knees with the ball.   Anyone tagged by the ball is also IT and helps tag others.

Kickers use inside of foot rather than toe, to avoid lofting ball.   Kickers may also dribble ball with small, short kicks in an effort to get closer to players.

Players may not touch ball with hands, but must block with body or feet.   Game continues until all are tagged.   Last player tagged is IT for next game and chooses other ITs to help him.

BOOT BALL

Behavioral goal: To kick and field successfully in a game situation.
Concept: Skills of overcoming inertia of external objects.

Biologic efficiency: Coordination; strength; endurance.
Movement skill: Kicking; fielding.

Children are divided into two teams, one at bat and the other in the field. Fielders scatter to cover playing area. First kicker places ball in circle and kicks it into the field, then runs to first base, and if possible, continues to second, third, and home. Base runners may stop on any base but only one runner may be on a base at a time. Runners may not pass other runners on the bases.

Foul balls are kicked over. Runners are out if:

(1) Fielder catches a fly ball;
(2) Fielder hits runner below waist with ball while runner is off base;
(3) Runner passes another runner, or goes to an occupied base, in which case, runner who makes the error is out;
(4) Fielder with ball touches base before runner gets there.

If runner reaches home, he scores one point for his team. Team continues at bat until each player has had one turn to be kicker. Then they become fielders and team in field comes to bat. Team with most scores at end of period wins.

ONE OLD CAT

Behavioral goal: To strike a ball successfully with a bat.
Concept: Newton's laws of motion; skill of batting.
Biologic efficiency: Coordination.
Movement skill: Batting.

Divide children into groups, with 6 to 10 per group. Play area has a home plate and first base. Two of the players are batters and others are fielders, numbered consecutively. Batters rotate catching position from one to the other.

Child at bat tosses ball into air and bats it into the field.   There are no fouls and all hits are good.   When batter hits ball, he must run to first base and home in one trip without being put out.   If he is successful he makes a score, and continues batting after serving as catcher for second batter.   If he is put out, he becomes last fielder and fielders rotate positions from last fielder consecutively to first fielder, and first fielder becomes batter.

Batter is out if he:

(1) Has 3 strikes at the ball and misses each time;

(2) Is tagged while running by fielder with the ball;

(3) Does not reach home plate before catcher tags home with ball;

(4) Hits a fly ball that is caught;

(5) Fails to touch bases while running;

(6) Throws his bat.

Any size of rubber ball may be used while children are learning to bat. After children have become successful in striking rubber balls, a spongy soft-ball may be substituted.

LONG BASE KICK-BALL

Behavioral goal: To punt for distance and score a home run.

Concept: Skill of kicking.

Biologic efficiency: Coordination; strength; speed.

Movement skill: Kicking.

Children are divided into two teams, one at bat and the other in the field.   Playing field has a home base and a long base, which is approximately 30 to 40 feet from home base.

First player of team at bat stands behind home base and punts soccer ball or football into field.   Then he tries to run to long base and home before fielders can throw the ball to the catcher.   If he succeeds, he makes a run for his team.

Kicker does not score if:

(1) Ball is returned to catcher before kicker gets home;

(2) Fly ball is caught;

(3) Kicker does not kick a fair ball in three trials. (A "fair" ball must be punted and must land within agreed upon boundaries.)

Batters stay at bat until each player has had a turn at bat. Then batters become fielders and fielders become batters. Team with higher score after even number of times at bat wins.

Variation: Game may be played with a pitcher, catcher, baseman, and fielders, using a softball and bat in place of soccer or football. Batter is out if he:

(1) Strikes out;

(2) Bats a fly ball that is caught;

(3) Is tagged off base by a fielder with the ball;

(4) Reaches long base after baseman has tagged base with ball;

(5) Throws his bat.

In this game, runners may be allowed to remain on long base if it is not safe to return home, and any number of runners may be on long base at same time.

BOUNCE NET BALL

Behavioral goal: To strike a volleyball over the net successfully.

Concept: Skills of overcoming inertia in external objects.
Biologic efficiency: Coordination.
Movement skill: Striking.

Divide children into two teams, each team on its own court on either side of net. Volleyball court should be about 25 × 50 feet, with top of net about 5 feet from ground.

Each team scatters on own side of net. Volleyball is given to one player, and on signal, "Go!" he tosses it into air and hits it with both hands over net into opponents' court. Ball must bounce once in opponents' court and then must be hit over net before it bounces again. Any number of players may hit ball any number of times.

When ball bounces more than once in a court after crossing net, it is a point for opposing team. Team which loses the point starts the ball in play again.

Fouls are:

(1) Ball bouncing more than once in court;
(2) Ball thrown rather than batted;
(3) Ball caught and held;
(4) Ball hit with fist;
(5) Out-of-bounds ball.

Penalty for fouls: one point awarded to opposing team. Play is started again on side where foul occurred. Team with most points at end of playing period wins.

Activities for Grades 5, 6

Ten, eleven, and twelve year olds are able to perform many kicking and striking activities successfully and are eager to participate in the traditional athletic games of softball, soccer, football, and volleyball. Boys are particularly motivated to excel in these areas, and girls are interested in exploring these skills because of their challenge and variety. The team games suggested here provide opportunities for boys and girls to participate together in a variety of activities using these movement skills.

PUNT AND CATCH

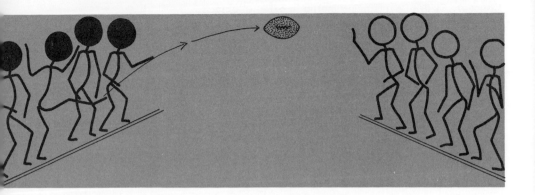

Behavioral goal: To punt a soccer ball, or football, over the opponents' line and to field punted balls successfully.

Concept: Levers of the body; skills of kicking.

Biologic efficiency: Coordination; strength.

Movement skill: Kicking; catching.

Divide children into two teams, each team on its own goal line. Goal lines are 30 to 60 feet apart, depending upon the skill of the players. Team members number off and take turns punting in order.

Number 1 player on one team punts ball from own goal line over opponents' goal line. Any member of opponents' team may try to catch the ball. If the ball is caught on the fly, there is no score. If ball touches the ground before it is stopped, the kicker's team receives a point.

If the ball does not go over the goal line, and receivers on opponents' team can catch it on the fly, a point goes to the receiver's team. Ball alternates from team to team until each player has punted. Team with most points wins.

If most balls are falling short of goal, shorten distance between goals; lengthen the distance if most children are able to punt well beyond the goal line.

FUNGO

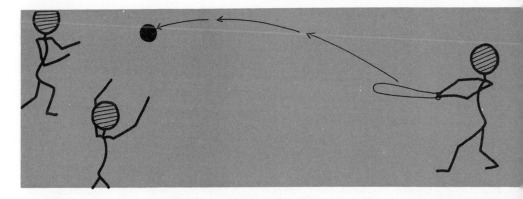

Behavioral goal: To bat a ball successfully into the field.
Concept: Levers of the body; Newton's laws of motion.
Biologic efficiency: Coordination.
Movement skill: Batting.

One player is batter and others are fielders. Batter tosses up ball and bats fly balls or grounders out into field. If a fielder can catch a fly ball or stop a grounder, he becomes batter and batter becomes fielder.

If no fielder succeeds in catching or stopping ball, first player to pick up ball calls, "Fungo!" Then batter lays bat on ground parallel to the fielder, who tries to roll ball over bat. If ball hits or jumps over bat, fielder who rolled ball becomes batter. If ball misses bat, same batter continues batting.

BEAT BALL

Behavioral goal: To kick ball successfully into field and circle bases before
fielders relay ball to base.

Concept: Overcoming inertia of external objects.

Biologic efficiency: Coordination; strength.

Movement skill: Kicking; running; throwing; catching.

Players divide into two teams, one in field, the other at bat. Softball diamond is used, with bases 30 feet apart. Fielders take regular softball positions.

Pitcher rolls ball to batter, who kicks it into field and tries to circle bases before fielders relay ball. If ball beats runner around the bases, the runner is out. If runner beats ball, he scores a point for his team.

When ball is fielded, it must be thrown, in order, to first baseman, second, third, and home. Each baseman must have one foot touching the base when he throws the ball to the next baseman. Batter is out if:

(1) Fly ball is caught;

(2) Ball beats him around the bases;

(3) He does not touch all bases as he rounds them;

(4) He kicks four fouls.

Three outs retire the side and fielders become batters. Team with most points at end of playing period wins.

KICKER'S CHOICE

Behavioral goal: To kick various types of balls for distance and accuracy.
Concept: Skills of overcoming inertia of external objects.
Biologic efficiency: Leg strength; coordination; endurance.
Movement skill: Kicking; running.

Children divide into two teams, one at bat and other in the field. Fielders play regular softball positions. A box of different types of balls that can be kicked—football, soccer ball, different sizes of rubber playground balls—is placed back of home plate. The kicker chooses any ball he wishes and any type of kick he wishes, and kicks the ball into the field. Then he runs bases consecutively, from first to home, without stopping on any base. If he gets home safely, he scores a point for his team.

Kicker is out if:

(1) Fielder catches a fly ball;

(2) Fielder throws the ball to a baseman before the runner reaches the base, with ball being passed in order from first to second, third, home and each baseman having one foot on the base as he throws to the next baseman;

(3) Kicker kicks 3 foul balls;

(4) Base runner neglects to touch base.

KICK BALL

Behavioral goal: To kick, run, and field successfully.
Concept: Overcoming inertia of external objects; rules of softball.
Biologic efficiency: Coordination; strength; endurance.
Movement skill: Kicking; running; catching.

This game is played with two teams, using a softball diamond and softball rules. A soccer ball is used in place of the softball, with the pitcher rolling the soccer ball to the batter, who kicks it into the field.

Batter is out if he:

(1) Strikes out by missing 3 balls that roll over home plate;
(2) Kicks 4 fouls;
(3) Kicks a fly ball that is caught;
(4) Is thrown out before he reaches base;
(5) Is tagged or thrown out before he returns to a base;
(6) "Leads off" a base;
(7) Steals a base, except on an overthrow.

ONE-BOUNCE VOLLEYBALL

Behavioral goal: To strike a volleyball over the net, either from a bounce or from a teammate's volley; to serve a volleyball.

Concept: Skills of overcoming inertia of external objects.

Biologic efficiency: Coordination.

Movement skill: Striking.

Players divide into two teams, one team on either side of the net. The volleyball court is about 25 × 50 feet, with top of net 6½ feet from ground.

First player on serving team serves ball (using the underhand volleyball serve) from behind serving line into opposite court. Server has two trials to make a good serve. If he succeeds, he serves until he fails to make a good serve, or until his team fails to return the ball (ball must be returned by contacting it with fleshy pads of all the fingers) to the opponents. Then the side is out and the opponents serve.

The team scores a point for each successful serve that opponents fail to return. After the side is out, players rotate positions for new server.

Each time ball crosses net, it must bounce once in the court before it is returned. No player may hit a ball more than twice in succession, but any number of players may hit the ball.

Fouls are:

(1) Failure to make a good serve in two trials;

(2) Striking ball on return before it has bounced once;

(3) Allowing ball to bounce more than once;
(4) Player hitting ball more than twice in succession;
(5) Hitting ball with fist;
(6) Failure to return ball over the net;
(7) Out-of-bounds ball.

Penalties for fouls: If serving team fouls, it is side out, and the ball goes to the opponents; if the receiving team fouls, the serving team scores a point, and the same server continues.

The winning team is the one with the most points at end of playing period, or the team which first reaches 21 points.

VOLLEYBALL NEWCOMB

Behavioral goal: To volley a ball successfully in a game situation.
Concept: Skills of overcoming inertia of external objects.
Biologic efficiency: Coordination.
Movement skill: Striking.

Players divide into two teams, one on either side of the net. The volley-ball court should be about 25 × 50 feet, with net 6½ feet from ground.

Ball goes to a player on one team, who tosses it into air and strikes it over net using both hands. Opponents try to hit ball back over the net. The game continues until the ball strikes the ground in one court, which gives a point to the opponents. The ball is started again on the side where it hit the ground. Any player on the team may start the ball by tossing it into the air and striking it with both hands. There is no rotation or serving order. Any number of players may hit the ball any number of times.

Fouls are:

(1) Ball caught and held;
(2) Ball hit with fist;
(3) Ball thrown rather than batted;
(4) Out-of-bounds ball.

Penalties for all fouls are 1 point awarded to the opponents. Play is started again on the side where the foul occurred. At the end of a given length of playing time, the team with the most points wins.

PADDLE BADMINTON

Behavioral goal: To serve and volley a shuttlecock with a paddle.
Concept: Skills of overcoming inertia of external objects.
Biologic efficiency: Coordination.
Movement skill: Striking.

Players divide into two teams, each team on its own side of the volleyball court; top of net is 5 feet from ground. First player on serving team serves shuttlecock while standing behind service line. One service is allowed with exception of "let" bird, which is re-served. (Shuttlecock that touches top of net as it goes over is "let.") Serve must be underhand, but any stroke may be used to return the shuttlecock. It may not be hit twice in succession by the same player, but any number of players may hit it. Shuttlecock landing on boundary line is good.

Scoring is same as for volleyball. If receiving side fails to return shuttlecock legally, serving side scores a point, and server continues to serve. If serving side fails, it is side out, and opponents serve. After side out, players rotate (see arrows in illustration), and new server serves.

Two 10-minute halves are played, and team with higher score wins.

SOFTBALL

Behavioral goal: To use batting skills in the game of softball.
Concept: Newton's laws of motion; levers of the body; rules of softball.
Biologic efficiency: Coordination; strength; endurance.
Movement skill: Batting; pitching; catching; throwing; running.

Players divide into two teams, one at bat and the other in the field. Play area is softball diamond with bases 45 feet apart.

The pitcher throws the ball to the batter, using an underhand pitch. Batter tries to score a run by hitting a fair ball and running the bases from first to home in succession. He may stop on any base, but only one runner may occupy a base at one time; runners may not pass each other.

The batter is out if he:

(1) Has three strikes;
(2) Is tagged or thrown out before reaching first base;
(3) Hits a fly ball that is caught;
(4) Throws the bat.

The base runner is out if he:

(1) Is tagged by a fielder with the ball when off a base;
(2) Is forced to run, and the fielder with the ball reaches the base ahead of him;
(3) Runs from a base before a fly ball is caught and is tagged before he returns to the base, or a fielder with the ball gets to the base before he returns;
(4) Leaves a base before the ball leaves the pitcher's hand;
(5) Fails to touch a base while running, or passes another base runner.

After 3 outs, the batting team exchanges places with the fielding team. Both teams have an equal number of times at bat, and the team with the higher score wins.

TOUCH FOOTBALL

Behavioral goal: To use passing, kicking, and running skills in a football game situation.

Concept: Skills of overcoming inertia of external objects; rules and strategy of football.

Biologic efficiency: Coordination; agility; endurance.

Movement skill: Passing; catching; kicking; running; dodging.

For description of game, see Chapter 17, p. 278.

PUNT BACK

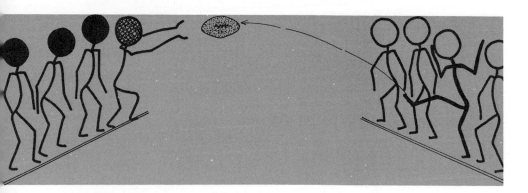

Behavioral goal: To punt and catch a football.
Concept: Skills of overcoming inertia of external objects.
Biologic efficiency: Coordination; strength.
Movement skill: Kicking.

Players divide into two teams. Each team has its own goal line, approximately 250 feet from opponents' goal. Ball is given to one player, who punts from his own goal toward opponents' goal. Other players on the punter's team stand behind own goal line.

Any player on the opposing team may receive the kick. The player who receives the ball punts from the point where he gained possession of it, with other members of his team scattered behind him. If the ball is caught on the fly, the player catching it may take two "giant" steps toward the opponents' goal before punting.

If the ball is punted over the opponents' goal line and is not caught on the fly, it scores a point for the punters. If the ball is caught on the fly, there is no score; the ball is returned to the goal line, and the player who caught the ball punts from his own goal line toward the opponents' line.

Out-of-bounds balls are punted from sideline at point where they went out.

Team with the most points at the end of a given playing period wins.

Summary

The activities described in this chapter emphasize the movement skills of: (1) kicking various types of balls, (2) striking balls with the hands, and (3) striking balls with a bat or paddle. Concepts related to the performance of these skills are presented in Chapters 2, "Human Movement," 3, "Mechanics of Movement," and 4, "Movement Analysis of Selected Skills." These activities contribute to the development of coordination, strength, and endurance.

19 AQUATICS

The increased number of swimming areas in our communities has stimulated an interest in learning to swim. The materials in this section include children's activities for learning to adjust to the water, and to propel oneself through the water by wading and swimming.[1]

Anatomic and physiologic barriers are not usually a problem in learning to swim, since many such limitations imposed on land are modified by the tendency of the water to support the individual in an almost weightless state. Moving in the water provides an excellent opportunity for satisfying movement experiences for children with reduced strength and endurance levels resulting from accidents or disease. They may operate effectively during learning despite a reduced energy output and minimal levels of strength and endurance.

The major barrier to performance in learning to swim is the psychologic adjustment that is necessary to become comfortable when the face and body are submerged. Once the child is at ease in the water, he can usually be taught to swim in very short order. Psychologic adjustment begins when the teacher can make the child understand that the water will "help" him swim. The activities in this chapter may be used with any age level; and techniques for helping a beginner learn to swim are suggested.

Adjusting to Water

The purposes of these activities are to help the child become familiar with the water medium, to learn how to move about in water, and to overcome the fear of water.

[1] Activities in this section are modified from ideas and unpublished materials contributed by Dorothy Govas, Long Beach Unified School District, Long Beach, Calif.

MR. CLEAN

Behavioral goal: To splash and pour water over one's head.
Concept: Movement and the biologic condition; psychologic barrier.
Biologic efficiency: Psychologic.
Movement skill: Splashing water.

Mr. Clean stands in shallow water and washes his arms, shoulders, neck, chest, head, and face. He fills a plastic container with water and "rinses" his hair.

Variation: Mr. Clean's bucket brigade—children form a bucket brigade, with each child in line receiving the full bucket, pouring it over his head and shoulders, refilling it, and passing it on to the next as rapidly as possible.

WALKING IN WATER

Behavioral goal: To walk across the width of the pool and back.

Concept: Human locomotion.
Biologic efficiency: Psychologic.
Movement skill: Walking in water.

Children, individually or with a partner, walk across the width of the pool, then turn and walk back.

They repeat several times, using various forms of locomotion, such as jumping, hopping on one foot, sliding, skipping, and running.

WATER RACE

Behavioral goal: To race others across the pool.
Concept: Human locomotion in water.
Biologic efficiency: Psychologic; endurance.
Movement skill: Moving in water.

Several children line up alongside the pool in shallow water. On signal, "Go!" they race across pool, using any means of locomotion. Winner is first child to reach opposite side of pool. After all have raced, the winners race each other for "water championship."

JUMPING DOLPHINS

Behavioral goal: To jump with others while holding hands in a circle.
Concept: Human locomotion; jumping in water.
Biologic efficiency: Psychologic; endurance.
Movement skill: Jumping in water.

Children form a circle in shallow water and join hands, closing in to-ward each other to avoid straining. On signal, "Jump!" they jump up and down in the water. If any children release hands, they must drop out of the circle. Winners are those who continue jumping, holding hands, until the signal, "Stop!" is given.

WATER TAG

Behavioral goal: To tag others and avoid being tagged.
Concept: Human locomotion in water.

Biologic efficiency: Psychologic; endurance; coordination.
Movement skill: Moving in water.

Children are in shallow water. One child is IT and attempts to tag another. The child tagged is the new IT, and must tag another.

If desired, safety zones may be designated, such as sides of pool.

HOLD TAG

Behavioral goal: To tag others and avoid being tagged.
Concept: Movement and the biological condition; psychologic barriers.
Biologic efficiency: Psychologic; endurance; coordination.
Movement skill: Moving in water.

Children are in shallow water. One child is IT and chases others. When he tags another, the child tagged must hold the part of his body where he was tagged as he chases the other players.

FISH TAG

Behavioral goal: To tag others and avoid being tagged.
Concept: Movement and biological condition; psychologic barriers.
Biologic efficiency: Psychologic; endurance; coordination.
Movement skill: Moving in water; submerging.

Children are in shallow water. One child is IT and chases others. When he tags another, that child becomes IT. A child may save himself from being tagged if he ducks under water; he is safe for as long as he is submerged. He may move under water if he chooses.

FISH EYES

Behavioral goal: To hold breath and open eyes in the water.
Concept: Psychologic barriers to performance.
Biologic efficiency: Psychologic.
Movement skill: Opening eyes underwater.

Each child has a partner. One of the partners is "fish eyes" and the other is IT. IT stands with his hands behind his back. "Fish eyes" takes a breath and puts his face in the water, and IT extends both hands underwater with one to ten fingers extended. If "fish eyes" counts the fingers correctly without lifting his head above water, he becomes IT and IT becomes "fish eyes."

BUBBLING WHALES

Behavioral goal: To blow bubbles underwater.
Concept: Psychologic barriers to performance.
Biologic efficiency: Psychologic; breath control.
Movement skill: Blowing bubbles underwater.

Children are whales, blowing bubbles. Standing in shallow water, they inhale through the mouth; then, placing their faces in water, they exhale, causing bubbles in the water.

POISON AIR

Behavioral goal: To hold breath underwater.
Concept: Breath control; psychologic.
Biologic efficiency: Breath control.
Movement skill: Holding breath underwater.

Children are standing in shallow water. When teacher calls, "Poison Air!" all children take a deep breath and place the face in water, holding breath until teacher claps her hands for "All clear!"

Variation: Children compete to see who can hold breath the longest.

DOUBLE BUBBLE

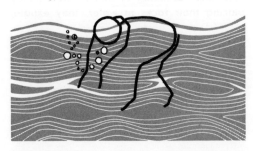

Behavioral goal: To blow bubbles in water, inhaling and exhaling rhythmically.

Concept: Psychologic.
Biologic efficiency: Breath control.
Movement skill: Bubbling rhythmically.

Children stand in shallow water. They inhale, then exhale under water, blowing bubbles; they raise their heads and inhale, then exhale again under water. After they can successfully bubble twice, they try for three, four, and five times.

ELEMENTARY BOBBING

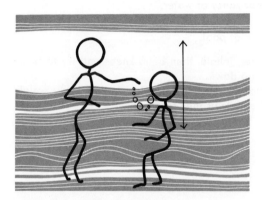

Behavioral goal: To inhale and exhale rhythmically while submerging in the water.
Concept: Psychologic; breath control.
Biologic efficiency: Psychologic; breath control.
Movement skill: Coordinated bobbing with rhythmic breathing.

Children stand in hip-deep water, each child with a partner. One of partners takes a breath, then bends his knees and submerges face, exhaling and bubbling as he submerges; then he straightens up and inhales, then exhales under water, continuing for several times. Other partner repeats performance.

Children then move into chest-deep water, and one partner bobs while other watches him. After all have bobbed in chest-deep water, children move to shoulder-deep water and bob, then to neck-deep, chin-deep, mouth-deep, and overhead water, bobbing rhymically.

Attention is directed to how light the pressure on the feet becomes when the body is submerged.

SIT ON THE BOTTOM

Behavioral goal: To sit on the bottom of the pool.
Concept: Psychologic barriers; buoyancy of water.
Biologic efficiency: Psychologic.
Movement skill: Sitting on bottom of pool.

Children stand in shallow water, inhale, then bend knees and try to sit on bottom of pool, exhaling as they go down.

Variation: Children jump into air and sit on water, letting body weight carry them down to bottom, and exhale as they go down.

TREASURE HUNT

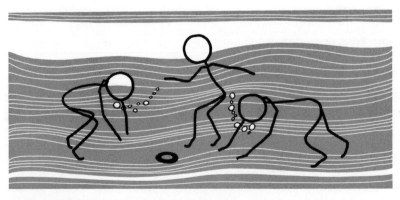

Behavioral goal: To pick up an object from the bottom of the pool.
Concept: Buoyancy of water; psychologic.
Biologic efficiency: Psychologic.
Movement skill: Submerging.

Children are in shallow water. A "treasure" such as a rubber ring, rubber heel, or shell, is placed on the bottom of the pool. Children submerge and try to bring up the treasure.

Variation: Children may be in two teams, and several treasures may be placed on bottom of pool. Team obtaining greater number of treasures wins.

Learning to Swim

These activities help the child to learn how to propel himself through the water in various ways, ending in the performance of the human stroke, a very elementary swimming skill. The human stroke is extremely effective, and easily learned, because it does not require a synchronized breathing technique. This stroke does not enjoy great popularity because it is not recognized as a style of swimming utilized in competition. It is, nevertheless, a fundamental propulsion pattern and progresses easily into the front crawl as the child develops more confidence and acquires skill in rhythmic breathing.

CORK

Behavioral goal: To float, face down, and regain standing position.
Concept: Buoyancy in water; psychologic adjustment.
Biologic efficiency: Psychologic; endurance.
Movement skill: Holding breath and floating face down.

Child inhales, places face in the water, then slides his hands down his legs toward his ankles. When he reaches the point (somewhere between the knees and ankles) at which it feels safe to do so, he grips himself there, allowing himself to float like a cork until he needs air.   Then he slides the hands back up the body, rests his feet on the bottom and raises his head.

It is important that the child's feet touch the bottom *before* he lifts his head.

THE ICEBERG

Behavioral goal: To float like an iceberg.
Concept: Buoyancy in water; psychologic adjustment.
Biologic efficiency: Psychologic adjustment.
Movement skill: Floating face down.

The iceberg floats with $\frac{4}{5}$ of its body underwater and $\frac{1}{5}$ out in the air. It does so because its body is lighter than the water.   Teacher tells children that they too are lighter than water, and if they fill their lungs with air, they too will float like the iceberg.

Child inhales, places face in water, draws his knees to his chest, and clasps his arms around his shins, floating like an iceberg.   To regain standing position, he places feet on bottom, then raises head.

TUG BOAT AND OCEAN LINER

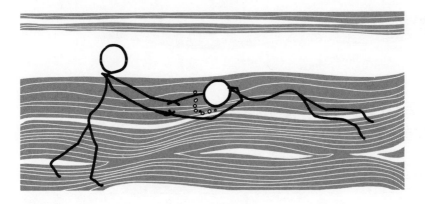

Behavioral goal: To float, face down, with body extended.
Concept: Buoyancy; psychologic adjustment.
Biologic efficiency: Coordination; psychologic.
Movement skill: Face float.

Children stand in shallow water, each child with a partner. Child who is ocean liner holds out both hands, palms down, and child who is tug boat grasps his wrists from the top. The liner takes a deep breath and lies face down on the water. Tug boat moves backward across the pool, towing the liner until he runs out of breath. Roles then change, and a return trip is made.

Caution child who is tug boat that he must keep his eyes on his ocean liner at all times, and that he should help him regain his feet when he runs out of breath.

After a few trips, the liner's motor starts, and he begins kicking his legs in a flutter kick. The legs are moved up and down so that the heels alternately come to the surface of the water, but care should be taken to keep the feet in the water and not make big splashes. The legs should be straight but not stiff and some slight movement at the knee is to be expected.

FLOATING LOG

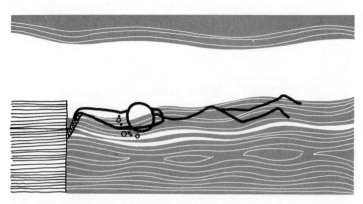

Behavioral goal: To float face down and regain standing position unaided.
Concept: Buoyancy; psychologic adjustment.
Biologic efficiency: Psychologic; coordination.
Movement skill: Floating face down; regaining standing position.

Child stands in shallow water, several feet from side of pool and facing it. He extends his arms toward side of pool, palms down and fingers relaxed. He inhales, puts face in water and drifts toward side of pool allowing feet to float up behind him. When his knuckles touch the side of the pool, he pushes down on the water with his hands, simultaneously drawing his knees to his chest in the iceberg position. Then he places his feet on the bottom, and finally lifts his head.

MOTOR BOAT

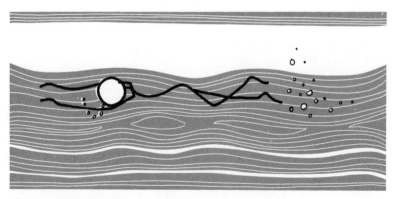

Behavioral goal: To float face down and move through the water by kicking.

Concept: Newton's laws of motion; human locomotion.
Biologic efficiency: Psychologic; endurance.
Movement skill: Kicking.

Child stands in shallow water, inhales, and places his face in the water, arms extended forward, palms down. He permits his legs to float up, then begins kicking his legs in a flutter kick, propelling himself forward through the water until he runs out of breath or reaches the side of the pool.

WADING AND PULLING

Behavioral goal: To wade and pull oneself through the water.
Concept: Newton's laws of motion; human locomotion.
Biologic efficiency: Coordination.
Movement skill: Wading and pulling.

Children stand in the shallowest water, then wade, with their arms out of the water. Children move to chest-deep water, and wade with arms out, noting difficulty in moving rapidly because of density of water. Then children make their hands into "cups," and as each step is taken they reach out with the opposite hand and pull a cup of water back to the body. Children continue wading and pulling, using hands and arms alternately.

If this is done properly the child will "feel" that he is pulling himself through the water.

When children can perform this skill effectively, they may race with each other as they wade and pull.

THE HUMAN STROKE

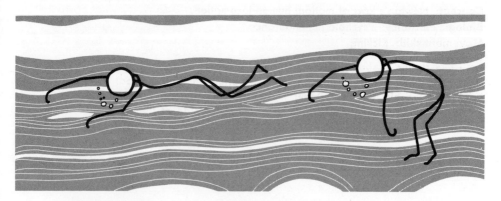

Behavioral goal: To swim, using the human stroke.
Concept: Newton's laws of motion.
Biologic efficiency: Psychologic; endurance.
Movement skill: Swimming.

Child stands in shallow water, leans forward at the waist, and begins pulling cups of water, alternating each hand, and pulling to the hip level. Hands are kept just *below* the surface of the water as they slide forward, reach for a new cup of water, and pull to the hip level.

As child pulls cups of water, he permits his feet to float up and kicks them in the flutter kick, holding his head above the surface of the water so that his eyes, nose, and mouth are out of water. If he pulls and kicks strongly, swimming will occur.

BALL TAG

Behavioral goal: To tag another with the ball and to avoid being tagged.

Concept: Human locomotion in water; overcoming inertia of external objects; Newton's laws of motion.
Biologic efficiency: Coordination; endurance; psychologic.
Movement skill: Wading; swimming; throwing; dodging.

One child is IT and holds a rubber ball. He throws the ball at the other players. If a player is hit by the ball, he becomes IT and the game continues. The players may swim, duck under water, walk, or run in the water to avoid being hit. The game may be played in either shallow or deep water, depending upon the skill and confidence of the players.

WATER KEEPAWAY

Behavioral goal: To pass the ball to one's own teammates and try to keep opponents from obtaining it.
Concept: Human locomotion in water; overcoming inertia of external objects.
Biologic efficiency: Coordination; endurance; psychologic.
Movement skill: Wading; swimming; throwing; catching.

Children divide into two teams. The ball is tossed to one child, who passes it to his teammates, while other team tries to intercept the ball. Game continues until teacher calls time. This game is vigorous and should be played for short periods.

COLLECTING CORKS

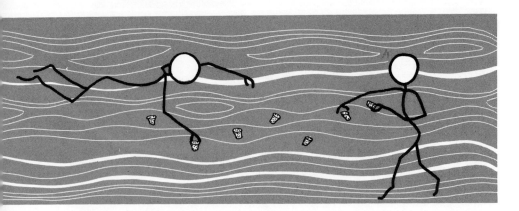

Behavioral goal: To collect more corks than opponents do.
Concept: Human locomotion; overcoming psychologic barriers.
Biologic efficiency: Coordination; endurance; psychologic.
Movement skill: Swimming; wading.

Children divide into two teams. A number of corks are tossed into the water. Teams try to collect more corks than their opponents do. A child may take only one cork at a time and must place it at a designated place on the pool deck. Team collecting most corks is the winner.

ADVANCED BOBBING

Behavioral goal: To bob rhythmically in deeper water.
Concept: Buoyancy of water.

Biologic efficiency: Psychologic adaptation.

Movement skill: Coordinated bobbing using body floatation.

Child takes face float position with the arms extended over the head, and legs and hips hanging comfortably in the water. The breath is held 20 to 30 seconds, and is then exhaled sharply through the nose and mouth. As the child exhales, he also presses hard against the water with hands and arms, which permits him to raise his head and take a full rapid inhalation. After inhaling, he will sink 6 to 10 inches below the surface; and as he relaxes and assumes the hanging position, he will bob back to the surface with his shoulders and neck slightly out of water. The 20 to 30-second relaxation period is followed by another breath recovery.

This sequence is practiced until it becomes almost effortless. Children may first practice in chest-deep water, and, as they become skillful, they may progress to deep water.

As a form of survival swimming, this technique enables persons to stay afloat for extended periods without excessive fatigue.

Summary

The materials in this chapter are focused on human movement in the water medium. Psychologic adjustment, the main barrier to successful performance in the water, was discussed in Chapter 12, "Movement and the Biologic Condition." Newton's laws of motion apply to the overcoming of body inertia in the water as well as on land; and Chapters 2, "Human Movement," and 3, "Mechanics of Movement," provide information that can be applied to movement in the water environment.

These activities contribute primarily to psychologic adjustment, coordination, and endurance.

Suggested Readings: Movement Activities for Children

Anderson, Marian, Margaret E. Elliot, and Jeanne La Berge, *Play With a Purpose.* New York: Harper & Row, Publishers, 1966.

Andrews, Gladys, Jeannette Saurborn, and Elsa Schneider, *Physical Education for Today's Boys and Girls.* Boston: Allyn & Bacon, Inc., 1960.

Bornell, Donald G., Ted H. Hucklebridge, and Evelyn Taix, *Administration of the Approved Physical Performance Tests in California.* Sacramento, Calif.: State Department of Education, 1965.

Fait, Hollis F., *Physical Education for the Elementary School Child.* Philadelphia: W. B. Saunders Co., 1964.

Halsey, Elizabeth, and Lorena Porter, *Physical Education for Children.* New York: Henry Holt and Company, 1958.

LaSalle, Dorothy, *Guidance of Children Through Physical Education.* New York: The Ronald Press Company, 1957.

Latchaw, Marjorie, *A Pocket Guide of Games and Rhythms for the Elementary School.* Englewood Cliffs, N.J.: Prentice-Hall, Inc., 1956.

————, and Jean Pyatt, *A Pocket Guide of Dance Activities.* Englewood Cliffs, N.J.: Prentice-Hall, Inc., 1958.

Miller, Arthur G., and Virginia Whitcomb, *Physical Education in the Elementary School Curriculum* (2nd ed.). Englewood Cliffs, N.J.: Prentice-Hall, Inc., 1963.

Salt, E. Benton, et al., *Teaching Physical Education in the Elementary School* (rev. ed.). New York: The Ronald Press Company, 1960.

Sehon, Elizabeth L., and Emma Lou O'Brien, *Rhythms in Elementary Education.* New York: A. S. Barnes & Co., Inc., 1951.

Vannier, Maryhelen, and Mildred Foster, *Teaching Physical Education in Elementary Schools* (rev. ed.). Philadelphia: W. B. Saunders Co., 1958.

Wallis, Earl L., and Gene A. Logan, *Exercise for Children.* Englewood Cliffs, N.J.: Prentice-Hall, Inc., 1966.

INDEX

Entries in boldface indicate movement activities described in Part Two.